helmut schmid
schmid typography
typografie

edited by
herausgegeben von

kiyonori muroga
nicole schmid

museum für gestaltung zürich
lars müller publishers

This German/English edition is
initiated by Lars Müller and
published by Lars Müller Publishers
in collaboration with the
Museum für Gestaltung Zürich.

For their generous support
the publishing house thanks:

Museum für Gestaltung Zürich /
　　Zurich University of the Arts
University of Applied Sciences and Arts
　　Northwestern Switzerland /
　　Basel Academy of Art and Design
Chikako Tatsuuma
Josef Schmid
Nicole Schmid
Lars Müller

Introduction	Einleitung — 005

1 **Experiment and practice:** Developments in the Basel era	**1** Experiment und Praxis: Entwicklungen in der Basler Zeit — 007
2 **In the internationalization of design:** Challenges at NIA	**2** Die Internationalisierung des Designs: Herausforderungen bei der NIA — 033
3 **White space and form:** The search for Japanese culture and aesthetics	**3** Weissraum und Form: Die Suche nach japanischer Kultur und Ästhetik — 055
4 **Organic and systematic:** Works in Sweden	**4** Organisch und systematisch: Arbeiten in Schweden — 087
5 **A political individual:** Works for the Social Democratic Party of Germany	**5** Ein politischer Mensch: Arbeiten für die Sozialdemokratische Partei Deutschlands — 099
6 **Character and philosophy:** Corporate and store identity	**6** Charakter und Philosophie: Corporate und Store Identity — 121
7 **Linking function and strategy:** Packaging for Otsuka	**7** Funktion und Strategie verbinden: Verpackungen für Otsuka — 141
8 **The essence of elegance:** Shiseido's brand logotypes	**8** Die Essenz der Eleganz: Markenlogos von Shiseido — 165
9 **A statement of attitude:** Publications and posters	**9** Eine Stellungnahme: Veröffentlichungen und Plakate — 183
10 **Lecture:** Design is Attitude	**10** Vortrag: Gestaltung ist Haltung — 225

Afterword from the publisher	Nachwort des Verlegers — 236
Afterword from the Museum für Gestaltung Zürich: Typography as visual poetry	Nachwort des Museum für Gestaltung Zürich: Typografie als visuelle Poesie — 237
References	Quellen — 238

Introduction

Born in Austria in 1942, Helmut Schmid was a typographer and graphic designer of German nationality. After beginning his career as a typesetter, he studied under Emil Ruder and others at the Allgemeine Gewerbeschule Basel in the 1960s. At the time, Basel, along with Zurich, was at the center of a movement that later became known in design history as "International Typographic Style" or "Swiss Typography."

Influenced by Ruder's creative typography, Schmid's desire to explore further, and the opportunities he was presented with, led him to work in Japan, Sweden, Canada and Germany during a period from the late 1960s to the late 1970s. He came to Japan in search of, among other things, the Eastern ideas that Ruder referred to often; the visit was a major turning point for Schmid. For the rest of his life from 1977 onwards, he based himself in Osaka.

Schmid worked in the field of typography, his work focusing mainly on publications, posters and logotypes. Some of his client work is very familiar to the Japanese public: examples include Otsuka Pharmaceutical's Pocari Sweat, and various brand logos in the Shiseido range. Schmid also continued to write and publish on typography throughout his life, introducing important works of contemporary typography to the world and acting as a gateway between Eastern and Western design.

In 2021, a retrospective exhibition of his working life, *Try Try Try: Helmut Schmid Typography*, was held at kyoto ddd gallery, attracting a large audience despite the prevailing corona pandemic.

This book introduces the activities of Helmut Schmid through his work. The projects discussed in the following chapters correspond roughly to the chronological changes that occurred to Schmid's place of residence. A change in location for Schmid also meant a change in the projects he committed himself to and the people he worked with.

Why was Schmid drawn to typography? And how exactly did he explore it? In order to understand questions like these, we need to refer to both the period in which he lived and the state of design at the time. After the Second World War, the 1950s and 1960s were a period of development in the field of graphic design. Printing technology had given rise to a field in which graphic elements – which until then had required the use of separate materials such as lead type, copperplate and woodblock – could be freely combined into a single plane. The professional field of graphic design came to be known as the art of controlling this field. Other older domains such as typography and illustration were also integrated into the world of graphic design.

In the 1950s and 1960s, Swiss graphic design had begun showing highly sophisticated ways of integrating text and graphics, but the designers behind them varied in their fields of expertise. They included artists, illustrators and typesetters. Basel's typography, which brought sense to the integration of words and form, can be interpreted as a response to this trend from the realm of typographers (metal type was still in use in the 1960s).

Through Basel, Schmid saw typography as a relationship between meaning and form, letterforms and counterforms, space and negative space. This awareness of the complementary relationship between factors – each simultaneously defining the other – led Schmid to the East (Japan), as a counter to the West. It was there that he also learned about duality in Japanese culture: kanji and kana, ideography and phonetic expression.

After that, time progressed from modernism to postmodernism, and then on to a global age where beliefs have no place. The spirit of the time that was Schmid's starting point has been relativized; the time when beliefs and ideals were associated with design and typography currently exists only in our imagination.

Despite this, Schmid's typography was always full of vitality; he continued to face his original intentions in the midst of contradictory dualities of meaning and form, base and figure, West and East, etc., which lay repeatedly in constant conflict and flux. Schmid's typography, therefore, was not grounded in any single method, but was repeatedly revitalized according to the times. This is where Schmid's motto "design is attitude" and his stance in "confronting the duality of informative and freeform" (stated in his biography), come together.

In this book, we will follow in Schmid's footsteps as he tackles the issues of each era and see the kind of attitude he adopted, while referring to his past comments. Schmid's attitude is his own, and cannot be imitated by others. However, in his past activities, clues lie dormant for modern-day designers to discover, in order to explore their own posture and capture ideas they have not yet seen. It is our hope that this book will serve as valid reference material for the next generation to see what Schmid left behind and what he desired to pass on.

Kiyonori Muroga

Einleitung

Helmut Schmid, 1942 in Österreich geboren, war ein deutscher Typograf und Grafikdesigner. Seine berufliche Laufbahn begann zunächst als Schriftsetzer; anschliessend studierte er in den 1960er Jahren unter anderem bei Emil Ruder an der Allgemeinen Gewerbeschule Basel. Zu der damaligen Zeit stand Basel zusammen mit Zürich im Zentrum einer Bewegung, die später als «International Typographic Style» oder «Schweizer Typografie» in die Geschichte des Designs einging.

    Beeinflusst von Ruders kreativer Typografie und getrieben von seinem Forschungsdrang ergriff Schmid zwischen Ende der 1960er und Ende der 1970er Jahre verschiedene Gelegenheiten, in Japan, Schweden, Kanada und Deutschland zu arbeiten. Nach Japan ging er, um unter anderem die östlichen Ideen, auf die sich Ruder oft bezog, kennenzulernen. Diese Reise markierte auch einen wichtigen Wendepunkt für Schmid, der sich ab 1977 für den Rest seines Lebens in Osaka niederliess.

    Schmid arbeitete als Typograf; seine Arbeit konzentrierte sich hauptsächlich auf Publikationen, Plakate und Logos. Einige seiner Auftragsarbeiten sind der japanischen Öffentlichkeit wohlbekannt, darunter das Logo von Pocari Sweat, einem isotonischen Erfrischungsgetränk des Pharmaunternehmens Otsuka Pharmaceutical, sowie verschiedene Logos der Marke Shiseido. Schmid schrieb und publizierte zeit seines Lebens über Typografie, stellte der Welt zeitgenössische typografische Werke von Bedeutung vor und fungierte als Vermittler zwischen östlichem und westlichem Design.

    2021 fand in der kyoto ddd gallery unter dem Titel *Try Try Try: Helmut Schmid Typography* eine retrospektive Ausstellung seines Schaffens statt, die trotz der anhaltenden Coronapandemie ein breites Publikum anzog.

    Das vorliegende Buch stellt das Tätigkeitsspektrum Helmut Schmids anhand seines Werks vor. Die in den folgenden Kapiteln besprochenen Projekte entsprechen in grober zeitlicher Reihenfolge seinen wechselnden Wohnsitzen. Ein Ortswechsel bedeutete für Schmid immer auch ein neues Projekt, dem er sich verschrieb, und andere Menschen, mit denen er zusammenarbeitete.

    Wieso war Schmid so von der Typografie fasziniert? Und wie genau erforschte er diese? Um solche Fragen zu verstehen, müssen wir sowohl die Zeit, in der er lebte, als auch den Stand des gestalterischen Schaffens in der damaligen Zeit betrachten. Nach dem Zweiten Weltkrieg waren die 1950er und 1960er Jahre eine Zeit der Entwicklung auf dem Gebiet des Grafikdesigns. Durch die Drucktechnik entstand ein Tätigkeitsfeld, bei dem grafische Elemente, die bis dahin nur mithilfe von Bleisätzen, Kupferplatten und Druckstöcken aus Holz verwendet werden konnten, sich frei auf einer einzigen Fläche kombinieren liessen. So entstand das Berufsfeld des Grafikdesigns. Andere, ältere Domänen wie Typografie und Illustration wurden ebenfalls in diesen Bereich integriert.

    In den 1950er und 1960er Jahren bewies das Schweizer Grafikdesign zunehmend eine grosse Kunstfertigkeit darin, Text und Grafik miteinander zu verbinden. Die Gestalter, die dafür verantwortlich zeichneten, kamen aus unterschiedlichen Fachgebieten; es waren Künstler, Illustratoren und Schriftsetzer. Die Basler Typografie, die Wort und Form auf sinnvolle Weise miteinander in Beziehung setzte, kann als Antwort auf diesen Trend aus dem Umfeld der Typografen interpretiert werden (in den 1960er Jahren waren immer noch Metallsätze in Gebrauch).

    Durch seine Basler Zeit betrachtete Schmid die Typografie als Beziehung zwischen Wortbedeutung und Form, Buchstabenformen und Gegenformen, Bedrucktem und Unbedrucktem. Das Bewusstsein für die komplementäre Beziehung zwischen Faktoren, die sich gegenseitig bedingen, führte Schmid in den Osten (Japan) als Gegenpol zum Westen. Dort lernte er auch das Prinzip der Dualität in der japanischen Kultur kennen: Kanji und kana, Ideografie und phonetischer Ausdruck.

    Seitdem ist die Zeit von der Moderne zur Postmoderne und dann weiter zu einem globalen Zeitalter vorangeschritten, in dem Überzeugungen keinen Platz mehr haben. Der Zeitgeist, der Schmids Ausgangspunkt war, hat sich relativiert; die Zeit, in der Überzeugungen und Ideale mit Design und Typografie verbunden waren, existiert heute nur noch in unserer Vorstellung.

    Nichtsdestotrotz war Schmids Typografie immer voller Vitalität; er verfolgte weiterhin seine ursprünglichen Absichten inmitten der widersprüchlichen Dualitäten von Wortbedeutung und Form, Grund und Bild, West und Ost etc., die sich immer wieder in einem ständigen Konflikt und Wandel befanden. Entsprechend war Schmids Typografie nicht auf eine einzige Methode festgelegt, sondern wurde zeitgemäss immer wieder neu belebt. An diesem Punkt treffen Schmids Motto «Gestaltung ist Haltung» und seine Überzeugung bezüglich der «Auseinandersetzung mit der Dualität von Information und Freiform», wie es in seiner Biografie heisst, aufeinander.

    In diesem Buch wandeln wir auf Schmids Spuren, beleuchten seine Auseinandersetzung mit den Themen der jeweiligen Zeit, betrachten die Haltung, die er vertrat, und beziehen uns dabei auf seine damaligen Äusserungen. Schmid hatte eine eigene Denkweise, die andere nicht nachahmen können. In seinem Werk schlummern jedoch Hinweise, die moderne Gestalterinnen und Gestalter finden können, um ihre eigene Haltung zu erforschen und Ideen zu entdecken, die sie noch nicht erkannt haben. Wir hoffen, dass dieses Buch der nächsten Generation als wertvolles Referenzmaterial dienen wird, um zu entdecken, was Schmid hinterlassen hat und was er weitergeben wollte.

Kiyonori Muroga

1 experiment and practice:
developments in the basel era

Experiment und Praxis:
Entwicklungen in
der Basler Zeit

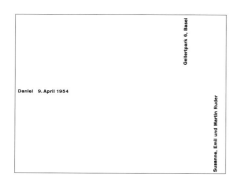

Birth announcement
Design: Emil Ruder, 1954

Geburtsanzeige
Design: Emil Ruder, 1954

Book cover for *Versunkene Kulturen*
(Lost Culture)
School assignment, 1964
135 × 206 mm

Buchcover für *Versunkene Kulturen*
Studienaufgabe, 1964

Helmut Schmid was born on February 1, 1942, in Ferlach, the southernmost town of Austria (under German rule at the time), as the oldest son of a German border guard and his wife. In 1957, when Schmid was 15 years old, his father was transferred to Weil am Rhein, a town on the east bank of the Rhine River in the southwestern corner of Germany, on the border between France and Switzerland. Schmid became an apprentice at a printing house and started to make a living as a typesetter.

One day in 1959, Schmid was caught by an illustration he happened to see in a printing trade journal. It was a greeting card announcing the birth of a child, in which each element (the name, date of birth and address) was spatially composed with a simple but unmistakable tension. The designer's name was Emil Ruder.

Arriving at the Allgemeine Gewerbeschule (AGS, later Basel School of Design) in 1942, Ruder had established himself as a pioneering typography teacher, practitioner and theorist. He spearheaded an educational program that enhanced the creativity of typesetters, aiming to "strive for a typography as an expression of our time," "rejection of formalism and mere imitation of earlier epochs" and "the feeling for material authenticity and material honesty as the basis of every typographic design."[*1]

In the common history of graphic design, it is often explained that escaping the ravages of World War II, Switzerland saw the emergence of a trend in graphic design in the 1950s and 1960s known as the "International Style," which was characterized by the use of sans-serif typefaces and grids, and was influenced by the pre-war modern design movement. Similar to the nature of Switzerland, however – a country with multiple cultures and languages – the reality was actually based on a variety of contexts.

One of the best known was the movement surrounding Zurich. Artists and designers such as Max Bill, Josef Müller-Brockmann and Richard Lohse had developed a rational modernism based on an awareness of industrialism and public nature. Another movement was occurring in the old cultural city of Basel. Students from all over the world had gathered at the AGS under the leadership of Emil Ruder and Armin Hoffmann, and the school had become "a place searching for living and rhythmical typography."[*2]

Fascinated by Ruder's typography, Schmid had asked personally and was allowed to study there as Ruder's personal student (i.e., not a regular student). From around 1960 to 1962, Schmid spent a few years riding his bicycle to Ruder's twice a week. After that, Schmid spent a year working as a layouter in Berlin as a substitute for military service, and then worked as a typesetter in Stockholm to earn money for his approaching studies in Basel.

Schmid eventually became an official student at the AGS in 1964, studying in the typography course under Ruder. The course was specifically designed for high-level typography and was only open to students who had both completed the foundation course as a typesetter and had practical experience. Schmid's encounters with his teachers, including Ruder, Robert Büchler (who taught typography at the school), Kurt Hauert (who taught lettering and drawing) and also the students he studied with, were a great source of inspiration, and he remained in contact with them throughout his life.

Wolfgang Weingart, in particular, became Schmid's lifelong friend and rival. While Schmid developed Ruder's typography, Weingart's graphic approach transcended conventional typographic means and greatly influenced postmodern typography after the 1980s. Discussion on typography between the two men, who respected each other despite their different directions, never ended.

Another noteworthy encounter would be with Axel Janås, the editor-in-chief of the trade journal *Grafisk Revy* in Stockholm, before Schmid officially entered the AGS. Schmid was given the opportunity to design covers and write articles for the magazine, which broadened his activities.

After graduating from the AGS, Schmid originally intended to work in Stockholm, but Ruder introduced him to Ernst Roch, a designer working in Montreal, Canada, for whom he would work as an assistant. The job at Roch's studio did not last long, however. While working as a freelancer in Vancouver on Canada's west coast, Schmid's mind had moved to his next destination: Japan.

[*1] Helmut Schmid, "Emil Ruder: Typography from the Inside," *Baseline,* No. 36, Bradbourne Publishing, 2002

[*2] Helmut Schmid, "Ruder typography, Ruder philosophy," *Idea,* No. 333, Seibundo Shinkosha, 2007

Helmut Schmid wurde am 1. Februar 1942 in Ferlach, der südlichsten Stadt Österreichs (damals unter deutscher Herrschaft), als ältester Sohn eines deutschen Grenzsoldaten und dessen Ehefrau geboren. 1957, als Schmid 15 Jahre alt war, wurde sein Vater nach Weil am Rhein versetzt, einer Kleinstadt am Ostufer des Rheins im Südwesten Deutschlands, an der Grenze zu Frankreich und der Schweiz. Schmid wurde Lehrling in einer Druckerei und begann, seinen Lebensunterhalt als Schriftsetzer zu verdienen.

Eines Tages im Jahr 1959 erregte eine Illustration, die er zufällig in einer Druckereifachzeitschrift sah, seine Aufmerksamkeit. Dabei handelte es sich um eine Glückwunschkarte zur Geburt eines Kindes, bei der alle Elemente, also Name, Geburtsdatum und Adresse, mit einer einfachen, aber unverwechselbaren Spannung räumlich angeordnet waren. Der Name des Gestalters war Emil Ruder.

Als Ruder 1942 an die Allgemeine Gewerbeschule (AGS, später Schule für Gestaltung Basel) kam, hatte er sich als progressiver Lehrer, Praktiker und Theoretiker der Typografie einen Namen gemacht. Er leitete ein Ausbildungsprogramm, das die Kreativität der Schriftsetzer förderte und darauf abzielte, «eine Typografie anzustreben, die unserer Zeit Ausdruck verleiht», «den Formalismus und die blosse Nachahmung früherer Epochen ablehnt» und «ein Gefühl für materielle Authentizität und Ehrlichkeit als Grundlage des typografischen Gestaltens zu wecken».[*1]

In der allgemeinen Geschichte des Grafikdesigns findet sich oft die Erklärung, dass in den 1950er und 1960er Jahren in der Schweiz, die den Verheerungen des Zweiten Weltkriegs entkommen war, ein Trend im Grafikdesign aufkam, der als «International Style» bekannt wurde. Dieser Stil zeichnete sich durch die Verwendung von serifenlosen Schrifttypen und Rastern aus und war von der modernen Designbewegung der Vorkriegszeit beeinflusst. Ähnlich dem Wesen der Schweiz – einem Land mit vielfältigen Kulturen und Sprachen – spielten in der Realität jedoch diverse Kontexte eine Rolle.

Zu den bekanntesten Einflüssen gehörte die Bewegung, die in Zürich stattfand. Künstler und Designer wie Max Bill, Josef Müller-Brockmann und Richard Lohse hatten einen rationalen Modernismus entwickelt, der auf einem Bewusstsein für den Industrialismus und die öffentliche Natur beruhte. Eine weitere Bewegung entstand in der alten Kulturstadt Basel. Studierende aus aller Welt kamen unter der Leitung von Emil Ruder und Armin Hoffmann zusammen und die Schule wurde zu einem «Ort, der eine lebendige und rhythmische Typografie anstrebte».[*2]

Schmid war fasziniert von Ruders Typografie und nachdem er persönlich vorgesprochen hatte, durfte er zwar nicht als regulärer Student, aber als Ruders persönlicher Schüler dort studieren. Von etwa 1960 bis 1962 fuhr Schmid zweimal wöchentlich mit dem Fahrrad zu Ruder. Danach verbrachte er im Rahmen des Wehrersatzdienstes ein Jahr als Layouter in Berlin und arbeitete anschliessend als Schriftsetzer in Stockholm, um Geld für sein bevorstehendes Studium in Basel zu verdienen.

1964 wurde Schmid schliesslich regulärer Student an der AGS und studierte Typografie unter der Leitung von Emil Ruder. Der Kurs war speziell auf Typografie auf hohem Leistungsniveau zugeschnitten und stand nur Studierenden offen, die sowohl den Grundkurs im Schriftsatz absolviert hatten, als auch über praktische Erfahrung verfügten. Schmids Begegnungen mit seinen Lehrern, darunter Ruder, Robert Büchler (der an der Schule Typografie unterrichtete) und Kurt Hauert (der Schrift und Zeichnen unterrichtete), aber auch mit seinen Kommilitoninnen und Kommilitonen, waren eine reiche Quelle der Inspiration, und er blieb zeitlebens mit ihnen in Kontakt.

Vor allem Wolfgang Weingart wurde für Schmid ein lebenslanger Freund und Rivale. Während Schmid die Typografie von Ruder weiterentwickelte, liess Weingart mit seinem grafischen Ansatz die konventionellen typografischen Methoden hinter sich und beeinflusste die postmoderne Typografie nach den 1980er Jahren massgeblich. Endlos waren die Diskussionen über Typografie, die die beiden Gestalter, die sich trotz ihrer unterschiedlichen Richtungen gegenseitig respektierten, miteinander führten.

Eine weitere bemerkenswerte Begegnung ergab sich mit Axel Janås, dem Chefredakteur der Fachzeitschrift *Grafisk Revy* in Stockholm, bevor Schmid offiziell das Studium an der AGS aufnahm. Schmid erhielt die Möglichkeit, für die Zeitschrift Titelseiten zu gestalten und Artikel zu schreiben, wodurch er sein Tätigkeitsspektrum erweiterte.

Ursprünglich wollte Schmid nach seinem Abschluss an der AGS in Stockholm arbeiten, aber Ruder stellte ihn Ernst Roch vor, einem im kanadischen Montreal tätigen Gestalter, für den er als Assistent arbeiten sollte. Der Job in Rochs Studio war jedoch nicht von langer Dauer. Während Schmid noch freiberuflich in Vancouver an Kanadas Westküste arbeitete, hatte er in Gedanken bereits sein nächstes Ziel im Visier: Japan.

Poster tower in the city (Basel, ca. 1965)

Plakatsäule in der Stadt (Basel, um 1965)

On Johanniter Bridge (Basel, ca. 1962)

Auf der Johanniterbrücke (Basel, um 1962)

[*1] Helmut Schmid, «Emil Ruder: Typography from the Inside», in: *Baseline*, Nr. 36, Bradbourne Publishing, 2002.

[*2] Helmut Schmid, «Ruder typography, Ruder philosophy», in: *Idea*, Nr. 333, Seibundo Shinkosha, 2007.

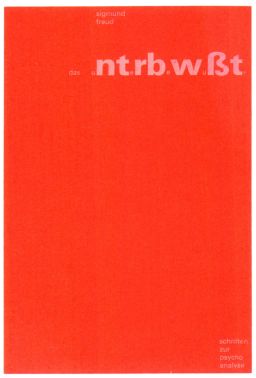
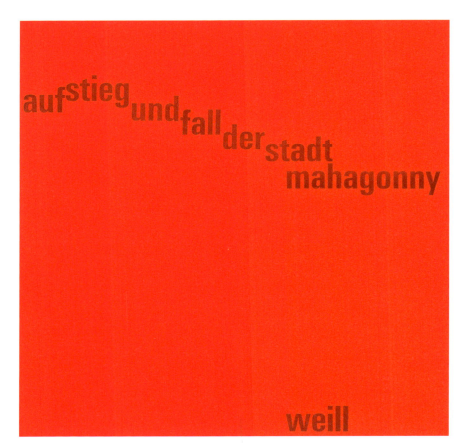

Book cover for *Das Unterbewusste*
(The Subconscious)
by Sigmund Freud
School assignment, 1964
136 × 208 mm

Buchcover für das Buch
Das Unterbewusste
von Sigmund Freud
Studienaufgabe, 1964

Record jacket for *Rise and Fall
of the City of Mahagonny*,
an opera by Kurt Weill
School assignment, 1964
208 × 208 mm

Schallplattenhülle für *Aufstieg und
Fall der Stadt Mahagonny*,
eine Oper von Kurt Weill
Studienaufgabe, 1964

Invitation card to a *Filmabend*
(film evening), an event of
the Printers' Association in Basel
School assignment, 1964
148 × 105 mm

Einladungskarte für einen Filmabend
der Drucker-Vereinigung in Basel
Studienaufgabe, 1964

"Rinner inte" (Doesn't run),
ad for a Swedish paint manufacturer
School assignment, 1964
208 × 208 mm

«Rinner inte» (Rinnt nicht),
Werbeanzeige für einen
schwedischen Farbenproduzenten
Studienaufgabe, 1964

Büchler was a generous teacher who often allowed students of the typography class to design posters for the Gewerbemuseum Basel (Museum of Crafts and Design). That is how my first (and until now last) two posters appeared on the Swiss poster site, *Kunstkredit 64* and *Shakespeare and German theater*.

    I put forward two proposals for the *Kunstkredit 64* poster, which Büchler then presented to the director, Mr. Grünigen. (At the time the post of director of the Basel school was announced, it was also the time of the awakening of typography in Basel, even before the palace revolution took place). To my disappointment, the director decided in favor of my traditionally designed poster.
(*TM,* No. 3, 2007)

Poster for the exhibition
Shakespeare und das deutsche Theater
(Shakespeare and German theater)
School assignment in actual use, 1965
905 × 1280 mm

Plakat für die Ausstellung
Shakespeare und das deutsche Theater
Studienaufgabe (tatsächlich verwendet),
1965

Büchler war ein grosszügiger Lehrer, der Plakataufträge für das Gewerbemuseum Basel oft von Schülern der typografischen Gestaltungsklasse ausführen liess. So kam auch ich zu meinen zwei ersten (und bis jetzt letzten) Plakaten an der Schweizer Plakatwand, Kunstkredit 1964 und Shakespeare und das deutsche Theater.

Für das Plakat Kunstkredit schuf ich zwei Versionen, die Büchler der Direktion, Herrn von Grüningen, präsentierte. (Um diese Zeit war die Stelle des Direktors der Basler Schule ausgeschrieben. Es war auch die Zeit des Aufbruchs der Typografie in Basel, die noch vor der Palastrevolution einsetzte.) Zu meiner Enttäuschung entschied sich die AGS-Direktion für mein klassisch gestaltetes Plakat.
(*TM*, Nr. 3, 2007)

Poster for *Kunstkredit 64* exhibition
School assignment, 1964

Poster for *Kunstkredit 64* exhibition
School assignment in actual use, 1964
905 × 1280 mm

Plakat für die Ausstellung
Kunstkredit 64
Studienaufgabe, 1964

Plakat für die Ausstellung
Kunstkredit 64
Studienaufgabe
(tatsächlich verwendet), 1964

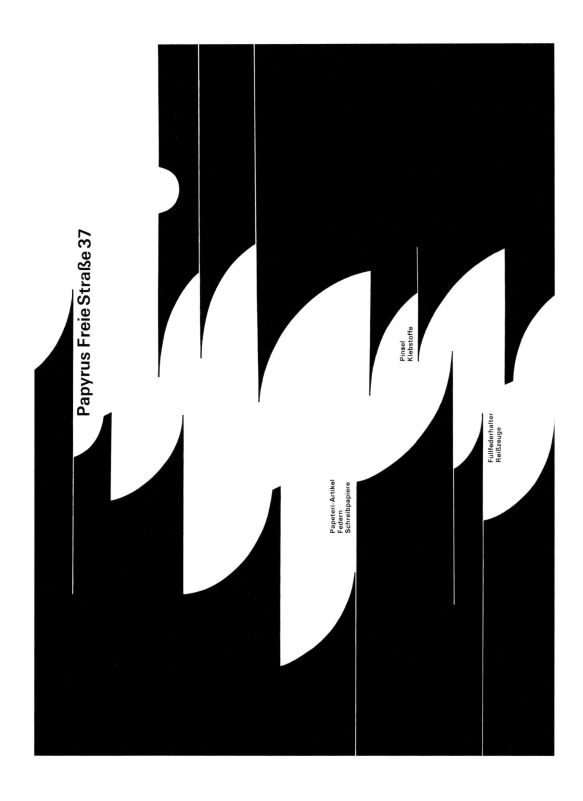

Poster for Papyrus,
stationery store in Basel
School assignment, 1964
A4

Plakat für Papyrus,
ein Schreibwarengeschäft in Basel
Studienaufgabe, 1964

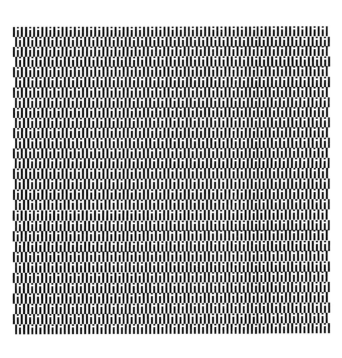

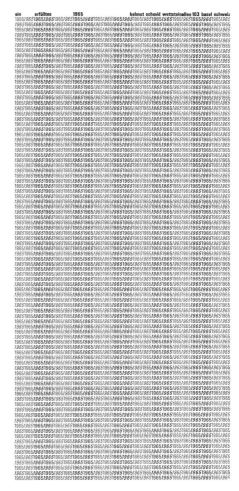

Poster for children's traffic week
School assignment, 1964
A4

Plakat für den Kinder-Verkehrsgarten
Studienaufgabe, 1964

i
School assignment, 1964
279 × 279 mm

i
Studienaufgabe, 1964

New Year's card, 1965
91 × 205 mm

Neujahrskarte, 1965

g	r a	p h	i s
		Internationale Monatsschrift für freie Graphik Gebrauchsgraphik und Dekoration	International monthly for Graphic and applied art
1964 No 5 6		Januar Februar März	January February March
		1. Jahrgang	Volume 1
		Herausgeber Dr. Walter Amstutz Walter Herdeg	Editiors Dr. Walter Amstutz Walter Herdig

		Index	
3	Dr. E. Wartmann	Edvard Munch, der Grafiker	Edvard Munch as a Graphic Artist
28	Serge Brignoni	Masken der Primitiven	Masks among Primitive Peoples
42	Hans Kasser	Gute Schweizer Plakate 1944	Good Swiss Posters 1944
51		Hauszeitschriften	Periodical Pamphlets and Internal Bulletins
59	Dr. Albert Baur	Giambattista Bodoni	
67		Die Basler Mustermesse als Experimentierfeld der Dekorateure	Decorative Experiment at the Basle Industries Fair
75	Hans Kasser	Eugen Haefelfinger, Papierplastiken	Paper Sculptures
95		Verschiedenes	Miscellaneous
97		Bücherchronik	Books
107		Ausstellungskalender	Exhibitions
		Umschlag dieser Nummer von Edvard Munch	Cover of this number by Edvard Munch
	Commentaire français voir Page 87-88		
		Aus dem Inhalt der nächsten zwei Nummern	Features from the next two numbers
	Dr. Erwin Grabmann	Maillol als Zeichner	Maillol as a Draughtsman
	A. Bruckner	Schweizerische Fahnen	Swiss Flags
		Alte Hotelwerbung	Hotel Advertising, Old Style
	Hans Kasser	Der Buchschutzumschlag	Dust Covers
		Photo und Graphiker zu den Arbeiten von Werner Bischof	The Artist and Photographer Wetner Bischof
	Dr. Hans Blösch	Gauklerplakate	Hand-bills of Town Fairs
	Karl Egender	Die Schweiz wirbt im Ausland	Swiss Tourist Propaganda Abroad
	Hans Kasser	Theater und Werbung	The Theatre and its Appeal to the Public
	Dr. Hans Strahm	Ein mittelalterliches Fabelbuch	A Medieval Book of Fables
		Der Zeitungskopf	The Newspaper Heading
	Dr. Albert Baur	Japanische Streichholzschachteln	Japanese Matchboxes
		E. J. Wolfensberger Vorkämpfer des Schweizer Künstlerplakates	E. J. Wolfsberger and his Work for the Swiss Art Poster

Published by
Amstutz & Herdeg
Graphis Press
Zürich 45 Switzerland
Nüschelerstrasse
Telephon 271215
Telegramme
Arherd Zürich
Postcheck VII 23071

Contents page of *Graphis* in two languages
School assignment, 1964
207 × 280 mm

Inhaltsverzeichnis von *Graphis* in zwei Sprachen
Studienaufgabe, 1964

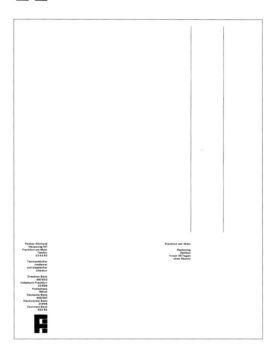

Logo and invoice
for Fischer-Bücherei
School assignment, 1964
215 × 280 mm

Logo und Rechnungsbogen
für Fischer-Bücherei
Studienaufgabe, 1964

Letterhead for *Grafisk Revy*
Swedish Association of Bookbinders /
Typographers, 1965
A4

Briefkopf für die Zeitschrift *Grafisk Revy*
Schwedischer Verband der
Drucker und Buchbinder, 1965

Cover for *Grafisk Revy*
(not used), 1965
A4

Titel für *Grafisk Revy*
(nicht verwendet), 1965

Experiment with wooden type *S*
School assignment, 1964

Experiment mit einem
hölzernen Buchstaben S
Studienaufgabe, 1964

Das Schweigen

Ingmar Bergmans
gewagtester Film

mit
Gunnel Lindblom
Ingrid Thulin
Birger Malmsten
Hakan Jahnberg
Jörgen Lindström

‹Der Schock,
die Provokation,
der Skandal
dieses Films
rütteln wach,
auch den,
der vielleicht
aus falscher
Spekulation
ins Kino gerät›
film-dienst

Cinema Royal
Basel
Telefon 25 44 21

Newspaper ad series for
Ingmar Bergman's *The Silence*
School assignment, 1964
279 × 208 mm

Serie von Zeitungsanzeigen für
Ingmar Bergmans Film *Das Schweigen*
Studienaufgabe, 1964

Gunnel Lindblom
Ingrid Thulin
Birger Malmsten
Hakan Jahnberg
Jörgen Lindström

in Ingmar Bergmans
gewagtestem Film

Das Schweigen

‹Der Schock,
die Provokation,
der Skandal
dieses Films
rütteln wach,
auch den,
der vielleicht
aus falscher
Spekulation
ins Kino gerät›
film-dienst

Cinema Royal
Basel
Telefon 25 44 21

‹Der Schock,
die Provokation,
der Skandal
dieses Films
rütteln wach,
auch den,
der vielleicht
aus falscher
Spekulation
ins Kino gerät›
film-dienst

Ingmar Bergmans
gewagtester Film

Das Schweigen

mit
Gunnel Lindblom
Ingrid Thulin
Birger Malmsten
Hakan Jahnberg
Jörgen Lindström

Cinema Royal
Basel
Telefon 25 44 21

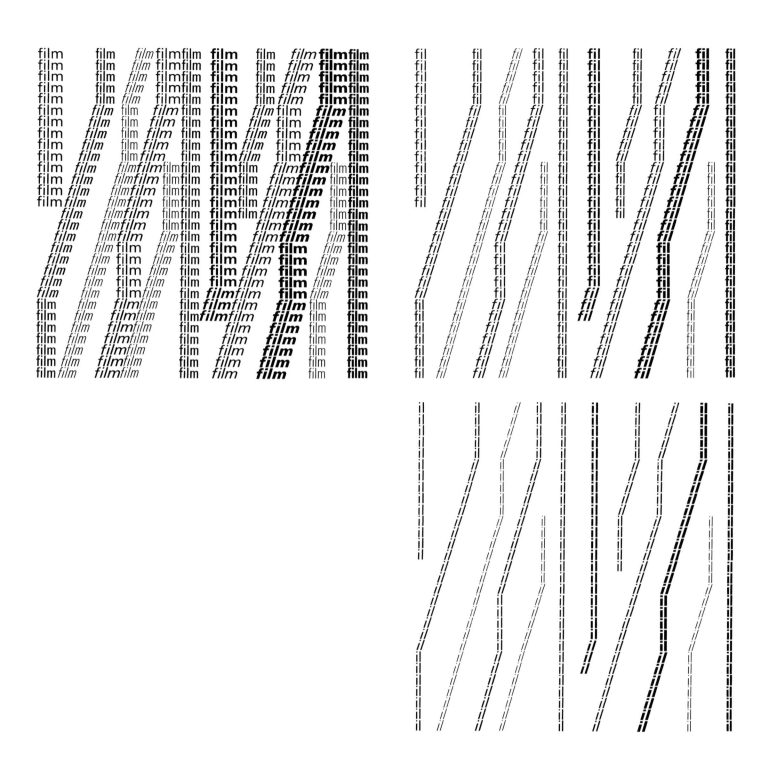

Experimental booklet visualizing the kinetic effect of film. 11 out of 21 fonts of the typeface Univers (Univers 47, 48, 57, 58, 67, 55, 56, 65, 66, 75, 76) are used to replicate movement. The kinetic effect is stressed by reducing the word to its smallest component, the dot on the *i*.
(*Typography Today*, New Edition)

Experimentelle Broschüre, die den kinetischen Effekt von Film visualisiert. 11 von den 21 Varianten des Univers-Schriftbilds (Univers 47, 48, 57, 58, 67, 55, 56, 65, 66, 75, 76) werden genutzt, um Bewegung auszudrücken. Der kinetische Effekt wird betont durch die Reduzierung des Worts auf die kleinste Komponente, den Punkt auf dem «i».
(*Typography Today*, neue Ausgabe)

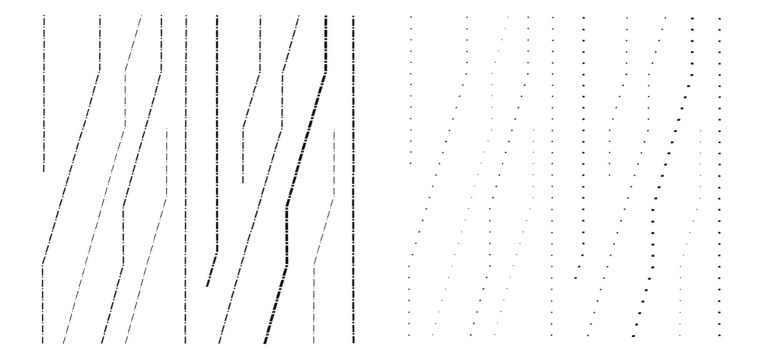

Kinetic / Film
School assignment, 1964
233 × 239 mm

Kinetik / Film
Studienaufgabe, 1964

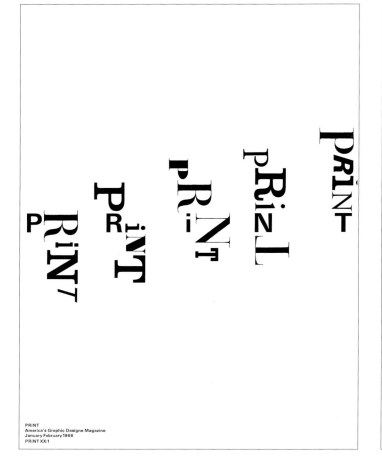

One project in the typography class under Emil Ruder was the designing of a series.
We could select the subject ourselves. Since I intended to try design in the world,
I chose to design covers for *Print*, the American bimonthly design magazine. The six themes selected for interpretation were: typeface, type size, type change, form and counter form, embossed, color. To stress the continuation of the series, the name *Print* remains in the same position, while the themes are interwoven.

"Typefaces" (January/February) makes use of the many available typefaces in the composing room of the Basel school. This will prove all those ignorant design critics wrong who maintain that Basel used only sans serif. There never existed any restriction on typefaces.

"Type change" (May/June) uses the large wooden letters that were available for designing posters. They were printed in the printing room in letterpress.

"Form and counterform" (September/October): Emil Ruder showed and explained this cover, intensified by cropping, in his magnum opus *Typography* on page 60:
"The line print is reduced to the internal spaces which are enclosed by a large quantity of black. In this way the white effect has been intensified to the limits of the optically tolerable."
(*Newwork Magazine*, No. 6, 2010)

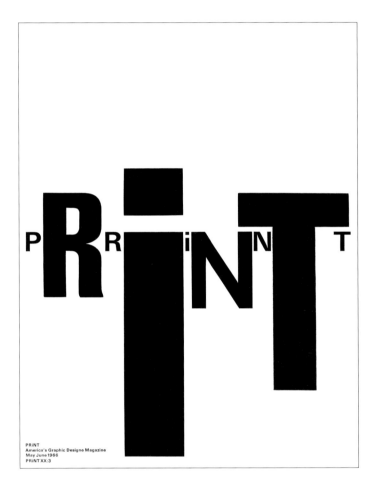
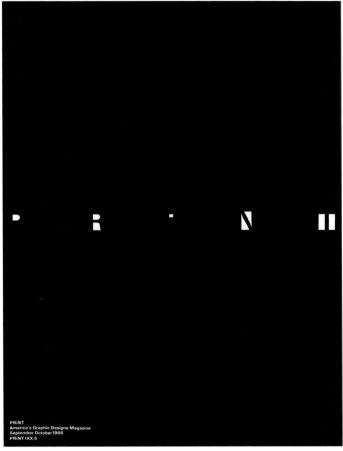

Eines der Projekte im Bereich Typografie unter Emil Ruder war die Gestaltung einer Serie. Das Thema konnten wir selbst wählen. Da ich etwas mit internationalem Design versuchen wollte, habe ich mich für die Gestaltung der Titel für das amerikanische zweimonatig erscheinende Designmagazin Print entschieden. Die für die Interpretation gewählten sechs Themen: Schrifttype, Schriftgrösse, Schriftwechsel, Form, Prägung, Farbe. Um die Fortsetzung der Serie zu betonen, bleibt der Name Print immer an der gleichen Stelle, während die Themen verflochten sind.

«Schrifttypen» (Januar/Februar) nutzt die vielen in der Setzerei der Gewerbeschule Basel vorhandenen Schrifttypen. Das allein demonstriert die Unwissenheit der Kritiker, die meinen, dass Basel nur serifenlose Schriften verwendet. Diese Restriktion hat es nie gegeben.

«Schriftwechsel» (Mai/Juni) benutzt grosse Holzbuchstaben aus dem Handsatz für Plakate, die in der Druckerei der Gewerbeschule gedruckt wurden.

«Form und Gegenform» (September/Oktober). Emil Ruder zeigte und erklärte diesen Umschlag auf Seite 60 in seinem Werk Typogrphie: «Die Schriftreihe ist auf die Zwischenräume reduziert und umrandet mit viel Schwarz. Auf diese Weise wird der weisse Effekt bis an die Grenze des optisch Akzeptablen intensiviert.»
(Newwork Magazin, Nr. 6, 2010)

Cover for *Print*,
American graphic design magazine
School assignment, 1964
220 × 300 mm

Titel für *Print*,
eine amerikanische Grafikdesignzeitschrift
Studienaufgabe, 1964

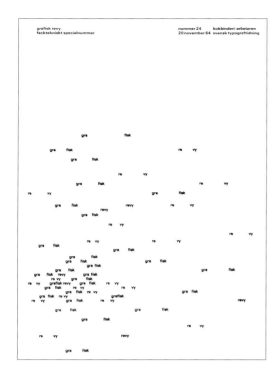
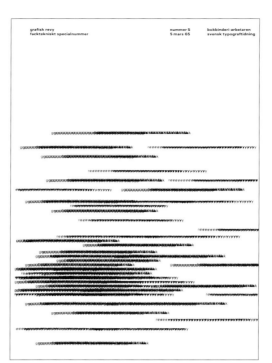
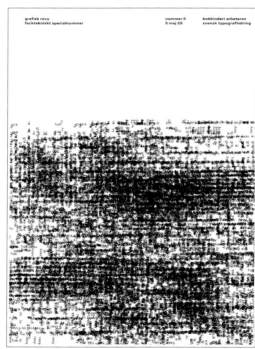
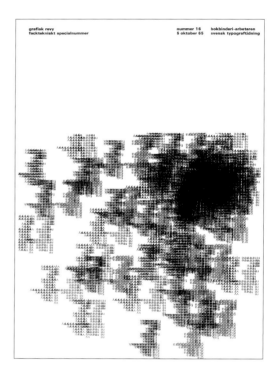

Cover for *Grafisk Revy*
No. 24, 1964,
No. 5, No. 9, No. 16, 1965
A4

Titel für *Grafisk Revy*
Nr. 24, 1964,
Nr. 5, Nr. 9, Nr. 16, 1965

Cover for *Grafisk Revy*
No. 24, 1965

Titel für *Grafisk Revy*
Nr. 24, 1965

Point Line Movement: Covers for *Grafisk Revy*
Grafisk Revy was published between 1960 and 1972 by the professional associations of the Swedish bookbinders and typographers. A4 in size, 20 issues annually, four of them as special issues.

Axel Janås, the editor and publisher responsible, shaped the content and appearance in a program of technically oriented and politically motivated information. A trained compositor, Janås followed with keen interest the revolutionary developments in printing techniques, and was also interested in typography.

I was living in Stockholm from 1963 to 1964 and during that time began a collaboration of continuous sincerity with an openminded, always helpful editor. For my first meeting with him I prepared three cover designs and left the editorial office with three covers accepted. Through Axel Janås and *Grafisk Revy*, I was able to work in Sweden in typography, before risking an involvement with Switzerland's *Typographische Monatsblätter*.

The cover series for the special issues of *Grafisk Revy* 1965 to 1966 originated in 1964 during my second study visit to the Basel school in Switzerland. They are practical applications of elementary theme exercises in typography under Robert Büchler. Using the name of the magazine, the covers illustrate the four dimensions: dot (dimensionless), line, plane, space, and movement, as well as variations such as horizontal–vertical or diagonal.

The covers took shape through direct proofing on the hand press in the school's composing room, where the typematter was progressively moved in several directions. The prints can be described as controlled coincidences with rhythmically positioned dots, longer and shorter lines, open and congested areas, static and movement.

Not only had the covers to pass up to 43 times through the press, but the typematter had to be set in a particular manner, in order to visualize the themes. It was not simply a case of moving the typematter a bit here and there in the press and waiting until something interesting happened, but a search for contemporary expression in typography.
(*Typographic Reflections 2*)

Punkt Linie Bewegung: Umschläge für *Grafisk Revy*
Grafisk Revy wurde zwischen 1960 und 1972 von den schwedischen Berufsverbänden der Buchbinder und Typografen herausgegeben. Format A4, zwanzig Hefte pro Jahr, vier davon als fachtechnische Nummern.

Axel Janås, Redakteur und verantwortlicher Herausgeber, prägte Inhalt und Aussehen in einem Programm von fachlich-bewachender und politisch-motivierender Information. Janås, der gelernte Setzer, verfolgte die revolutionierende Entwicklung in der grafischen Industrie sorgfältig und interessierte sich auch für typografische Gestaltung.

1963/64 hielt ich mich in Stockholm auf, und in dieser Zeit begann eine Zusammenarbeit von anhaltender Aufrichtigkeit mit einem aufgeschlossenen, immer hilfsbereiten Redakteur. Zur ersten Begegnung brachte ich drei Umschlagentwürfe mit und ich verliess die Redaktion mit drei akzeptierten Umschlägen. Durch Axel Janås und *Grafisk Revy* konnte ich mich in Schweden typografisch betätigen, noch bevor ich mich an die *Typographischen Monatsblätter* in der Schweiz wagte.

Die Umschlagserie für die fachtechnischen Nummern der *Grafisk Revy* 1965/66 entstanden 1964 während meines zweiten Studienaufenthalts an der Basler Schule. Es sind praktische Anwendungen von im Fach Typografie unter Robert Büchler erarbeiteten elementaren Themen. Die Umschläge schildern mit dem Namen der Zeitschrift die vier Dimensionen: Punkt (dimensionslos), Linie, Fläche, Raum und Bewegung sowie Variationen wie horizontal–vertikal oder diagonal.

Die Umschläge nahmen Gestalt an durch direkte Abzüge mit der Handpresse in der Setzerei der Schule. Druckformen wurden progressiv in verschiedene Richtungen verschoben. Die Drucke sind beschreibbar als kontrollierte Zufälle mit rhythmisch platzierten Punkten, mit längeren und kürzeren Linien, mit offenen und gedrängten Flächen, mit lesbarer und unlesbarer Schrift, mit Statik und Bewegung.

Die Umschläge mussten nicht nur bis zu 43-mal durch die Handpresse, sondern es mussten zuerst Basisformen erarbeitet und gesetzt werden, mit denen sich die Themen darstellen liessen. Es war nicht ein die Druckform ein wenig in der Presse herumschieben und warten, bis etwas Interessantes passiert, sondern es war ein Suchen nach dem zeitgemässen Ausdruck in Typografie.
(*Typographische Reflexionen 2*)

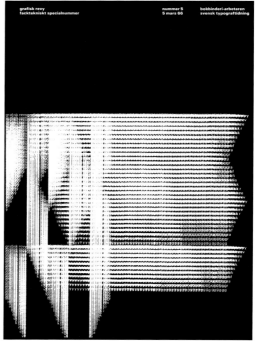

Cover for *Grafisk Revy*
No. 24, 1965
No. 5, 1966

Titel für *Grafisk Revy*
Nr. 24, 1965
Nr. 5, 1966

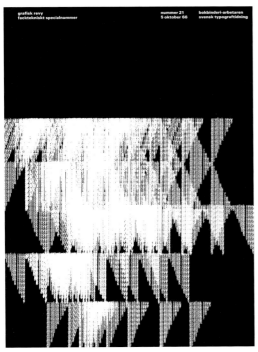

Cover for *Grafisk Revy*
No. 9, No. 21, No. 24, 1966

Titel für *Grafisk Revy*
Nr. 9, Nr. 21, Nr. 24, 1966

Cover for *Format*,
a Canadian design journal
Society of Typographic Designers
of Canada, 1965
A4

Titel für *Format*,
eine kanadische Designzeitschrift
Society of Typographic Designers
of Canada, 1965

Calendar
Hoffmann-La Roche (Montreal), 1965
149 × 148 mm

Kalender
Hoffmann-La Roche (Montreal), 1965

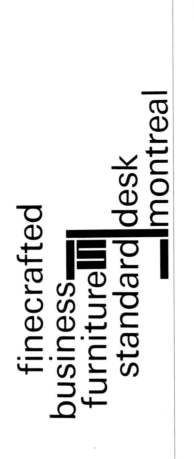

Magazine ad for furniture maker
Logo: Ernst Roch
Standard Desk, 1965
A4

Zeitschriftenanzeige für einen Möbelproduzenten
Logo: Ernst Roch
Standard Desk, 1965

Cover for *Graphische Revue Österreichs*, No. 5/6, 1965
Gewerkschaft der Arbeiter der Graphischen und Papierverarbeitenden Gewerbe, 1965
230 × 323 mm

Titel für *Graphische Revue Österreichs*, Nr. 5/6, 1965
Gewerkschaft der Arbeiter der Graphischen und Papierverarbeitenden Gewerbe, 1965

Cover for *Graphische Revue Osterreichs*, No. 5/6, 1966

Titel für *Graphische Revue Österreichs*, Nr. 5/6, 1966

New Year's greeting from Montreal
Typeface: New Alphabet, 1966
93 × 211 mm

Neujahrsgrüsse aus Montreal
Schrift: New Alphabet, 1966

After World War II, the word "design" had become central to capitalist society, and the ideas surrounding modern design in the early twentieth century had been applied and developed further into a discipline for designing visual information in a society where there was rapid development in the area of communication media. The name "International Style," which had been given to typography in the 1950s and 1960s, symbolized the role that Swiss graphic design had played in this trend.

In the postwar reconstruction of Japan, designers and businesspeople had begun to recognize the importance of design, and had started taking various steps that would establish the field of design in Japanese society. In the manufacturing industry especially, with its ties to the international market, it had become a priority to raise the level of design in products and marketing-related areas to the same level as Western countries.

2
in the internationalization of design:
challenges at NIA

Internationalisierung des Designs:
Herausforderungen
bei der NIA

Nach dem Zweiten Weltkrieg war das Wort «Design» zu einem zentralen Begriff in der kapitalistischen Gesellschaft geworden. Die Ideen des modernen Designs des frühen 20. Jahrhunderts wurden umgesetzt und weiterentwickelt zu einer Wissenschaft für die Gestaltung visueller Informationen in einer Gesellschaft, in der eine rasante Entwicklung im Bereich der Kommunikationsmedien stattfand. Die Bezeichnung «International Style», die der Typografie in den 1950er und 1960er Jahren gegeben wurde, steht für die Rolle, die das Schweizer Grafikdesign bei dieser Entwicklung gespielt hatte.

Im Zuge des Wiederaufbaus Japans nach dem Krieg hatten Designer und Geschäftsleute allmählich die Bedeutung von Design erkannt und unternahmen verschiedene Schritte, um das Thema Design in der japanischen Gesellschaft zu etablieren. Insbesondere in der verarbeitenden Industrie mit ihren Verbindungen zum internationalen Markt war es zu einer vorrangigen Aufgabe geworden, das Design für Produkte und im Marketing auf das Niveau westlicher Länder anzuheben.

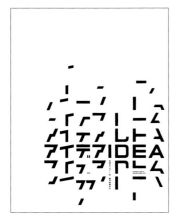

Cover proposal for *Idea*, 1966

Titelvorschlag für *Idea*, 1966

Cover for *Idea*, No. 78
Seibundo Shinkosha, 1966
225 × 297 mm

Titel für *Idea*, Nr. 78
Seibundo Shinkosha, 1966

It was in the midst of this era that Schmid set his sights on Japan, though it was Emil Ruder who initially sparked Schmid's interest. In explaining the aesthetics of asymmetric typography, Ruder cited Tenshin Okakura's writing, *The Book of Tea*, and found deep similarities between asymmetric typography and the aesthetics of the East. It was only natural that Schmid's interest in further exploring Basel's typography should lead him to Japan.

It was when he was working in Montreal that his interest grew into actions. Schmid saw a greeting card from Hiroshi Ohchi, a Japanese art director, that had been delivered to the Roch design office where he was working at the time. Ohchi was the first art director of *Idea* magazine, which began circulation in 1953, and through his journalistic activities he was in contact with the international graphic design community.

After moving to Vancouver, Schmid picked up *Idea* for the first time at the city library and tried to contact Ohchi and other leading designers of the time – names such as Hiromu Hara, Ikko Tanaka, and Ryuichi Yamashiro – to see if there was any place that would hire him to work in Japan while he learned about Japanese characters and culture.

At the time, Japan was in the midst of an era of rapid economic growth after the 1964 Tokyo Olympics, which had become a symbol of postwar reconstruction. Even now, the design of the Olympics is still talked about as a glowing achievement of modern graphic design in Japan, but it was also a time when the professional field of design was beginning to receive a great deal of attention from society. In 1965, the *Persona* exhibition was held by young designers from the postwar generation, including Ikko Tanaka and Tadanori Yokoo; this signaled the arrival of an era of diversification in design culture.

Even so, it was not easy to find a Japanese company that could meet Schmid's demands. He did, however, receive a very welcome reply from Hiroshi Ohchi. Ohchi explained how it happened in the pages of *Idea*.

"Later I received a letter from him, requesting me to have a look at a large collection of his work, and also to introduce him to an employer in Japan, where he wished to study Japanese type and characters. No enterprise in Japan, I was afraid, could afford him such a chance. So it seemed very difficult to grant his wish. But I felt his passion, and saw the truth in his works, and I hoped that Japanese type and its new typographic frontiers could be brought to life by the talent and passion of a man like Schmid, who sees typography as a vocation and is devoted to the field, rather than other busy Japanese graphic designers. I tried every available means to invite him to Japan, with the result that he was contracted to work for Nakamoto International Agency (NIA) for two years, and also given the chance at Japanese typography."
(Hiroshi Ohchi, "Helmut Schmid, Young Designer of Typography,"
Idea, No. 78, Seibundo Shinkosha, 1966 [original text modified by the editor])

In other words, Ohchi had sensed the need to develop the field of typography in Japan, and he thought that inviting Schmid would be a plus for the Japanese design community. He also introduced many of his past activities in the pages of *Idea*.

Reality however, is not something that can be managed by wishes alone. Schmid's visit to Japan was also the result of luck and timing. NIA, the recipient of Schmid's visit, was a new design agency founded in 1964 by Tadao Nakamoto, president of the long-established Osaka printing company and advertising agency Yarakasukan (now YRK&), who had brought many young designers together from abroad with the aim of producing high-quality international designs. Schmid's inquiry came at a time when one of the company's designers was looking for a successor to return to his home country. Moreover, the designers who reviewed the proposal had an eye for understanding Schmid's past work and career.

Thus, Schmid came to Japan on June 3, 1966, at the age of 24. What Schmid witnessed on arrival was a hectic Japan during a heightened economic period. Soon after, in 1968, Japan's GNP surpassed that of West Germany to become the second largest in the world, and in 1970, the Japan World Exposition was held in Osaka under the theme of "Progress and Harmony for Mankind." Working side by side with young designers from various countries, Schmid created numerous product logos, advertisements, packages and booklets for companies such as Sanyo Electric, Taiho Pharmaceutical and Otsuka Pharmaceutical. He was also involved in the graphics for the Sanyo Pavilion at the Osaka World Exposition.

Genau zu dieser Zeit richtete Schmid sein Augenmerk auf Japan, wobei es anfänglich Emil Ruder zu verdanken war, dass Schmids Interesse daran geweckt wurde. Als Ruder die Ästhetik der asymmetrischen Typografie erläuterte, zitierte er Tenshin Okakuras Werk *The Book of Tea* und stellte grosse Ähnlichkeiten zwischen der asymmetrischen Typografie und der Ästhetik des Ostens fest. So war es nur natürlich, dass Schmids Interesse an der weiteren Erforschung der Basler Typografie ihn nach Japan führte.

Als Schmid in Montreal arbeitete, wurde aus reinem Interesse konkretes Handeln. Er sah eine Grusskarte von Hiroshi Ohchi, einem japanischen Art Director, die an das Designbüro von Roch, in dem er zu der damaligen Zeit arbeitete, geschickt worden war. Ohchi war der erste Art Director der ab 1953 erscheinenden Zeitschrift *Idea*, und durch seine journalistische Tätigkeit stand er in Kontakt mit der internationalen Grafikdesign-Community.

Nach seinem Umzug nach Vancouver besorgte sich Schmid in der Stadtbibliothek zum ersten Mal die Zeitschrift *Idea* und nahm Kontakt zu Ohchi und anderen führenden Gestaltern der damaligen Zeit auf, wie Hiromu Hara, Ikko Tanaka und Ryuichi Yamashiro, um auszuloten, ob jemand ihn während seines Studiums der japanischen Kultur und Schriftzeichen in Japan anstellen würde.

Nach den Olympischen Spielen 1964 in Tokio, die zu einem Symbol des Wiederaufbaus nach dem Krieg geworden waren, befand sich Japan inmitten einer Ära rasanten Wirtschaftswachstums. Noch heute wird das Design der Olympiade als glanzvolle Errungenschaft des modernen Grafikdesigns in Japan bezeichnet, aber es war auch eine Zeit, in der der Berufszweig des Grafikdesigns immer grössere Aufmerksamkeit in der Gesellschaft erlangte. 1965 veranstalteten junge Designer der Nachkriegsgeneration, darunter Ikko Tanaka und Tadanori Yokoo, die Ausstellung *Persona*; diese war der Auftakt für eine Ära der Diversifizierung in der Designkultur.

Dennoch war es nicht leicht, eine japanische Firma zu finden, die Schmids Anforderungen erfüllte. Von Hiroshi Ohchi erhielt er aber eine sehr warmherzige Antwort; im Magazin *Idea* erzählt Ohchi, wie es dazu kam:

At NIA with colleagues
(Osaka, 1966)

Mit Kollegen und Kolleginnen bei der NIA (Osaka, 1966)

«Später erhielt ich einen Brief von ihm, in dem er mich bat, eine grosse Sammlung seiner Arbeiten zu begutachten und ihn bei einem Arbeitgeber in Japan vorzustellen, wo er japanische Schriftzeichen studieren wollte. Ich befürchtete, dass kein Unternehmen in Japan ihm eine solche Chance bieten könnte. Es schien also sehr schwierig, seinem Wunsch zu entsprechen. Aber ich spürte seine Leidenschaft und sah die Wahrheit in seinen Werken, und ich hoffte, dass die japanische Schrift und ihre neuen typografischen Grenzen zum Leben erweckt werden könnten durch das Talent und die Leidenschaft eines Mannes wie Schmid, der die Typografie als Berufung sieht und sich diesem Gebiet mehr als die anderen vielbeschäftigten japanischen Grafikdesigner widmet. Ich habe also mit allen Mitteln versucht, ihn nach Japan einzuladen, mit dem Ergebnis, dass er für zwei Jahre bei der Nakamoto International Agency (NIA) unter Vertrag genommen wurde und die Chance bekam, japanische Typografie zu studieren.»
(Hiroshi Ohchi, «Helmut Schmid, Young Designer of Typography»,
in: *Idea*, Nr. 78, Seibundo Shinkosha, 1966 [Originaltext vom Herausgeber angepasst])

Mit anderen Worten, Ohchi hatte die Notwendigkeit erkannt, den Bereich der Typografie in Japan weiterzuentwickeln, und er dachte, dass es für die japanische Grafikdesign-Community ein Gewinn sein würde, Schmid einzuladen. So stellte er in der Zeitschrift *Idea* auch viele von Schmids vergangenen Arbeiten vor.

Die Realität lässt sich jedoch nicht durch Wunschdenken allein steuern. Vielmehr war es das Ergebnis von Glück und gutem Timing, dass Schmid Japan besuchen konnte. Die NIA, bei der Schmid unterkam, war eine neue Designagentur, die 1964 von Tadao Nakamoto, dem Präsidenten der alteingesessenen Druckerei und Werbeagentur Yarakasukan (heute YRK&) in Osaka, gegründet worden war. Tadao Nakamoto hatte viele junge Gestalter aus dem Ausland geholt mit dem Ziel, internationale, hochwertige Designs herzustellen. Schmids Anfrage kam zu einem Zeitpunkt, als einer der Designer des Unternehmens aufgrund seiner geplanten Rückkehr in sein Heimatland nach einem Nachfolger suchte. Darüber hinaus hatten die Designer, die Schmids Bewerbung prüften, ein Auge für Schmids Arbeiten und vermochten seine Qualifikation einzuschätzen.

So kam Schmid am 3. Juni 1966 im Alter von 24 Jahren nach Japan. Bei seiner Ankunft erlebte er ein geschäftiges Land in einer Zeit des wirtschaftlichen Aufschwungs. Bald darauf, im Jahr 1968, übertraf Japans Bruttosozialprodukt das der Bundesrepublik Deutsch-land und wurde zum zweitgrössten der Welt. 1970 schliesslich wurde in Osaka die Weltausstellung unter dem Motto «Fortschritt und Harmonie für die Menschheit» veranstaltet. In Zusammenarbeit mit jungen Designern aus verschiedenen Ländern entwarf Schmid zahlreiche Produktlogos, Werbeanzeigen, Verpackungen und Broschüren für Unternehmen wie Sanyo Electric und die beiden Pharmaunternehmen Taiho Pharmaceuticals und Otsuka Pharmaceuticals. Er war auch am Grafikdesign für den Sanyo Pavillon auf der Weltausstellung in Osaka beteiligt.

**With Ivor Kaplin and Sumi Schmid
(Sumiko Tanaka) at NIA**
(Osaka, 1970)

Mit Ivor Kaplin und Sumi Schmid (Sumiko Tanaka) bei der NIA (Osaka, 1970)

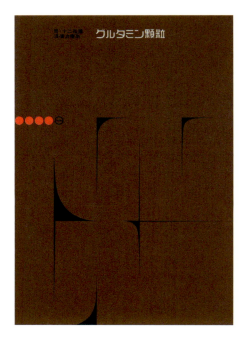
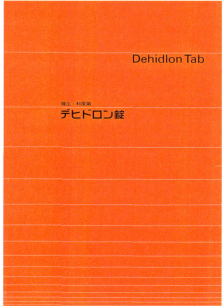

Brochures of ethical pharmaceuticals
Taiho Pharmaceutical, 1967
153 × 226 mm

Broschüren für ethische Pharmazeutika
Taiho Pharmaceutical, 1967

Magazine ad for Glutamine Granules
Taiho Pharmaceutical, 1967
220 × 280 mm

Zeitschriftenanzeige für Glutamingranulat
Taiho Pharmaceutical, 1967

Cover for the promotional
magazine *4527* (yokozuna)
No. 1, No. 3, No. 6, No. 7
Taiho Pharmaceutical, 1967
220 × 280 mm
Photo: Kenji Narumiya

Titel für die Werbezeitschrift
4527 (yokozuna)
Taiho Pharmaceutical, 1967
Foto: Kenji Narumiya

Logotype of *4527*
Taiho Pharmaceutical, 1967

Logo für *4527*
Taiho Pharmaceutical, 1967

Packaging of Ambezim Injection
Taiho Pharmaceutical, 1966
154 × 154 × 73 mm

Verpackung für Ambezim Injection
Taiho Pharmaceutical, 1966

Magazine ad for Neophagen
As always, there were stipulations, there were expectations.
I had an idea and thought about a model: about the waitress from the cafe next door
with a face like one of Utamaro's woodcuts. We took a photo and over the soft-focus photo
I repeated the three differently spaced headlines in red.
　　For me it was an advertisement where everything worked – the idea, the typography,
the photo, the model. I presented the advertisement. I advertised for the ad (secretly for the model).
I advertised in vain...
　　Afterwards I printed the advertisement at my own expense and showed the printed ad
without any expectations. The result: the advertisement was accepted and appeared
(with additional product information) over many months.
(HQ, No. 30, 1994)

Zeitschriftenanzeige für Neophagen
Wie immer – es gab keine Vorgaben, es gab Erwartungen. Ich hatte eine Idee und dachte an
ein Modell – an die Bedienung vom Café nebenan mit einem Gesicht wie aus Utamaros Holzschnitten.
Wir machten ein Foto, und über das in Softfokus belichtete Mädchengesicht repetierte ich
die Schlagzeilen in drei unterschiedlichen Spationierungen in Rot.
　　Für mich war es eine Anzeige, bei der alles stimmte – die Idee, die Typografie,
das Foto, das Modell. Ich präsentierte die Anzeige. Ich warb für die Anzeige (insgeheim für das Modell).
Ich warb vergebens ...
　　Ich habe die Anzeige dann auf meine Kosten drucken lassen und so nebenbei, also ganz ohne
irgendwelche Erwartungen, vorgezeigt. Resultat: Sie wurde akzeptiert und erschien
(mit zusätzlicher Produktinformation) viele Monate lang.
(HQ, Nr. 30, 1994)

Magazine ad for Neophagen
Taiho Pharmaceutical, 1967
220 × 280 mm
Photo: Kunihiro Kanasaki

Zeitschriftenanzeige für Neophagen
Taiho Pharmaceutical, 1967
Foto: Kunihiro Kanasaki

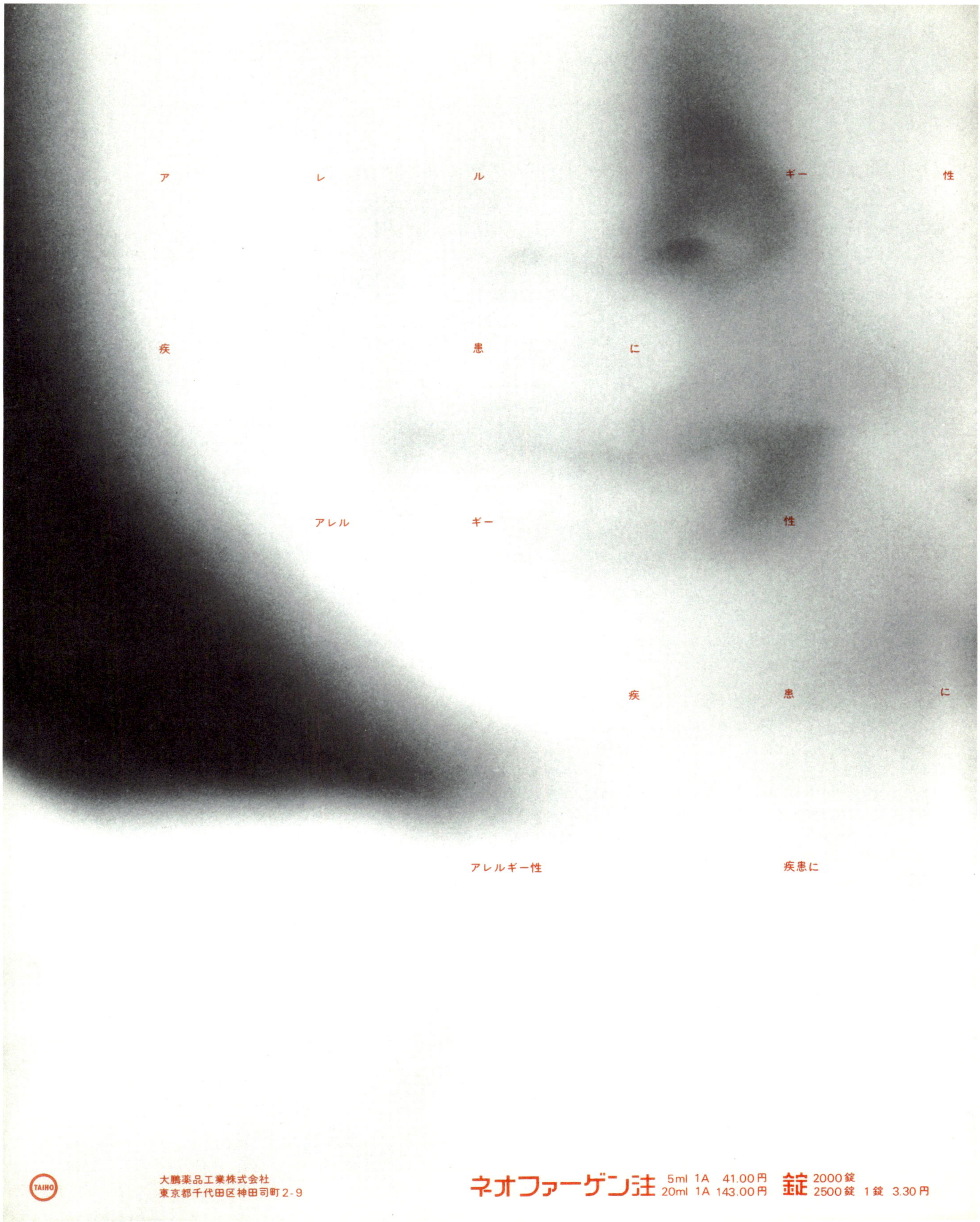

アレルギー性

疾患に

アレルギー性

疾患に

アレルギー性　　　　　　疾患に

大鵬薬品工業株式会社
東京都千代田区神田司町2-9

ネオファーゲン注　5ml 1A　41.00円　錠 2000錠
　　　　　　　　20ml 1A 143.00円　　2500錠 1錠 3.30円

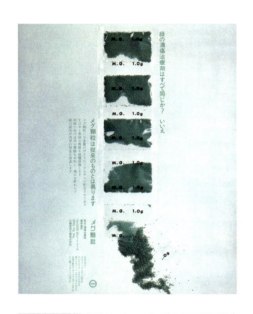
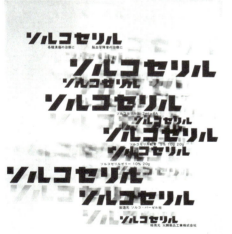

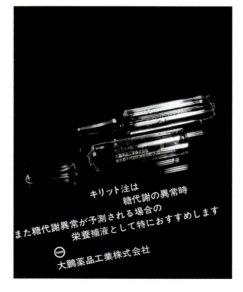

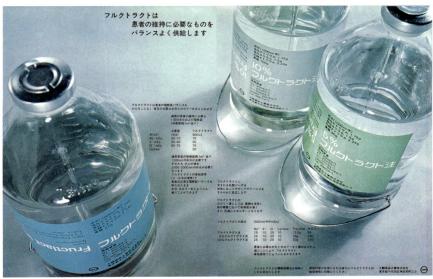

Magazine ads for
ethical pharmaceuticals
Taiho Pharmaceutical, 1968
220 × 280 mm

Werbeanzeigen für
ethische Pharmazeutika
Taiho Pharmaceutical, 1968

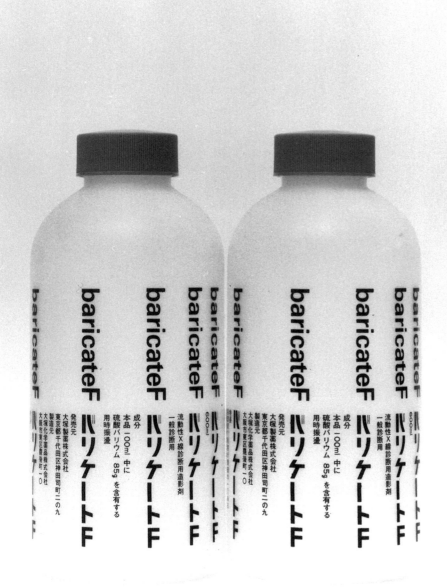

Packaging for Baricate F
Otsuka Pharmaceutical, 1966

Verpackung für Baricate F
Otsuka Pharmaceutical, 1966

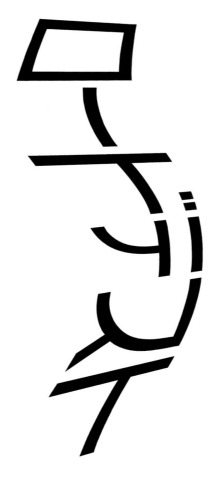

Cover for *Sudachi*, No.1,
promotional magazine
Otsuka Pharmaceutical, 1970
214 × 298 mm

Titel für das Werbemagazin
Sudachi, Nr. 1
Otsuka Pharmaceutical, 1970

Logo for *Road Test*
1968

Logo für *Road Test*
1968

Title logo of *Akinai*,
promotional magazine for
liquor manufacturer
Godo Shusei, 1969

Titellogo für *Akinai*,
ein Werbemagazin für den
Spirituosenproduzenten
Godo Shusei, 1969

Logo and ad for Trans World,
radio and tape recorder brand
Sanyo Electric, 1969
182 × 257 mm

Logo und Anzeige für Trans World,
eine Radio- und Kassettenrecorder-Marke
Sanyo Electric, 1969

Package for FT-860,
8-track car-stereo
Sanyo Electric, 1969

Verpackung für FT-860,
ein 8-Spur-Stereogerät für Autos
Sanyo Electric, 1969

Lithium

MORGEN

Logo and leaflet for
Proto, television
Sanyo Electric, 1967

Logo und Broschüre
für das Fernsehgerät Proto
Sanyo Electric, 1967

Logo for Eck, electric shaver
Sanyo Electric, 1967

Logo für den Elektrorasierer Eck
Sanyo Electric, 1967

Logo for Lithium
Sanyo Electric, 1967

Logo für Lithium
Sanyo Electric, 1967

Logo for Morgen, electric shaver
Sanyo Electric, 1967

Logo für den Elektrorasierer Morgen
Sanyo Electric, 1967

Logo and letterhead for advertising
agency Yarakasukan, 1969

Logo und Briefkopf für die
Werbeagentur Yarakasukan, 1969

Building signage for Yarakasukan,
1969

Schriftzug am Gebäude
von Yarakasukan, 1969

Logo and letterhead for NIA
(Nippon International Agency), 1967

Logo und Briefkopf für NIA
(Nippon International Agency), 1967

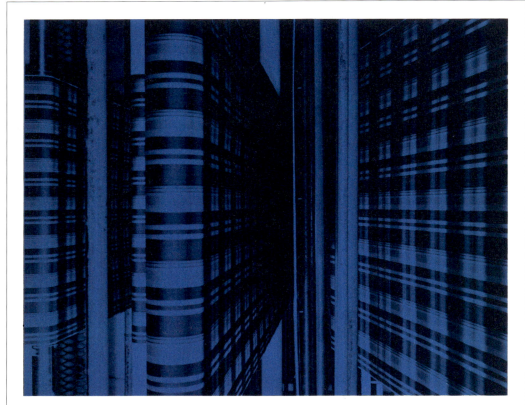

Brochure for Toyobo Osaka Plant
Toyobo, 1967
210 × 220 mm

Broschüre für das Toyobo-Werk Osaka
Toyobo, 1967

**Toyobo Co., Ltd.
Osaka plant**

24 Honjo Higashidori 4-chome
Oyodo-ku, Osaka, Japan
Established October 1896

Land and Building
Total Land Area 14.70 acres
Buildings Floor Space 7.17 acres
Works 2.49 acres
Auxiliary Buildings 0.68 acres
Warehouses 1.07 acres
Welfare Facilities 2.91 acres

Characteristics
Color fast dyeing of fabrics
made of cotton and man-made
fibers and bleaching of
man-made fabrics are done in
this plant.
In addition, the following
are performed:
May1956 Sanforizing
and everglazing treatment
March1959 Toyobo-set
treatment
July1959 Treatment of
synthetic fabrics
August1965 Permanent press
finish·Durable Press finish
May1966 Bonding process

Personnel

Numbers of Employees
Male
Female
Total

Average Age
Workers:
Male 34 years
Female 20 years

Average Years of Service
Workers:
Male 17 years
Female 3 years

Welfare Facilities
Dormitories
Company Housing Facilities
Dining-room, Club
Commissary Store
Mutual Aid Association
Hospital
Vocational High School

Monthly Productive Capacity

Cotton Fabric
Color-fast, Sanforized
Color-fast, Creaset

Rayon Fabric
Bleached, Toyobo-set
Color-fast, Toyobo-set

Polyester and Cotton Blends
Color-fast, crease resistant
finish and Toyobo Cure
bonded goods.

Total: 2,600,000 yards

Machinery and Equipment
3 sets Singeing Machines
1 set Continuous Desizing Range
11 sets Pressure Jiggers
Scouring
1 range Continuous Bleaching
1 set Pad Roll Bleaching Machine
1 set Heat Setter
2 sets Mercerizing Machines
1 set Short Loop Dryer
1 set Shearing Machine
4 ranges Continuous Dyeing
3 sets Pressure Jiggers
Dyeing
8 sets Jiggers
2 ranges Resin Finishing
for Creaset or Toyobo set
2 sets Compressive Shrinking
Machines
1 set Tenter Palmer
2 sets Calenders
1 set Bonding Machine

Continuous Dyeing Range

Product name	Fabric	Treatment	Treatment
Flying Dragon 8500	Twill	Color fast	Sanforized
Flying Dragon 8330	Corkscrew twill	Color fast	Creaset
Flying Dragon 3000	Broadcloth	Color fast	Sanforized
Flying Dragon 7930	Sateen	Color fast	Creaset
Toyobo Z 1000	Lawn	Color fast	Toyobo-set
Toyobo 3471	Gingham	Yarn dyed	Creaset, Stretched
Toyobo P 1860	Polypropylene blended twill	Color fast	Pre-shrunk
Toyobo S 7700	Polyester blended twill	Color fast	Resin treated, durable press finish
Toyobo S 1400	Polyester blended poplin	Color fast	Sanforized
Toyobo S 9605	Polyester blended lawn	Color fast	Resin treated
Bonfeel 9500	Cotton Corduroy/Rayon Gingham	Bonding	
Bonfeel 9550	Cotton Corduroy/mixed	Bonding	
	Nylon and Rayon Tricot Combined		

Resin Finishing Range

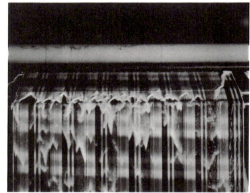

Toyobo Co., Ltd.

C.P.O. Box 277, Osaka, Japan
Established 1882
Capital: ¥17,992,000,000
(approx. $50,000,000)
Chairman, Board of Directors:
T. Taniguchi
President: K. Kawasaki

Overseas Offices:
Toyobo New York Office
1 Whitehall street
New York, N.Y. 10004, U.S.A.
Telephone WHitehall 3-9070 to 74

Toyobo Hamburg Office
Bergstrasse 14, 2 Hamburg 1
West Germany
Telephone 32-0458

Toyobo Sydney Office
5th Floor, Haughton House
24 Jamison Street
Sydney,N.S.W. Australia
Telephone BU 7550

Toyobo Hongkong Office
Room 142, 14th Floor
Jardine House
20 Pedder Street, Hongkong
Telephone 225-869

Main Lines of Business

Fibers, Yarns and Fabrics
Made-up Goods
Furnishings
Industrial Materials
and others

Toyobo Nylon
Toyobo Polyester
Exlan (Acrylic Fiber)
Toyobo Pylen
(Polypropylene Fiber)
Espa (Polyurethane
Elastomeric Yarn)
Tufcel (High Polymeric
Cellulosic Fiber)
Rayon
Cotton
Wool

Production Facilities

Cotton, Spun Rayon and Synthetic Spinning 1,198,000 spindles
Worsted Spinning 131,272 spindles
Woolen Carding 11 sets
Twisting 284,154 spindles
Textured Yarn Processing Machine 7,320 spindles
Cotton, Spun Rayon Loom 10,679 looms
Synthetic Loom 62 looms
Woolen Loom 525 looms
Tire Cord Loom 50 looms
Dyeing and Finishing Machines for Fabrics 55.6 sets
Dyeing and Finishing Machines for Wool Fabrics 4 sets
Rayon Filament Yarn 29.037 tons per day
High Tenacity Rayon Yarn 19.96 tons per day
Rayon Staple 104.829 tons per day
Pulp 78.1 tons per day
Polypropylene (Toyobo Pylen) 6.569 tons per day
Polypropylene Film 2.5 tons per day
Polyurethane Elastomeric Yarn (Espa) 0.5 ton per day
Polyester (Toyobo Polyester) 27.875 tons per day
Nylon (Toyobo Nylon) 35.4 tons per day
Yeast 10 tons per day
Nucleic Acid 0.45 ton per day
Lignin 66 tons per day

入口
非常出口
受付
事務所
御手洗

喫茶
食堂
切符

世界の水
予洗
洗浄
乾燥

Interior signs and graphics
for Sanyo Pavilion in the
Japan World Exposition, Osaka
Sanyo Electric, 1970

Innenbeschilderung und -grafik
für den Sanyo Pavilion auf der
Weltausstellung Expo'70, Osaka
Sanyo Electric, 1970

Badge for Sanyo Pavilion
Sanyo Electric, 1970
ø 60 mm

Ansteckbutton für den Sanyo Pavilion
Sanyo Electric, 1970

entrance
emergency exit
information
office
rest room

tea room
restaurant
tickets

waters of the world
pre-washing
washing
drying

Leaflet for *EXPO '70*,
photo exhibition by Takeji Iwamiya
Hanshin Department Store, 1970
128 × 182 mm

Informationsblätter für *EXPO '70*,
eine Fotografieausstellung von Takeji Iwamiya
Kaufhaus Hanshin, 1970

3 white space and form:
the search for japanese culture and aesthetics

Weissraum und Form:
Die Suche nach japanischer
Kultur und Ästhetik

Ryoanji (Kyoto, 2003)

Ryoanji (Kyoto, 2003)

In 1966, Schmid came to Japan to find the typographic inspiration he was looking for. However, the Japanese culture that Schmid had in mind was already nonexistent in everyday life in the 1960s. Schmid desired to find more "Japan" in Japan. The stage was set for this when he wrote a series of articles entitled "Japan japanisch" (Japan Japanese) in the Swiss typography magazine *Typografische Monatsblätter* (or "Typography Monthly," hereafter *TM*).

Schmid was asked by the magazine's editor-in-chief, Rudolf Hostettler, to write a series of articles introducing Japanese form and utensils used in daily life as seen through the eyes of a typographer. Through this series, Schmid deepened his knowledge of Japan and expanded his personal network. In 2012, a quarter of a century later, the series was published in book form, and an exhibition was held at kyoto ddd gallery in 2015.

Schmid's exploration of Japan can also be found in his work. One of the biggest challenges he faced was working with Japanese characters. Schmid started out at NIA designing katakana logos for electronics and pharmaceuticals, but soon began working on his own original typeface.

The result was the katakana typeface Eru. Eru was designed based on a vision that in the future Japanese would be written horizontally and used in combination with the Latin alphabet. As the name was taken from his former teacher's name, Emil Ruder, it was intended to be set together with Univers, a typeface synonymous with Ruder's typography.

Schmid describes the typeface as "a study in designing Japanese characters in an aesthetic way like the latin alphabet."[*1] Eru emerged out of Schmid's sense of form, which abstracts the history of katakana and the fluid movement of handwritten characters. Schmid submitted Eru to the 3rd Japan Lettering Design Exhibition in 1971 and won the award for great effort.

In the same competition, Schmid also won the award in the typography category for the record jacket of Toshiro Mayuzumi's *Nirvana Symphony*. Musicality is another important factor in Schmid's typography. For Schmid, who had loved music ever since he was a boy, a letter is a "sound sculpture"[*2] and typography can be seen as a musical analogy.

This typographic representation of Mayuzumi's masterpiece *Nirvana Symphony*, which incorporates Buddhist chanting, is the culmination and fusion of Schmid's perspective of the Orient and his sense of typography. Through Toshiro Mayuzumi, Schmid became acquainted with Kohei Sugiura, an influential graphic designer. Sugiura's design philosophy, deeply rooted in scientific and cultural perspectives, was a great inspiration to Schmid.

There is a visual identity in Japan that is not confined to Japonism and traditional cultures; this has been a major problem for graphic designers in Japan to date. While Schmid used his foreign upbringing as a starting point, his final approach to a very central point in Japanese culture came through the formal and linguistic thinking that only a typographer could achieve. Schmid's stance provides an important suggestion on how to deal with history and culture in a global society.

[*1] "Typefaces and Script Designed by Helmut Schmid,"
Gebrauchsgraphik, December 1971, Verlag F. Bruckmann KG, 1971

[*2] "Typography and Typography,"
Idea special issue: *Typography in Japan*, Seibundo Shinkosha, 1982

1966 reiste Schmid nach Japan, um dort die typografische Inspiration zu finden, die er suchte. Die Kultur, die Schmid vorschwebte, war jedoch im japanischen Alltag der 1960er Jahre bereits nicht mehr existent. Schmid wünschte sich, mehr «Japan» in Japan zu finden. Die Weichen dafür wurden gestellt, als er in der Schweizer Typografiezeitschrift *Typografische Monatsblätter (TM)* eine Artikelserie mit dem Titel «Japan japanisch» schrieb.

Schmid war vom Chefredakteur der Zeitschrift, Rudolf Hostettler, gebeten worden, einige Artikel zu verfassen, in denen japanische Form und Gebrauchsgegenstände des täglichen Lebens aus der Sicht eines Typografen vorgestellt werden. Durch diese Serie vertiefte Schmid sein Wissen über Japan und erweiterte sein persönliches Netzwerk. Ein Vierteljahrhundert später, im Jahr 2012, wurde die Serie in Buchform veröffentlicht, und 2015 gab es in der kyoto ddd gallery eine Ausstellung darüber.

Schmids Beschäftigung mit Japan findet sich auch in seinem Werk wieder. Zu den grössten Herausforderungen zählte für ihn die Arbeit mit japanischen Schriftzeichen. Bei der NIA fing Schmid zunächst damit an, Logos in der Silbenschrift Katakana für Elektronik- und Pharmaunternehmen zu gestalten, begann jedoch bald mit der Arbeit an seiner eigenen Schrift.

Das Ergebnis war die Katakana-Schrift Eru. Eru basierte auf der Idee, dass Japanisch in Zukunft horizontal geschrieben und in Kombination mit dem lateinischen Alphabet verwendet werden würde. Da die Bezeichnung der Schrift dem Namen seines ehemaligen Lehrers, Emil Ruder, entliehen war, sollte sie zusammen mit Univers gesetzt werden, einer Schrift, die für Ruders Typografie stand.

Schmid beschreibt die Schrift als «eine Studie, japanische Zeichen in ästhetischer Weise zum Alphabet zu setzen»[*1]. Eru ist aus Schmids Formsinn entstanden; dabei berücksichtigte er die Geschichte von Katakana und die fliessende Bewegung handgeschriebener Zeichen. Schmid reichte Eru bei der 3rd Japan Lettering Design Exhibition 1971 ein und gewann den Award for Great Effort.

Im selben Wettbewerb gewann Schmid auch den Preis in der Kategorie Typografie für die Gestaltung der Hülle der Schallplatte *Nirvana Symphony* von Toshiro Mayuzumi. Die Musikalität ist ein weiterer wichtiger Faktor in Schmids Typografie. Für Schmid, der seit seiner Kindheit Musik liebte, ist ein Buchstabe eine «Klangskulptur»[*2], und die Typografie kann als musikalische Analogie betrachtet werden.

Die typografische Darstellung von Mayuzumis Meisterwerk *Nirvana Symphony*, das buddhistische Gesänge enthält, ist der Höhepunkt und die Verschmelzung von Schmids Blick auf den Orient und seinem Sinn für Typografie. Durch Toshiro Mayuzumi lernte Schmid Kohei Sugiura, einen einflussreichen Grafikdesigner, kennen. Sugiuras Gestaltungsphilosophie, die tief in wissenschaftlichen und kulturellen Perspektiven verwurzelt ist, war eine grosse Inspiration für Schmid.

In Japan gibt es eine visuelle Identität, die sich nicht auf den Japonismus und die traditionellen Kulturen beschränkt, was für Grafikdesigner in Japan bis heute ein grosses Problem darstellt. Schmid nutzte zwar seine ausländische Prägung als Ausgangspunkt, aber seine endgültige Annäherung an einen sehr zentralen Punkt der japanischen Kultur erfolgte durch das Form- und Sprachdenken, das nur ein Typograf erreichen konnte. Schmids Haltung liefert einen wichtigen Impuls für den Umgang mit Geschichte und Kultur in einer globalen Gesellschaft.

[*1] «Typografie und Schriftdesign von Helmut Schmid», in: *Gebrauchsgraphik*, Dezember 1971, Verlag F. Bruckmann KG, 1971

[*2] «Typography and Typography», in: *Typography in Japan,* Sonderausgabe *Idea,* Seibundo Shinkosha, 1982

With Toshiro Mayuzumi (Nara, 1969)

Mit Toshiro Mayuzumi (Nara, 1969)

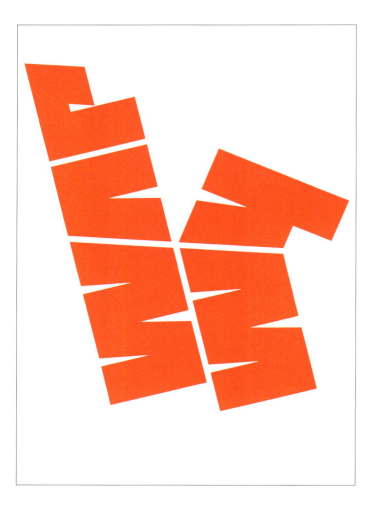

War Why
Antiwar poster (study), 1966
728 × 1030 mm

War Why
Antikriegsposter (Entwurf), 1966

In the first exhibition of Japan
Lettering Designers' Association
(Tokyo, 1968)

In der ersten Ausstellung der
Japan Typography Association
(Tokio, 1968)

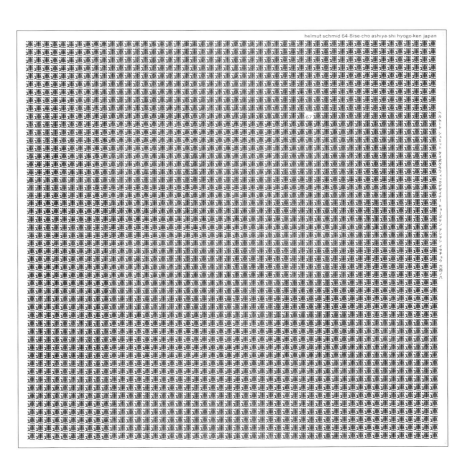

Un (luck)
New Year's card, 1967
238 × 238 mm

Un (Glück)
Neujahrskarte, 1967

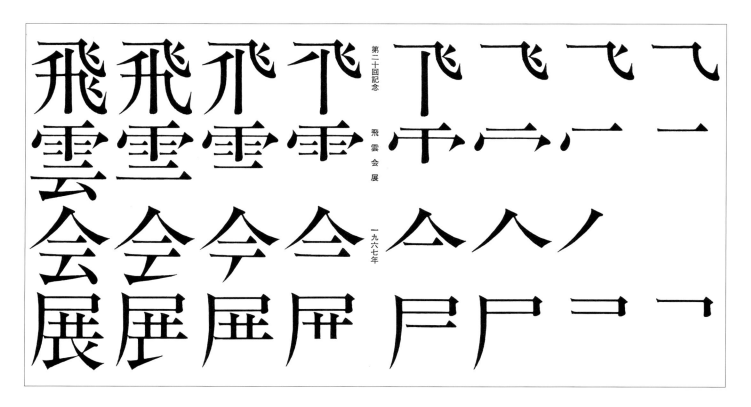

Catalog cover for an exhibition
by the calligraphic society
Hiunkai, 1967
200 × 218 mm

Titel des Katalogs für eine Ausstellung
der kalligrafischen Gesellschaft
Hiunkai, 1967

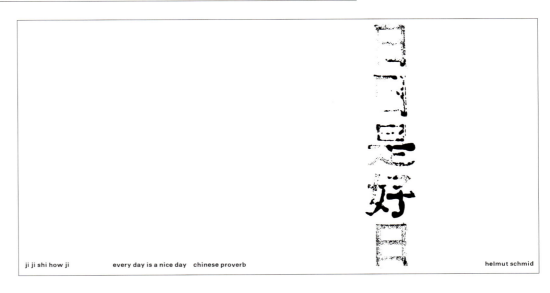

Seiki ni michita (full of energy)
Two ancient poems by Tang Dynasty
poet Wang Jian, overprinted in
blue letters
New Year's card, 1968
210 × 107 mm

Seiki ni michita (voller Energie)
Zwei Gedichte des Dichters Wang Jian
aus der Tang-Dynastie, überlagert
mit blauen Schriftzeichen
Neujahrskarte, 1968

Nichi nichi kore kojitsu
(Every day is a nice day)
New Year's card, 1969
229 × 115 mm

Nichi nichi kore kojitsu
(Jeder Tag ist ein schöner Tag)
Neujahrskarte, 1969

春

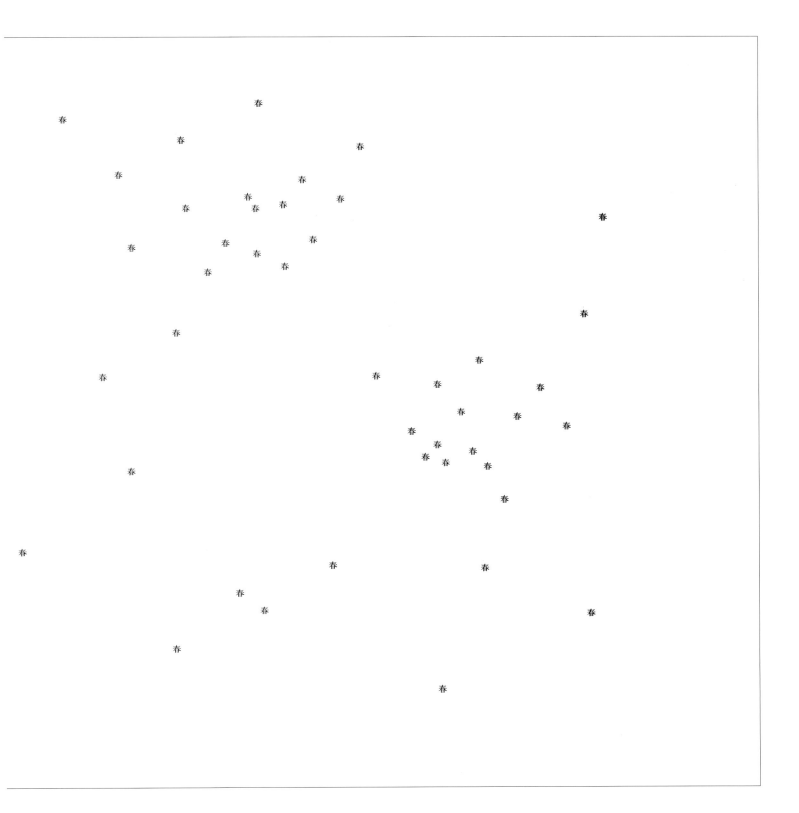

The composition of nature is open, crowded, accidental. A lasting impression
of a visit to the tiny Japanese island of Manabeshima is the white marguerites in the
green of the hills. This seemingly easy, natural, spontaneous sprinkling of nature
is typographically interpreted here by the ideogram *Haru* (spring).
(*TM,* No. 1, 1989)

Die Komposition der Natur ist offen, gedrängt, ist zufällig. Ein anhaltender
Eindruck eines Besuches der kleinen japanischen Insel Manabeshima ist das Weiss
der Margeriten im Grün der Hügel. Dieses scheinbar leichte, natürliche, spontan
Gestreute der Natur ist hier links mit dem Wortzeichen *haru* (Frühling)
typografisch interpretiert.
(*TM,* Nr. 1, 1989)

夏	夏	夏	夏	夏	夏	夏	夏	夏	夏	夏
夏	夏	夏	夏	夏	夏	夏	夏	夏	夏	夏
夏	夏	夏	夏	夏	夏	夏	夏	夏	夏	夏
夏	夏	夏	夏	夏	夏	夏	夏	夏	夏	夏
夏	夏	夏	夏	夏	夏	夏	夏	夏	夏	夏
夏	夏	夏	夏	夏	夏	夏	夏	夏	夏	夏
夏	夏	夏	夏	夏	夏	夏	夏	夏	夏	夏
夏	夏	夏	夏	夏	夏	夏	夏	夏	夏	夏
夏	夏	夏	夏	夏	夏	夏	夏	夏	夏	夏
夏	夏	夏	夏	夏	夏	夏	夏	夏	夏	夏
夏	夏	夏	夏	夏	夏	夏	夏	夏	夏	夏

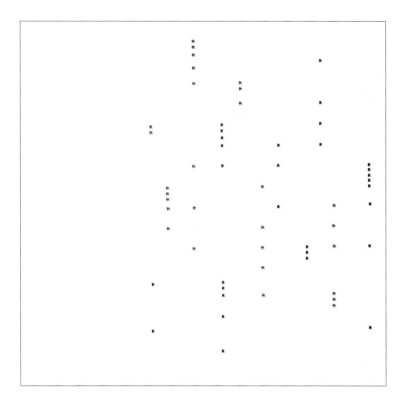

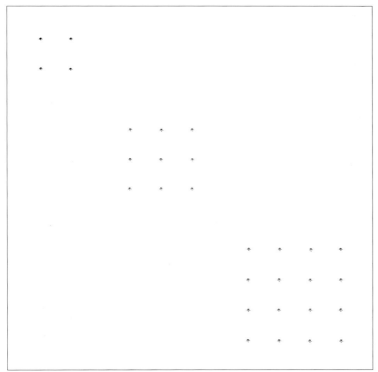

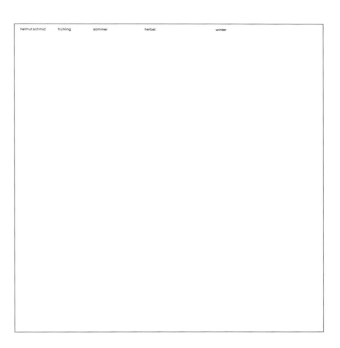

Spring Summer Autumn Winter
Brochure, 1968
210 × 215 mm

Frühling Sommer Herbst Winter
Broschüre, 1968

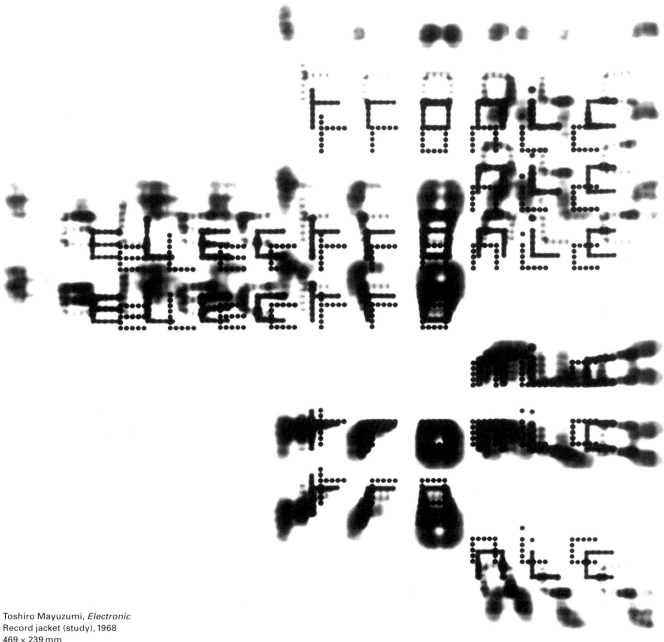

Toshiro Mayuzumi, *Electronic*
Record jacket (study), 1968
469 × 239 mm

Tosihio Mayuzumi, *Electronic*
Schallplattenhülle (Entwurf), 1968

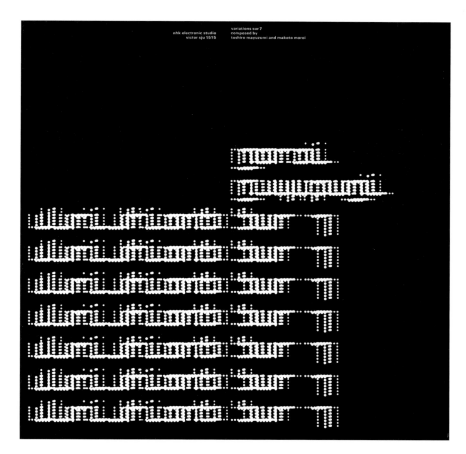
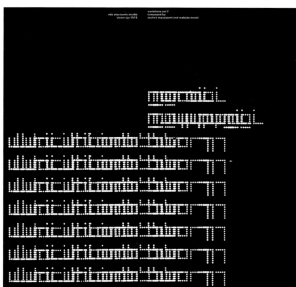
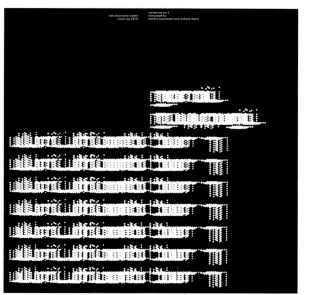

Toshiro Mayuzumi and
Makato Moroi, *Variations sur 7*
Record jacket (studies), 1968
136 × 136 mm

Toshiro Mayuzumi und
Makato Moroi, *Variations sur 7*
Schallplattenhülle (Entwürfe), 1968

アイウエオ
カキクケコ
サシスセソ
タチツテト
ナニヌネノ
ハヒフヘホ
マミムメモ
ヤユヨ
ラリルレロ
ワヲン

カタカナ エル

stockhausen	シュトックハウゼン
mixtur	ミクストゥール
ensemble	アンサンブル
hudoba doneska	フドバ ドネスカ
ladislav kupkovitc	ラディスラフ クプコヴィツ
dirigent	シキ
johannes fritsch	ヨハネス フリッチュ
harald boje	ハラルド ボイエ
rolf gehlhaar	ロルフ ゲールハール
david johnson	デイヴィッド ジョンソン
sinusgeneratoren	セイゲンハッセイキ
stockhausen	シュトックハウゼン
klangregie	オンキョウカントク

```
アメニモマケズ
カゼニモマケズ
ユキニモナツノアツサニモマケヌ
ジョウブナカラダヲモチ
ヨクハナク
ケッシテイカラス
イツモシズカニワラッテイル
イチニチニゲンマイヨンゴウト
ミソトスコシノヤサイヲタベ
アラユルコトヲ
ジブンヲカンジョウニイレズニ
ヨクミキキシワカリ
ソシテワスレズ
ノハラノマツノハヤシノカゲノ
チイサナカヤブキノコヤニイテ
ヒガシニビョウキノコドモアレバ
イッテカンビョウシテヤリ
ニシニツカレタハハアレバ
イッテソノイネノタバヲオイ
ミナミニシニソウナヒトアレバ
イッテコワガラナクテモイイトイイ
キタニケンカヤソショウガアレバ
ツマラナイカラヤメロトイイ
ヒデリノトキハナミダヲナガシ
サムサノナツハオロオロアルキ
ミンナニデクノボートヨバレ
ホメラレモセズ
クニモサレズ
ソウイウモノニ
ワタシハナリタイ
```

stockhausen	シュトックハウゼン
prozession	プロゼッション
alfred alings	アルフレッド アリングス
tam tam	タムタム
rolf gehlhaar	ロルフ ゲールハール
tam tam	タムタム
johannes fritsch	ヨハネス フリッチュ
viola	ヴィオラ
harald boje	ハラルド ボイエ
electronium	エレクトロニウム
aloys kontarsky	アロイス コンタルスキー
piano	ピアノ
stockhausen	シュトックハウゼン
filters	フィルター
potentiometers	ポテンショメーター

stockhausen	シュトックハウゼン
stimmung	シュティムング
collegium vocale	コレギュウム ヴォカレ
dagmar apel	ダグマール アペル
sopran	ソプラノ
gaby rodens	ガビー ロデンス
sopran	ソプラノ
helga albrecht	ヘルガ アルブレヒト
mezzosopran	メゾソプラノ
wolfgang fromme	ウォルフガング フロメ
tenor	テノール
siegfried bernhoft	シーグフリード ベルンホフト
tenor	テノール
alderich billig	アルデリッヒ ビリグ
bass	バス

Katakana Eru
(with Univers 45, 55, 65)
1968–1971
296 × 295 mm

Katakana-Silbenschrift Eru
(mit Univers 45, 55, 65)
1968–1971

Katakana Eru
A typeface, isolated from its function, its purpose, its readability, becomes pure form.
It was this vision of pure form that made me go to Japan. I was particularly attracted by the
syllabic writing katakana, one of the three radically distinct systems united in Japanese writing.
It is used for the names of foreigners, foreign firms and products.
 Katakana incorporates certain elements of Chinese ideography. It dates back to about the
eighth century and was first used to phonetically render works of Chinese literature and Buddhist
sutras. Today, the system comprises 46 signs that dance in print between the well-balanced
quadrangular ideographs. I attempted to discipline these dancing signs, which still seem to be
under the spell of the brush that originally created them, by lending them definitive
x-, descender- and ascender-heights.
 By way of maximum abstraction, as in the philosophy of Anton Webern, whose music
ends as soon as the tones have been played. Although letters are intimately connected with the act
of writing, I decided to do without a brush, for the modern Japanese also use markers, ballpoints,
fountain pens and pencils far more frequently than the brush. In a not-too-distant future
Japan will be compelled to recognize English as a second language, but it will never give up
its complicated system of writing. My Katakana Eru – I named it after my teacher Emil Ruder –
is an attempt to translate Japanese signs into an aesthetic alphabet.
(*Gebrauchsgraphik*, No. 12, 1971)

Katakana-Silbenschrift Eru
Schrift, wenn sie ihre Aufgabe aufgibt, wenn ihr Zweck, wenn die Lesbarkeit wegfällt, wird Form.
Diese Form, die jungfräuliche Form, führte mich nach Japan. Von den drei grundverschiedenen
Schriften, die das japanische Schriftsystem vereint, beschäftigte mich die Silbenschrift Katakana.
In ihr werden ausländische Namen geschrieben, Firmen- und Produktnamen.
 Katakana sind Teile chinesischer Ideografie. Sie entstand etwa im 8. Jahrhundert und
diente zuerst als Lautschrift zur chinesischen Literatur und zu buddhistischen Sutras. Heute sind es
46 Zeichen, die in der Druckschrift zwischen den quadratisch wohlbalancierten Ideogrammen tanzen.
Diese tanzenden Zeichen, die ausserdem noch zu sehr dem Pinsel nachträumen, versuchte ich
durch definitive Ober-, Mittel- und Unterlängen zu straffen.
 Durch maximal mögliche Abstraktion etwa in Gedanken an die Philosophie Anton Weberns,
dessen Musik endet, sobald seine Töne abgespielt sind. Obwohl Schrift von Schreiben kommt,
wurde auf das Phänomen des Pinsels verzichtet, denn heute schreibt auch Japan mit Filzstift,
Kugelschreiber, Füllfederhalter, Bleistift und eigentlich äusserst selten mit dem Pinsel. In nicht allzu
ferner Zukunft wird Japan zwar nicht sein kompliziertes Schriftsystem aufgeben, aber es wird
gezwungen sein, Englisch als Zweitsprache durchzusetzen. Meine Katakana Eru, ich nannte sie nach
meinem verstorbenen Lehrer Emil Ruder, ist eine Studie, japanische Zeichen in ästhetischer
Weise zum Alphabet zu setzen.
(*Gebrauchsgraphik*, Nr. 12, 1971)

Nirvana Symphony
Nirvana Symphony by Mayuzumi impressed me with its delicate tone structures and
bold sound clusters. After having met the composer, I decided to translate the work into typography.
After trying different directions I applied the *Sūtra Śūraṅgama*, which is integral to the symphony.
The composition of the chanted sutra in the varying voice pitch style of Buddhist priests and the composition
of the temple bell effects inspired me to interpret the symphony with the newly typeset sutra.
 To me, the multi-stroke Chinese ideographs (kanji), and the tiny Japanese reading guide (katakana),
express the dark and light tone structures of the sonorous *Nirvana Symphony*. What Mayuzumi achieved
by creating tone clusters with a full orchestra and male chorus, I tried to form typographically by
spontaneous inking, by sprinkling ink cleaner on the printing block of the sutra, by different proofing
speeds of the letterpress.
 All improvised in the composing room of Yarakasukan Inc. in Osaka in 1970.
In search of a different expression, I also experimented in the darkroom, using two negatives of the sutra
exposed directly on the silver gelatine paper (photogram).
(*Typographic Reflections* 7)

Nirvana Symphony
Die *Nirvana Symphony* von Mayuzumi hat mich mit ihren abwechselnd delikaten und
kräftigen Tonstrukturen sehr beeindruckt. Nach einem Treffen mit dem Komponisten habe ich mich
entschlossen, sein Werk durch Typografie auszudrücken. Nach einigen Versuchen unterschiedlicher
Richtungen habe ich *Sūtra Śūraṅgama* gewählt, ein integraler Teil der Symphonie. Die Komposition
des Singsangs in den unterschiedlichen Stimmlagen der buddhistischen Mönche und die Komposition
der Tempelglocken-Effekte hat mich inspiriert, die Symphonie mit der neu gesetzten Sutra
zu interpretieren.
 Das mehrstrichige chinesische Ideogramm (Kanji) und die winzige japanische Leselenkung
(Katakana) drücken für mich die dunkle und helle Tonstruktur der klangvollen *Nirvana Symphonie* aus.
Was Mayuzumi mit der Schaffung von tonalen Anhäufungen durch ein volles Orchester und einen
Männerchor erreicht hat, versuchte ich typografisch zu schaffen, indem ich spontan einfärbte, Farbreiniger
auf den Sutra-Druckblock sprühte und mit unterschiedlichen Geschwindigkeiten beim Drucken.
 All das geschah 1970 in der Setzerei der Yarakasukan Inc. in Osaka. Auf der Suche nach anderen
Lösungen habe ich auch in der Dunkelkammer experimentiert, indem ich zwei Negative der Sutra
direkt auf Silbergelatine abgezogen habe.
(*Typographische Reflexionen* 7)

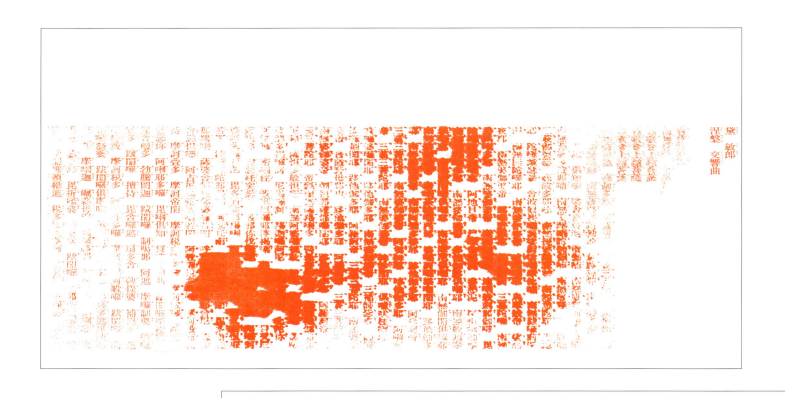

Toshiro Mayuzumi, *Nirvana Symphony*
Record jacket (study), 1970
592 × 296 mm

Toshiro Mayuzumi, *Nirvana Symphony*
Schallplattenhülle (Entwurf), 1970

Iroha
Poster (study), 1969
728 × 1030 mm

Iroha
Plakat (Entwurf), 1969

"The wild geese do not intend to
cast their reflection; The water has
no mind to retain their image"
New Year's card, 1972
100 × 212 mm
This Zen poem is printed on both
sides of the transparent paper.

«Die Wildgänse wollen kein
Spiegelbild werfen; Das Wasser will
ihr Bild nicht festhalten»
Neujahrskarte, 1972
Das Zen-Gedicht ist auf beide Seiten des
transparenten Papiers gedruckt.

ryoanji

five two three two three
fifteen
perfection completion
fifteen years
manhood
jugo ya no tsuki
fifteenth moonlit night
full moon

group one
five contrasting blocks of rock
dominating
broad high leaning back
uncertain
soothing
exuding calm
scarcely
out of the water out of the sand
floating blocks of ice

group two
dot stroke
group three four five

white pebble
groups of stone blocks
nothing
shifted from the centre
shifted away from the veranda
asymmetrical
rhythmical musical

observed sitting
experienced in stillness
thirteen
fourteen

ryoanji
garden of emptiness
garden of the ma
garden
which does not come
which allows one to come
the first time small
the second time blaring
the third time

five two
three two three

(*TM,* No. 8/9, 1973)

Next spread:
"Ryoanji"
Typographische Mönatsblatter,
No. 11, 1971
230 × 297 mm

Folgende Doppelseite:
«Ryoanji»
Typographische Monatsblätter,
Nr. 11, 1971

ryoanji

fünf zwei drei zwei drei
fünfzehn
perfektion vollendung
fünfzehn Jahre
mannesalter
jugo ya no tsugi
fünfzehnte mondnacht
vollmond

gruppe eins
fünf kontrastierende felssteinblöcke
dominierend
breit hoch zurücklehnend
unsicher
besänftigend
ruhe ausstrahlend
kaum
aus dem wasser aus dem sand
schwimmende eisblöcke
gruppe zwei
punkt strich
gruppe drei vier fünf

weisser kiesel
steinblockgruppen
nichts
aus der mitte gerückt
von der veranda weggerückt
asymetrisch rhythmisch musikalisch

sitzend betrachtet   ryoanji
in stille erlebt   garten der leere
dreizehn   garten der ma
vierzehn   garten
    der nicht kommt
    der kommen lässt
    das erstemal klein
    das zweitemal lärmend
    das drittemal
    fünf zwei
    drei zwei drei

Japan is also a living museum. The court music we hear there today has remained
unchanged for a thousand years. Ever since the emergence of the tea master,
Sen no Rikyu, the activation of space – asymmetry – has been cultivated there. For many
centuries, Japanese architecture has been dominated by a modular order.
It is the home of such impractical jewels as the Shinto temples in Ise, which are
rebuilt every 20 years for purely aesthetic reasons. Or there are indescribable gardens
such as the Ryoan-ji in Kyoto, the garden of nothing whose 15 flagstones are
arranged so that they are never all visible at the same time from a sitting position.
15 is the number of perfection. Perfection is like symmetry, static; it is lifeless.
(*TM*, No. 11, 1971)

Visiting Ryoanji in Kyoto, the garden with the 15 rhythmically placed stones,
I always have the feeling of meeting Emil Ruder. No photograph can take
the essence and beauty of Ryoan-ji. Upon my first return
from Japan in 1971, I made an attempt to compose the atmosphere
of Ryoan-ji with typographical material (brass). It appeared in the same
year in *TM* together with words that came to my mind.
(*Newwork Magazine*, No. 6, 2010)

Japan ist gleichzeitig ein lebendes Museum. Dort kann die Hofmusik noch heute
gehört werden wie vor tausend Jahren. Dort pflegt man seit den Tagen des Teemeisters
Senno Rikyu die Aktivierung des Raumes, die Asymmetrie. Dort sind die Bauten
seit Jahrtausenden von modularer Ordnung beherrscht. Dort werden so funktionslose
Kostbarkeiten errichtet wie die Shinto-Tempel in Ise, alle zwanzig Jahre neu und nur
der Ästhetik dienend. Dort werden so unbeschreibbare Gärten gepflegt wie Ryoan-ji
in Kyoto, der Garten des Nichts, dessen fünfzehn Steine so angelegt sind, dass,
sitzend betrachtet, nie alle Steine sichtbar werden. Fünfzehn ist die Zahl der Perfektion.
Perfektion ist wie Symmetrie, ist statisch, ist leblos.
(*TM*, Nr. 11, 1971)

Bei jedem Besuch von Ryoan-ji in Kyoto, dem Garten der 15 rhythmisch
platzierten Steine, habe ich das Gefühl, Emil Ruder zu begegnen.
Keine Fotografie kann das Wesen und die Schönheit von Ryoan-ji einfangen.
Nach meiner ersten Rückkehr aus Japan 1971 unternahm ich einen Versuch,
die Atmosphäre von Ryoan-ji mit typografischem Material (Messing)
nachzubilden. Er wurde im selben Jahr in *TM* veröffentlicht, zusammen
mit Worten, die mir in den Sinn kamen.
(*Newwork Magazine*, Nr. 6, 2010)

"Japan Japanese,"
a series of contributions in
Typographische Monatsblätter

"Kushi" (No. 3, 1968)
"Noren" (No. 10, 1968)
"Sumo" (No. 3, 1969)
"Yunomi Chawan" (No. 6/7, 1969)
"Sake" (No. 8/9, 1969)
"Rogotype" (No. 3, 1970)
230 × 310 mm

"Chasen" (No. 2, 1971)
"Tetsungen Tripitaka" (No. 2, 1976)
"Chozubachi" (No. 3, 1979)
230 × 297 mm

«Japan japanisch»,
eine Reihe von Beiträgen in den
Typographischen Monatsblättern

«Kushi» (Nr. 3, 1968)
«Noren» (Nr. 10, 1968)
«Sumo» (Nr. 3, 1969)
«Yunomi Chawan» (Nr. 6/7, 1969)
«Sake» (Nr. 8/9, 1969)
«Rogotype» (Nr. 3, 1970)

«Chasen» (Nr. 2, 1971)
«Tetsungen Tripitaka» (Nr. 2, 1976)
«Chozubachi» (Nr. 3, 1979)

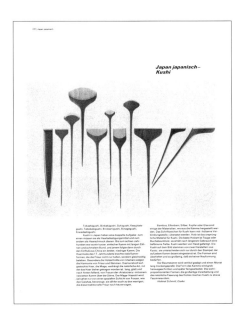

Japan japanisch – Kushi

Noren

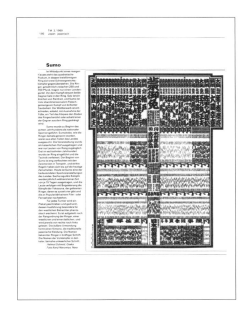

Sumo

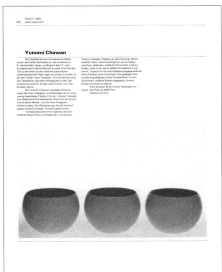

Yunomi Chawan

Sake

Rogotype

Chasen

Tetsugen Tripitaka

Chouzubachi

My first attempt to introduce Japanese typography was done under Rudolf Hostettler.
At that time I could choose between letterpress and offset, and I choose letterpress.
The cover, set in Katakana Eru, states: *The new typography starts with the new typeface.*
The 32-page issue includes the article "The Heart of Metal Type (Katsuji no Kokoro)"
by Toko Shinoda, "Typeface Design of Today's Japan" by Keinosuke Sato,
"The Feature of Kanamoji Form" by Miki Isamu and "The Line" by Helmut Schmid.
(*Newwork Magazine*, No. 6, 2010)

Meinen ersten Versuch, japanische Typografie einzuführen, machte ich unter Rudolf Hostettler.
Zu der Zeit konnte ich wählen zwischen Buchdruck und Offset, ich habe mich für Buchdruck entschieden.
Der Titel, gesetzt in Katakana Eru, lautet: *Die neue Typografie beginnt mit einer neuen Schrifttype.*
Die 32-seitige Ausgabe enthält den Artikel «Das Herz der Metallschrift (Katsuji no Kokoro)»
von Toko Shinoda, «Schriftdesign des heutigen Japans» von Keinosuke Sato, «Die Besonderheit
von Kanamoji» von Miki Isamu und «Die Linie» von Helmut Schmid.
(*Newwork Magazine*, Nr. 6, 2010)

Spreads and cover of
Typographische Monatsblätter
No. 8/9, 1973,
featuring typography in Japan
230 × 297 mm

Doppelseiten und Titel von
Typographische Monatsblätter
Nr. 8/9, 1973,
zum Thema Typografie in Japan

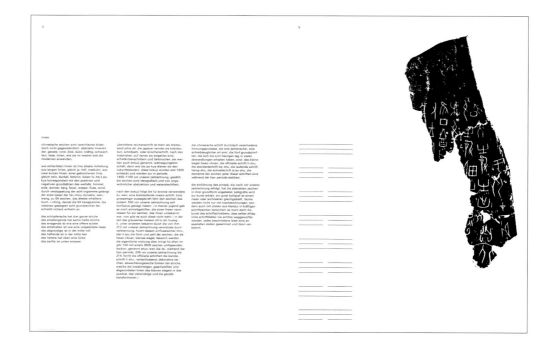

tm

sgm

70

アタラシイタイポグラフィハ

8/9

アタラシイタイプフェイストトモニ

ハジマルノデアル

kalligrafie ist die kunst der linie. es heisst, schwarz vereinigt fünf farben in sich. die dicke der farbe wird vom schreiber selbst bestimmt. durch kreisförmiges reiben einer tuschstange auf einem schwarzen tuschstein, unter zuhilfenahme von wasser, sucht der schreiber den ihm passenden ton. diese tuschzubereitung gibt ausserdem gelegenheit zu innerem sammeln. die vielen farbtöne im schwarz entstehen allein durch die rhythmische pinselführung. die strichfolge der zeichen ist bestimmt: waagrecht vor senkrecht, links vor rechts. seite 14 zeigt einen ausstellungskatalog, in dem die zeichen nach ihrer schreibfolge zerlegt sind. die stärke der kalligrafie liegt im weglassen. charaktere werden rhythmisch und in einem pinselzug geschrieben. die linie ist nicht korrigierbar. sobald sie auf dem papier steht, sie lebt von der frische des jetzt, vom überwachten zufall. der freien kalligrafie, die heute in japan sehr gepflegt wird, stehen eine vielzahl von pinseln zur verfügung, um die linie passioniert, leichtfertig, kraftvoll, weich, trocken, nass erscheinen zu lassen. auch spachtel, kartonstreifen, papierklumpen oder reisstroh werden verwendet.

inkoku, der siegelschnitt, wird vom mehr vom material bestimmt, vom chinesischen stein, marmor oder holz. die siegel, in china und japan heute noch die rechtskräftige unterschrift, darf als vorstufe der druckschrift betrachtet werden. es erscheint in china in der zeit des kaisers ch'in shi huang-ti und ersetzt die bis dahin übliche methode des zweiteilens eines bambus- oder jadestöckes bei abschlüssen von verträgen. in japan ist das siegel im rōnengi, 720, erwähnt.

das hier gezeigte siegel formte der japaner senro kawai. es lebt vom kontrast senkrecht und waagrecht fliessender linien, vom runden kreis, von der spannung der linien zu- und gegeneinander. von sikan aus ist die nebenstehende kalligrafie. ihre aussage ist unmittelbar fallende blätter, herbst, aki.

japan bleibt bis ins dritte jahrhundert ohne schrift. mit einführung des buddhismus aus china durch korea kommt die schrift nach japan. gegen ende drei jahrhunderte später, obwohl sich die struktur des japanischen wesentlich von chinesischen unterscheidet. übernimmt man unverändert die chinesischen zeichen. ändert aber deren laute. schwierigkeiten werden durch phonetische zeichen umgangen, gewöhnlich steht ein zeichen für ein wort.

ノノノノ
クククク
ウウウウ
シシシシ

die buchstabenbreite des alphabets variiert, die zeichenbreite der kana dagegen sind gleich. von der phonetischen betrachtung her muss das so sein, weil jedes zeichen immer eine silbe ergibt. unter diesen vorausstellungen wurde die druckschrift für kana konzipiert. ihre schriftformen sind mit halbem gewicht, zweidrittelgewicht, geviert und mit expand gelöst. linke, für lichtsatzmaschinen wurden schriftscheiben angefertigt. schreibmaschinen für kana wurden hergestellt. kana ersetzt das alphabet.

der gebrauch phonetischer zeichen in der japanischen sprache bringt das erdringen des alphabets mit sich. bei simultaner anwendung verwendet man eine respektive kana-schrift für horizontales schreiben ist einem exzentierenden alphabet. die mit kana harmoniert. auf der schreibmaschine ist die kapazität der zahl der buchstaben, zahlen und zeichen beschränkt; sie liegt zwischen 54 und 96. ausser den katakana-schreibmaschine gibt es die kombinationsschreibmaschine, eine kombination von katakana und alphabet.

verglichen mit der schreibmaschine, gibt es viele arten von computern. aber auch viele lippmethoden. die schriftflächen sind eng, daher ist die schriftbild für den computer normalerweise so erarbeitet worden, dass die punzen breiter aussehen. aus mechanischen gründen werden nur versalien verwendet.

wie gesagt, hat katakana keine grossen und kleinen buchstaben. es findet sich aber die sogenannte waagrechte führungsiinie, die den horizontalen optischen effekt ergeben. die schrifteinheit. kana kann, übernimmt die rolle der überlänge der alphabets. nach dem amerikaner stickney lässt man das alphabet mit der oberen hälfte, das kann von katakana gesagt werden.

in katakana kann man in grunde genommen die horizontalen waagrecht und die vertikalen senkrecht, aber an den kanten die horizontalen linien folgen respektive kurven, um die steifheit der katakana zu lockern. die verbindung der zeichen untereinander beginnt mit dem einfachsten no und entwickelt sich durch anfügen von punkten und strichen. im bestimmten kurve muss für an zeichen muss die unterscheidbarkeit gegenüber den übrigen zeichen beachtet werden. die kurve verändert sich in der ordnung von a ne su me ku va ne ro.

(rechts: zeigt die von miki isamu entworfene schreibmaschinenschrift für ibm 72. die zeichen für stimmhaft und halb stimmhaft sind im unteren text als ersatzdruck fügeriger und behandelt. seite 21. die 46 katakana.)

miki isamu, tokio
übersetzung: kiyomi yamada

カク゛ギジュタ トインサウ キジュタ トハ
マヤタタ ペヒノ フタラン モノテ゛ アリ、タヒ゛ニ アイイレル コトタク
シヨタ゛ツテ タ゛ンミニ゛ニ ウケラ メカレルヘ゛キ モノテ゛ アル
トイク ネツ゛ライ カンカ゛エカタテ゛ アル。
カセモシノヘ、クタクテ゛ コシンチキ ユウチキキ シヒ゛ルハセイチキテ゛
トラシンン モノテ゛ アル。タカ゛ノ セイカクケ゛ ハ゛ーソリリティーハ モテロン
ソノトキノ カタチノ シンキョウ チモ ハユエイ スル。
トコロカ゛、インサウ テレタ モシノ ホウハ
イカ゛ カラ イクラテ゛ ヒョウシ゛ウリ チュウリワ テ゛テチ セイカク
カタ フヘンノ カタチテ゛ クリカエシ ラカウレル。
ツマリ、ソレレシ゛テ ホンコシセイチキテ゛ チュウリリチキ キャッカンチキテ゛ アル。
タイタ゛ウラフォーカ ソレラ フヘンテ゛ キ ラカラテ゛
インタケトハ タウウリ ヘンカ オセチュルノモ、インクラモシ゛ン モラ
コノ トクシウスニ ヨル。エミール ルータ゛ー

カク゛ギジュタ トインサウ キジュタ トハ
マヤタタ ペヒノ フタラン モノテ゛ アリ、タカ゛ノ アイイレル
コトタク、シタカ゛ツテ ケ゛ンミニ゛ニ ウケラ
メカレルヘ゛キ モノテ゛ アル。トイク ネツ゛ヨイ カンカ゛エカタテ゛ アル。
カセモシ゛ハ、タクワテ゛モ コシ゛ンテキ
ユウチキキ シヒ゛ルハセイキチテ゛ トラシンン モノテ゛ アル。
タカ゛ノ セイカクケ゛ ハ゛ーソリリティーハ モテロン
ソノトキノ カタチノ シンキョウ チモ ハユエイ スル。
トコロカ゛゛、インサウ サレタ モシ゛ノ ホウハ、イカ゛ タカイ
イクラテ゛モ ヒョウシ゛ウリリチキ テ゛キチ セイカク カラ
フヘンノ カタチテ゛ クリカエシ ラカウレル。
ツマリ、ソレラレシ゛テ ホ゛ンコシセイチキテ゛ チュウリワチキテ゛ セイカク カラ
キトラカンテキテ゛ アル。タイタ゛ウラフォーカ ソレラ フヘンテ゛キニ
ラカラテ゛ インタケトハ タウウリ ヘンカ サセチュルノモ、
インクラモシ゛ン モラ コノ トクシウスニ ヨル。エミール ルータ゛ー

there is a remarkable variation in the angles which the upper lines and their continuous strokes make, the angle changes in the order from a no su me ku wa ro do. unification and variation are important in drawing. the lines which may be common should be as uniform as possible. a particular line which makes a letter characteristic should be as different from the rest of the letters as possible. these points can save the wordform from falling into monotony.

roman alphabet can be read by the upper half, kanamoji has the same feature. there are several letters in kanamoji which can be related to one another by the upper line. in order to make these letters easy to read we have suggested putting a line over the upper line, as eda, like in u ke ki se and shita eda, a stroke below the shita sen, the basic line, like the one in n.

in katakana there are 23 letters which have one or more leftwards descending strokes, such as a we ka ku ka. some say that katakana is therefore inconvenient for horizontal writing from left to right. there is also another opinion against it, but they are all questions about handwriting, so they will not be referred to here. the association among the letters starts with the simplest, no, and it develops by adding dots and strokes. the simplicity of kanamoji structure with only a few strokes gives limitless possibilities to designers, but in developing the possibilities a limit to the legibility will be found, where reading speed is concerned, the letters must be easy to distinguish. zo could be taken for n or a in oriental writing, that is why n is given clearly paralleled vertical lines and n quite horizontal lines. the same trouble is in sh/ and tsu. both are given serifs to show the beginning of the strokes.

it is possible to design kanamoji theoretically so as to be suitable for horizontal writing. the final question is the individual tendency of the letters. of course such elements as bulk, curve, balance and so on are variable according to the usage of the letters, and besides, in order to meet individual foundries it is inevitable to change a small part in the details.

(right: kanamoji typed with ibm 72, designed by miki isamu, the signs for voiced and halfvoiced letters are in the lower copy separate units. page 21. the 46 kanamoji.)

miki isamu, tokio
translation: sumi tanaka

あいうえおごぞと のほ。
がぎぐげせてねへもき、
さしすせぞとのへめ
だちつてぬふむよを
なにぬねのほまみゆる
はひふへほやゆりれ
まみむめもゃょん
やゆよらりるれろわをん

Hiragana Eru
1972–1976

Hiragana Eru
1972–1976

Ikuma Dan, *Yuuzuru*
Record jacket (study), 1976
278 × 278 mm

Ikuma Dan, *Yuuzuru*
Schallplattenhülle (Entwurf), 1976

はてしもないよるのなかを　せかいじゅうを
あのくらいひび　わたしはあるきつづけた
なみだをかみにかきつらねて
みをやつし　すがたをかえて
わたしは　けいさつにおわれる
おたずねものだった
すきとおったよふけ
こどくなほしのまたたく　おおぞらのしたを
わたしは　まちをよぎり　もりをぬけ
はたけのなかをあるき　みなとまちをとおり
とぐちから　とぐちへと
ひとのてからてへと　わたりあるいた
よるはつらいものだ　しかし　ひとびとは
きょうだいのあいずをおくってくれた

Hiragana Eru shown in
Pablo Neruda's poem "The Fugitive."

Hiragana Eru am
Beispiel von Pablo Nerudas Gedicht
«Der Flüchtling»

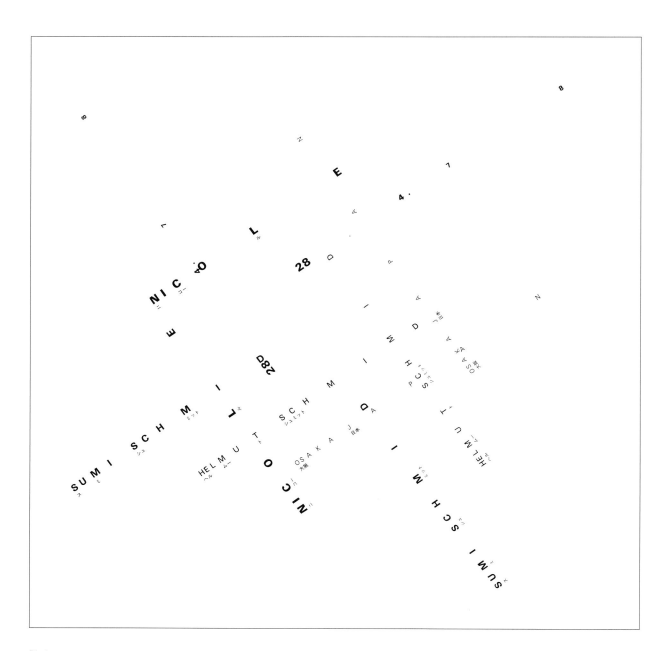

Birth announcement
of Nicole, 1978
210 × 210 mm

Anzeige der Geburt
von Nicole, 1978

In designing this birth announcement, I felt the need to free myself from self-imposed restrictions in my typography: for one thing, the use of capital letters, and for another, the formalistic spacing of words by ignoring the immediate readability.
By overlapping the message and by over-emphasizing the spacing, the birth announcement evokes associations with new life, with the notation of new music, or with a starry sky.
(*TM*, No. 1, 1989)

Das Gestalten dieser Geburtsanzeige brachte den passenden Anlass, meine mir selbst auferlegten Restriktionen in der Typografie zu sprengen: einerseits die Verwendung von Versalien, andererseits das formalistische Sperren ohne Rücksicht auf die unmittelbare Lesbarkeit. Durch die Überlagerungen der Information und durch das extreme Sperren weckt die Geburtsanzeige Assoziationen mit neuem Leben, mit neuer Musik, mit dem Sternenhimmel.
(*TM*, Nr. 1, 1989)

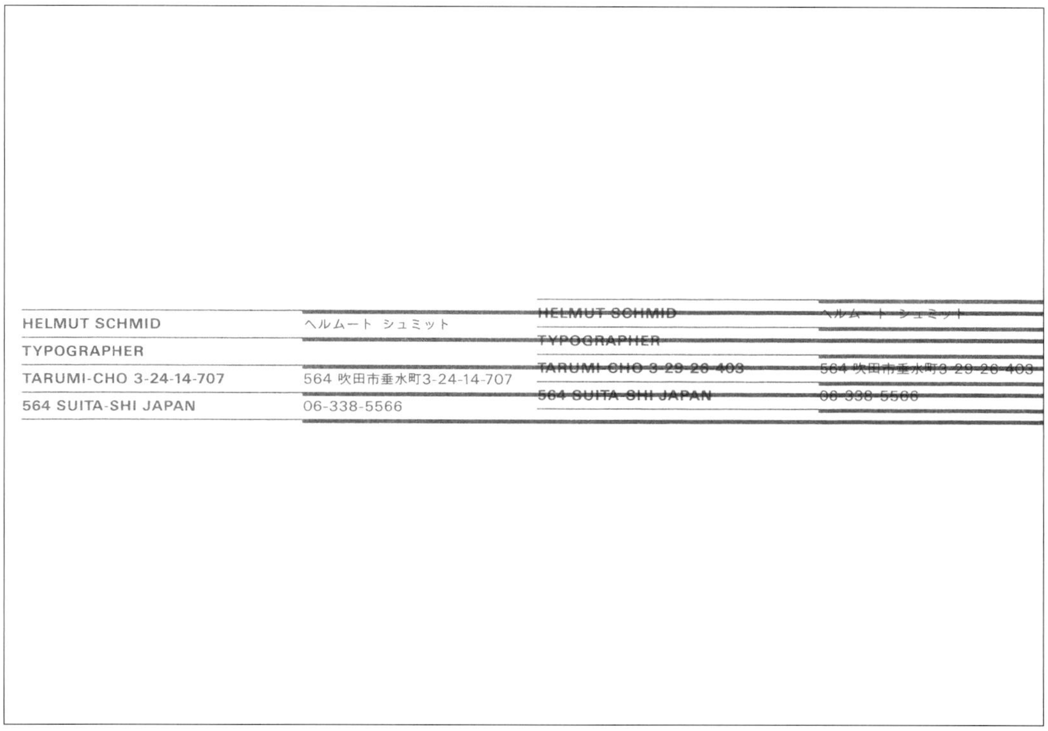

HELMUT SCHMID	ヘルムート シュミット	~~HELMUT SCHMID~~	~~ヘルムート シュミット~~
TYPOGRAPHER		~~TYPOGRAPHER~~	
TARUMI-CHO 3-24-14-707	564 吹田市垂水町3-24-14-707	~~TARUMI-CHO 3-29-28-403~~	~~564 吹田市垂水町3-29-28-403~~
564 SUITA-SHI JAPAN	06-338-5566	~~564 SUITA-SHI JAPAN~~	~~06-338-5566~~

New Year's greeting and
moving announcement, 1985
148 × 105 mm

Neujahrskarte und
Ankündigung eines Umzugs, 1985

4 organic and systematic: works in sweden

Organisch und systematisch:
Arbeiten in Schweden

During his four-year stay in Japan, Schmid garnered a lot of experience and achievements. However, he left Japan in 1971 and headed for Stockholm, Sweden. In the newsletter of the Japan Lettering Designers' Association (later renamed Japan Typography Association), Schmid answered the question of why he was leaving Japan as follows:

> "I came to Japan and entered the world of advertising design, but I found it difficult to remain independent from general trends. I have no choice but to return home. I'm always willing to come back if there's a place to work. If I could, I would like to work in Tokyo."
> ("Designer Interview: Helmut Schmid," *Lettering & Typography*, No. 3, the Japan Lettering Designers' Association, 1971)

The 1970 Osaka World Expo can be seen as a symbolic event in which Japan's postwar design lost its ideological, enlightened nature and was swallowed up by a world led by corporations and marketing. The "general trend" that Schmid sensed may have been something similar to this.

However, Schmid's interest in Japan and his interaction with the people there remained intact, and in the December 1971 issue of the German design magazine *Gebrausgraphik* he wrote an article on his work related to text and typography during his time in Japan. In the August/September 1973 issue of *TM*, he edited and wrote a major special issue on Japan; this was the culmination of his research.

Schmid's trip to Stockholm was probably due to the connections he had made through *Grafisk Revy*; he had initially envisioned the city as his first destination after graduating from the AGS Basel. Throughout his stay in Japan, Schmid also continued to design covers and write articles for the magazine.

His covers for *Grafisk Revy* included a series of Basel-style typographic experiments, a series that incorporated the sensibilities and methodologies of ink painting and calligraphy, a series that used speculative experimental typefaces (such as Wim Crowel's New Alphabet), and a series dedicated to his teacher, Emil Ruder, who passed away in 1970. The works directly reflect Schmid's interests at the time.

After arriving in Stockholm, however, his cover series had become a kind of formal exercise in which the typography was developed under certain constraints and forms. In these designs, which can be seen as a kind of return to his roots, one can sense his attitude of re-examining the basics after leaving Japan.

With friends (1964)
Mit Freunden (1964)

Helmut Schmid, "Renowned typographer Emil Ruder is new dean at Basel School of Design"
Grafisk Revy, No. 9, 1965

Helmut Schmid, «Renommierter Typograf Emil Ruder ist neuer Rektor der Kunstgewerbeschule Basel»
Grafisk Revy, Nr. 9, 1965

Room in Stockholm with
Shiko Munakata's wood-cut prints
on the wall
(Stockholm, 1971)

Zimmer in Stockholm, an der Wand
Holzschnitte von Shiko Munakata
(Stockholm, 1971)

Während seines vierjährigen Aufenthalts in Japan sammelte Schmid viele Erfahrungen
und Erfolge. Dennoch verliess er Japan 1971 und ging nach Stockholm. Im Newsletter der
Japan Typography Association antwortete Schmid auf die Frage, warum er Japan verliess:
«Ich kam nach Japan und trat in die Welt des Werbedesigns ein, aber es fiel mir
schwer, mich von allgemeinen Trends unabhängig zu machen. Ich habe keine andere
Wahl, als nach Hause zurückzukehren. Ich bin immer bereit zurückzukommen,
wenn es eine Arbeitsstelle gibt. Wenn ich könnte, würde ich gerne in Tokio arbeiten.»
(«Designer Interview: Helmut Schmid», in: *Lettering & Typography*, Nr. 3,
the Japan Lettering Designers' Association, 1971)

Die Weltausstellung in Osaka 1970 kann als symbolisches Ereignis betrachtet werden,
bei dem das japanische Nachkriegsdesign seinen ideologischen, aufgeklärten Charakter
verlor und von einer von Konzernen und Marketing gelenkten Welt verschluckt wurde.
Der «allgemeine Trend», den Schmid wahrgenommen hat, könnte etwas Ähnliches
gewesen sein.

Schmids Interesse an Japan und seine Beziehungen zu den Menschen dort blieben
jedoch intakt. In der Dezember-Ausgabe 1971 der deutschen Designzeitschrift *Gebrausgraphik* schrieb er einen Artikel über seine Arbeit mit Text und Typografie während seiner
Zeit in Japan. Im August/September 1973 war er Herausgeber und Autor einer grossen
Sonderausgabe der Zeitschrift *TM* über Japan – dies war der Höhepunkt seiner Forschung.

Schmids Reise nach Stockholm erfolgte wahrscheinlich aufgrund seiner Beziehungen,
die er durch *Grafisk Revy* geknüpft hatte; ursprünglich hatte er die Stadt als erstes Ziel
nach seinem Abschluss an der AGS Basel anvisiert. Während seines gesamten Aufenthalts
in Japan entwarf Schmid weiterhin Titelseiten und schrieb Artikel für die Zeitschrift.

Zu den von ihm gestalteten Titelseiten für die *Grafisk Revy* gehörten eine Serie mit
typografischen Experimenten im Basler Stil, eine Serie, die sich mit den Feinheiten und
Methoden des Zeichnens mit Tusche und der Kalligrafie befasste, eine Serie, die spekulative
experimentelle Schriftarten (wie Wim Crowels New Alphabet) behandelte, und eine Serie,
die seinem 1970 verstorbenen Lehrer Ruder gewidmet war. Diese Arbeiten spiegeln
Schmids damalige Interessen unmittelbar wider.

Nach seiner Ankunft in Stockholm waren seine Titelseitenserien jedoch zu einer Art
formalen Übung geworden, bei der die Typografie unter gewissen Zwängen und Formen
entwickelt wurde. In diesen Arbeiten, die als eine Art Rückkehr zu seinen Wurzeln betrachtet
werden können, spürt man seine Haltung, die Grundlagen neu zu überdenken, nachdem
er Japan verlassen hatte.

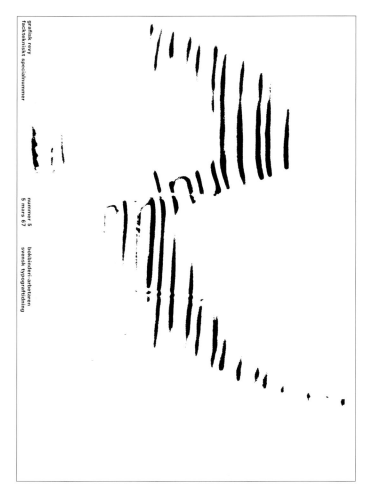

Cover for *Grafisk Revy*
No. 5, No. 9, No. 16, No. 19, 1967
Swedish Association of
Bookbinders / Typographers
A4

Titel für *Grafisk Revy*
Nr. 5, Nr. 9, Nr. 16, Nr. 19, 1967
Schwedischer Verband der
Drucker und Buchbinder

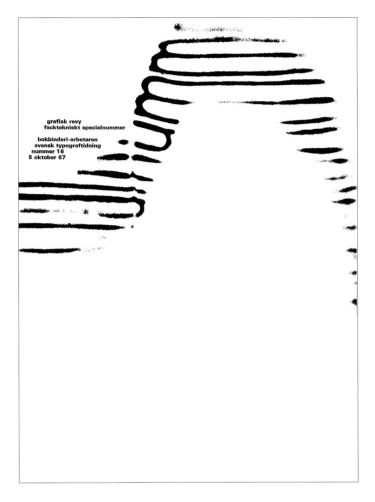

grafisk revy
faktekniskt specialnummer

bokbinderi-arbetaren
svensk typograftidning
nummer 16
5 oktober 67

grafisk revy
faktekniskt specialnummer

bokbinderi-arbetaren
svensk typograftidning
nummer 19
20 november 67

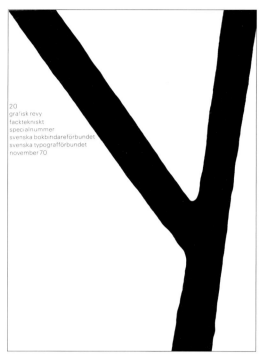

Cover for *Grafisk Revy*
No. 16, No. 20, 1970
A4

Titel für *Grafisk Revy*
Nr. 16, Nr. 20, 1970

Cover for *Grafisk Revy*
No. 5, No. 9, 1968

Titel für *Grafisk Revy*
Nr. 5, Nr. 9, 1968

Dedicated to Emil Ruder*
The linear shape of the letters *v* and *y*, relieved by the soft edges produced by
a combination of enlargement and letterpress printing, is placed in clearly defined
proportions within the format of the journal. This results in areas of tension
between the printed and unprinted surface and between the fine informative lines
of type and the bold graphic lines.
(*TM*, No.1, 1989)

* Ruder died in March, 1970

Emil Ruder gewidmet*
Die linearen Buchstaben V und Y, die durch die extreme Vergrösserung sichtbar
gemachter Buchdruck-Quetschränder entspannt werden, sind in klaren Proportionen
in das gegebene Format der Zeitschrift platziert. Es entstehen Spannungsfelder
von bedruckt und unbedruckt, von feinen informierenden Schriftzeilen und
kräftigen grafischen Linien.
(*TM*, Nr.1, 1989)

* Ruder ist im März 1970 verstorben.

Cover for *Grafisk Revy*, No. 16, 1968
Typeface: New Alphabet

Titel für *Grafisk Revy*, Nr.16, 1968
Schrift: New Alphabet

Cover for *Grafisk Revy,* No. 19, 1968
Typeface: Romat

Titel für *Grafisk Revy,* Nr. 19, 1968
Schrift: Romat

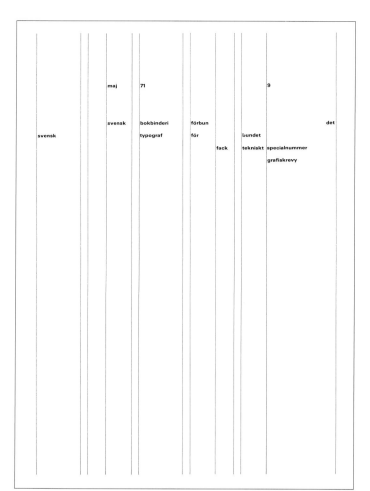

Study of cover series
for *Grafisk Revy*
No. 5, No. 9, No. 16, No. 19, 1971
A4

Studie einer Serie von Titeln
für *Grafisk Revy*
Nr. 5, Nr. 9, Nr. 16, Nr. 19, 1971

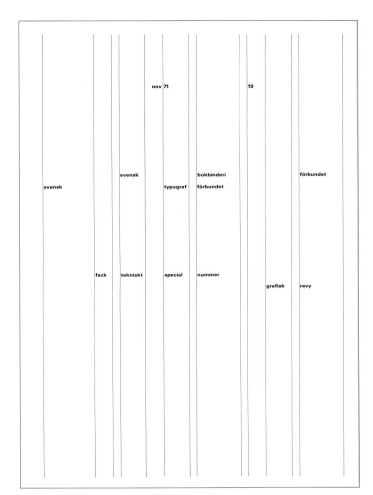

Cover designs for special issues of the journal *Grafisk Revy*
The book, the book page, have remained unchanged since Gutenberg. Only the cover
has always been adapted to the style of the time. Nevertheless, the cover is not a playground
for decorations of the designer. The cover is the signet of the title and the publishing house;
wrapping and salesman at the same time. The function of a book title differs from that of a
magazine title. The book has to attract attention through the author, title and design.
A journal, particularly a professional one, addresses an occupational group, and does not
have to sell.

My nine-year cooperation with the Swedish journal *Grafisk Revy* was a form-searching task.
The magazine understood itself to be not form-oriented but rather socio-politically oriented.
The obvious form for the cover of a journal is an interpretation of its name. The cover consists of
the title and the publishing date. The designs for the four *Grafisk Revy* covers take up this
possibility. Lines are also added, resulting in the contrast of points and lines, of terse
and open, of strict and playful.
(*TM*, No. 3, 1977)

Umschlagentwürfe für die fachtechnischen Nummern der *Grafisk Revy*
Das Buch, die Buchseite sind seit Gutenberg unverändert geblieben. Nur der Umschlag hat sich
stets den Zeitströmungen angepasst. Trotzdem ist der Umschlag kein Tummelplatz für Dekorationen
der Designer. Der Umschlag ist das Signet des Titels und des Verlages, er ist Verpackung und
Verkäufer. Die Funktion des Buchtitels unterscheidet sich von der des Zeitschriftentitels dadurch,
dass das Buch erst durch den Autor, den Titel oder die Gestaltung auf sich aufmerksam machen muss,
während der Zeitschriftentitel, speziell der Fachzeitschriftentitel, sich an ein bestimmtes Publikum
wendet und sich also nicht eigentlich verkaufen muss.

Meine neunjährige Mitarbeit für die schwedische Fachzeitschrift *Grafisk Revy* war ein formales
Suchen, obwohl sich diese Zeitschrift nicht eigentlich formal, sondern bewusst sozialpolitisch
versteht. Die naheliegende Form für einen Umschlag ist die Interpretation des Zeitschriftentitels.
Der Umschlag besteht aus dem Titel der Zeitschrift und dem Datum. Die vier *Grafisk Revy*-Umschläge
greifen diese Möglichkeit auf. Die Linie ist als Zusatzelement eingesetzt. So ergeben sich Kontraste
von Punkt und Linie, von gedrängt und offen, von streng und verspielt.
(*TM*, Nr. 3, 1977)

Covers for the Swedish journal *Grafisk Revy* are variations using one typeface and one type size. The cover announces the main contents like a poster. The grid of the inside pages is applied in the arrangement of the headlines, making it possible to design some of the covers by telephone. The cooperation with Axel Janås, the editor, was essential for continuing the series throughout the year. A German magazine commented: "Helmut Schmid's cover designs, created at a minimum of cost, are imaginative masterpieces of contemporary typography." (*Idea*, No. 156, 1979)

Die Titel der schwedischen Publikation *Grafisk Revy* sind Varianten einer Schrifttype in einer Grösse. Der Titel verkündet den Hauptinhalt wie ein Plakat. Das Raster der Innenseiten orientiert sich an der Anordnung der Überschriften und macht es somit möglich, einige der Titel über das Telefon zu gestalten. Die Kooperation mit Axel Janås, dem Herausgeber, war massgebend für die Kontinuität der Serie über das Jahr. Ein deutsches Magazin kommentierte: «Helmut Schmids Titelgestaltungen, kreiert mit minimalen Kosten, sind erfinderische Meisterwerke der zeitgemässen Typografie.» (*Idea*, Nr. 156, 1979)

Cover for *Grafisk Revy*,
No.1– No. 20/21, 1972
A4

Titel für *Grafisk Revy*,
Nr.1– Nr. 20/21, 1972

5
a political individual:
works for the social democratic party of germany

Ein politischer Mensch:
Arbeiten für die Sozialdemokratische
Partei Deutschlands

Private election postcards, 1972
A6

Private Wahlpostkarten, 1972

At the end of the 1960s, West Germany was undergoing a major policy shift from conservatives to reformers after the postwar reconstruction and reconciliation with the West that occurred in the 1950s. This period also saw a spread of student criticism of the previous regime and a global anti-war movement; in West Germany there was a growing protest movement against the previous Nazi party. This background had awakened a political consciousness in Germany's youth. Schmid, as a young man of the postwar generation, was also active in his own political intentions. This eventually led him to participate in actual political campaigns as a designer.

While living in Stockholm after leaving Japan in 1971, Schmid sent personal message cards to the people of West Germany in support of the Social Democratic Party (SPD) and Chancellor Willy Brandt during the 1972 parliamentary elections in West Germany. Willy Brandt was a politician who lived in exile from the Nazis during the war and served as mayor of West Berlin after the war ended. In 1969, Brandt became the first postwar West German chancellor from the SPD, and promoted a policy of easing tensions with the Soviet Union and Eastern European countries, for which he was awarded the Nobel Peace Prize in 1971. In 1972, the SPD won the election with the highest percentage of votes in its history, based on support for its policies and confidence in Brandt.

Schmid's pro-Brandt message cards caught the attention of SPD election officials, and from 1973 to 1976 he worked in Düsseldorf, Germany, as a designer for ARE, an advertising agency that handled government publications and SPD election campaigns. The agency employed about 30 people under the direction of Harry Walther and creative director Nils Johannisson.

In the design of public relations materials for political parties and governments, a wide variety of sequential printed material must be both individually characterized while providing a common overall image. Schmid and his colleagues responded to this need with a typographic and color design program.

In 1974, Brandt resigned due to the turmoil in the government and an incident in which it was discovered that his personal secretary was a spy for the East, and was subsequently replaced by a person called Helmut Schmidt (with the same name as Schmid, but spelled with a *t*). Thus the typographer Helmut Schmid designed the election campaign for the SPD, now led by the politician Helmut Schmidt.

The SPD's election campaign logo was originally commissioned to the designer Otl Aicher, but since the design did not meet with the approval of the party, it was handed over to ARE, and Schmid took over the task. The campaign, using a waveform symbol with the colors of the German flag (black, red and gold), was widely publicized through magazine advertisements, posters and other related materials. In the general election, the SPD lost its first parliamentary seat to the Christian Democratic Union (CDU), but remained in power by maintaining a coalition with the Free Democratic Party (FDP).

In addition to his work for ARE, Schmid also produced a series of political posters between 1974 and 1977 titled *15 Politypographien*. The term *politypographien* was coined from the words "politics" and "typography," and the typographic works consisted of typewritten text from the SPD platform and the words of Brandt and other politicians of the party. The series was originally exhibited at the Warsaw Biennial in 1976 and continued to be produced, culminating in Schmid's own solo exhibition, *15 Politypographien*, which was held at Print Gallery in Amsterdam in 1978.

These poster works, with their poetic beauty, were criticized by some for the divergence between their literal content and form. Schmid, however, included such criticism in his article on the work in *TM*, No. 1, 1980. For Schmid, this divergence might have been created out of necessity, since he was both a typographer and a political subject; seen from this perspective, it transcended what was otherwise valid criticism.

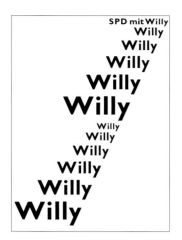

"SPD with Willy"
Postcard, 1972
A6

«SPD mit Willy»
Postkarte, 1972

Nach dem Wiederaufbau der Nachkriegszeit und der Aussöhnung mit dem Westen in den 1950er Jahren vollzog sich Ende der 1960er Jahre in der Bundesrepublik Deutschland ein grundlegender politischer Wechsel von der konservativen zur Reformpolitik. Diese Periode war auch von studentischer Kritik an der Vorgängerregierung und einer weltweiten Antikriegsbewegung gekennzeichnet. In der Bundesrepublik Deutschland gab es eine wachsende Protestbewegung gegen Beamte mit nationalsozialistischer Vergangenheit. Vor diesem Hintergrund war in der deutschen Jugend ein politisches Bewusstsein geweckt worden. Auch Schmid, als junger Vertreter der Nachkriegsgeneration, war politisch aktiv. So beteiligte er sich schliesslich als Designer an konkreten politischen Kampagnen.

Als Schmid nach seiner Ausreise aus Japan 1971 in Stockholm lebte, verschickte er persönliche Grusskarten an die Menschen in der Bundesrepublik Deutschland zur Unterstützung der Sozialdemokratischen Partei (SPD) und des Kanzlers Willy Brandt bei den Bundestagswahlen 1972. Willy Brandt war ein Politiker, der während des Kriegs im Exil lebte und nach Kriegsende unter anderem als Bürgermeister von Westberlin amtierte. 1969 wurde Brandt der erste bundesdeutsche Nachkriegskanzler der SPD und setzte sich für eine Politik der Entspannung mit der Sowjetunion und den osteuropäischen Ländern ein, wofür er 1971 den Nobelpreis erhielt. 1972 gewann die SPD die Wahlen mit dem höchsten Stimmenanteil ihrer Geschichte, was auf die Unterstützung ihrer Politik und das Vertrauen in Willy Brandt zurückzuführen war.

Schmids Grusskarten, mit denen er für Willy Brandt warb, erregten die Aufmerksamkeit der SPD-Wahlhelfer, sodass er von 1973 bis 1976 in Düsseldorf als Designer für Allgemeine Reklame (ARE) arbeitete, einer Werbeagentur, die mit Regierungspublikationen und Wahlkampagnen der SPD befasst war. Die Agentur beschäftigte etwa dreissig Mitarbeitende unter der Leitung von Harry Walther und dem Kreativdirektor Nils Johannisson.

Bei der Gestaltung von Materialien für die Öffentlichkeitsarbeit von politischen Parteien und Regierungen muss eine Vielzahl von nacheinander erscheinenden Drucksachen individuell gestaltet werden, die gleichzeitig ein einheitliches Gesamtbild ergeben. Schmid und seine Kollegen erfüllten diese Anforderung mit einem Programm zur typografischen und farblichen Gestaltung.

1974 trat Brandt nach Unruhen in der Regierung von seinem Amt als Bundeskanzler zurück, nachdem aufgedeckt worden war, dass sein persönlicher Sekretär ein DDR-Spion war. Sein unmittelbarer Nachfolger war Helmut Schmidt. So gestaltete der Typograf Helmut Schmid die Wahlkampagne für die SPD, die nun von dem Politiker Helmut Schmidt geführt wurde.

Ursprünglich war der Gestalter Otl Aicher mit dem Logo für die Wahlkampagne der SPD beauftragt worden, aber nachdem sein Entwurf nicht die Zustimmung der Partei fand, wurde der Auftrag an die ARE übergeben, und Schmid übernahm die Aufgabe. Die Kampagne, bei der ein wellenförmiges Symbol in den Farben der deutschen Flagge (Schwarz, Rot, Gold) zum Einsatz kam, wurde mit Zeitschriftenanzeigen, Plakaten und anderen Werbemitteln breit gestreut. Bei der Bundestagswahl verlor die SPD ihre Position als stärkste Bundestagsfraktion an die Christlich Demokratische Union (CDU), blieb jedoch an der Macht, indem sie eine Koalition mit den Freien Demokraten (FDP) einging.

Neben seiner Arbeit für ARE schuf Schmid zwischen 1974 und 1977 auch eine Serie von politischen Plakaten mit dem Titel *15 Politypographien*, einer Verschmelzung der Begriffe «Politik» und «Typografie». Die typografische Arbeit bestand aus maschinengeschriebenen Texten aus dem Parteiprogramm der SPD und Äusserungen von Brandt und anderen Politikern der Partei. Die Serie wurde ursprünglich 1976 auf der Internationalen Plakatbiennale in Warschau ausgestellt und weiter produziert. Ihren Höhepunkt fand sie schliesslich in der Einzelausstellung *15 Politypographien*, die 1978 in der Print Gallery in Amsterdam gezeigt wurde.

Diese Plakatarbeiten mit ihrer poetischen Schönheit wurden von einigen wegen ihrer Divergenz zwischen dem wörtlichen Inhalt und der Form kritisiert. Schmid ging in seinem Artikel über die Serie in der Ausgabe Nr. 1 von 1980 der Zeitschrift *TM* auf diese Kritik ein. Bei dieser Divergenz handle sich um eine Notwendigkeit für ihn als Typograf und politischer Mensch, die sogar logisch korrekte Kritik übersteige.

Working at ARE
(Düsseldorf, 1976)

Tätigkeit bei ARE
(Düsseldorf, 1976)

Among the many changes the SPD have brought about in today's Federal Republic of Germany, the most significant is a heightened political awareness in the minds of its citizens, who after the war became unpolitical and lethargic. It was Willy Brandt, once a refugee from the Nazis, who first gave the Germans back their pride. In 1972, when the SPD became the strongest party in parliament, the election slogan was: "Germans. You can be proud of your country."

Politics is not only for politicians. Politics is for the people and by the people. But in a country where the media is largely conservative in bias, it is difficult to inform the citizens of the activities of its social-liberal government. As Willy Brandt wrote: "Most news reaches the citizen in truncated form, often only as intimations. In the dialogue with the citizen it is necessary that correlations be explained, intentions and interests made clear, necessities interpreted – and that the ideas are carried forward."

To fill the gap between the media and the government, the government has its own press and information office. This office not only prepares campaigns in newspapers and magazines, it also issues a tremendous number of smaller publications in book or pamphlet form. They can be obtained either directly from the press office or picked up from party display stands.

Between 1973 and 1976, the government press office published a series of information leaflets and ads, black and white, and purely typographic. Black and white as the most definitive message.
They were produced by two Düsseldorf advertising agencies, ARE and GGK, under the direction of Dr. Werner Muller, chief of the press office.
(*Idea*, No. 147, 1978)

Leistungen der Jugendhilfe. Beide zusammen sollen sicherstellen, daß die erforderlichen Einrichtungen, Dienste und Veranstaltungen zur Verfügung stehen. Dazu gehören zum Beispiel Kindergärten, Erziehungsberatungsstellen und Einrichtungen für behinderte Kinder.

Es ist ein weiteres Anliegen der Bundesregierung, durch familienunterstützende und familienergänzende Hilfen die Heimerziehung weitgehend überflüssig zu machen. Außerdem ist beabsichtigt, erzieherische Maßnahmen aus dem Jugendgerichtsgesetz in das neue Jugendhilferecht zu übernehmen: Strafen sollen dann gegen junge Menschen unter 16 Jahren gar nicht mehr ausgesprochen werden können, gegen 16- bis 18jährige nur in ganz außergewöhnlichen Fällen.

Mehr Geld für den Bundesjugendplan.

Die Bundesregierung stellte 1973 für den **24. Bundesjugendplan** 74,5 Millionen DM für laufende Maßnahmen bereit. Für 1974 sind 77,6 Millionen DM vorgesehen. Nach den seit 1971 geltenden Richtlinien für den Bundesjugendplan wird die politische Bildung der Jugend verstärkt gefördert. Das neu geschaffene Programm **Sportliche Jugendbildung** wurde 1973 mit 0,5 Millionen DM unterstützt.

Mehr Mittel für die Bildung.

Die Ausgabenpolitik des Bundes geht in ihrer Bildungspolitik von 2 Zielen aus: Sie will dem einzelnen durch Entwicklung seiner individuellen Begabungen und Neigungen eine chancenreiche Zukunft eröffnen und den gesellschaftlichen Bedarf an qualifiziertem Nachwuchs sichern, um auch in der Welt von morgen Arbeitsplatz und Konkurrenzfähigkeit zu gewährleisten. Dazu bedarf es eines demokratischen und leistungsfähigen Bildungssystems, das jedem Bürger von der Vorschulerziehung bis zur Erwachsenenbildung während seines ganzen Lebens offensteht.

Die Ausgaben des Bundes für Bildung und Wissenschaft haben sich in den Jahren 1970 bis 1973 verdreifacht. Auch in Zukunft werden die Mittel weiter angehoben: gegenüber 3.355 Milliarden DM im Jahre 1973 sind für das Jahr 1974 Mittel in Höhe von 3.829 Milliarden DM vorgesehen.

Chancengleichheit und individuelle Förderung.

Am 20. Juni 1970 legte die Bundesregierung den **Bildungsbericht 70** vor. Er beschreibt das Ziel der Bildungspolitik: ein demokratisches, leistungs- und wandlungsfähiges Bildungssystem, das Chancengleichheit und individuelle Förderung gewährleistet.

Am 25. Juni 1970 schloß die Bundesregierung zur Durchführung einer **langfristigen** gesamtstaatlichen Bildungsplanung ein Verwaltungsabkommen mit den Ländern über die Errichtung einer gemeinsamen „Bund-Länder-Kommission für Bildungsplanung". Ihre Aufgabe: einen für alle Bundesländer verbindlichen „Bildungsgesamtplan" für die Jahre bis 1985 zu erarbeiten.

den 3 Themenbereichen der Konferenz – Wirtschafts- und Währungsunion und sozialer Fortschritt; Außenbeziehungen der Gemeinschaft und ihre Verantwortung in der Welt; Stärkung der Institutionen und Fortschritte im politischen Bereich – wurden Orientierungen festgelegt und ein konkretes Arbeitsprogramm in Form von Aufträgen an die Gemeinschaftsorgane verabschiedet. Die Verwirklichung einer Europäischen Union vor Ablauf dieses Jahrzehnts wurde als vornehmstes Ziel der Mitgliedstaaten bezeichnet. Die Bundesregierung trug durch aktive Teilnahme an der Konferenzvorbereitung und im Rahmen einer Reihe von bilateralen Gesprächen maßgebend zum Erfolg der Konferenz bei. Sie unterbreitete der Konferenz zahlreiche Initiativen, unter anderem ein Memorandum zur europäischen Sozial- und Gesellschaftspolitik.

Aus 6 werden 9: Die Gemeinschaft wird erweitert.

Am 30. Juni 1970 begannen die Verhandlungen über den Beitritt Großbritanniens, Irlands, Dänemarks und Norwegens zu den Europäischen Gemeinschaften. Das Vertragswerk wurde am 22. Januar 1972 in Brüssel unterzeichnet. In Volksabstimmungen in Irland und Dänemark fand der Beitritt zur EG eine Mehrheit. Das britische Parlament stimmte nach langen und gründlichen Erörterungen ebenfalls zu. Der Bundestag billigte das Zustimmungsgesetz zu den Beitrittsverträgen einstimmig am 21. Juni 1972.

In Norwegen erhielt der Vertrag über die Erweiterung in einer Volksabstimmung am 24./26. September 1972

nicht die erforderliche Mehrhe[...] schen ein eigenes Freihandelsa[...] das seit 1. Juli 1973 in Kraft ist[...] einer Freihandelszone in gewe[...] ber 1972 Abkommen mit den s[...] willigen Ländern (Großbritannie[...] wurden mit Wirkung vom 1. Ja[...] der Europäischen Gemeinschaf[...] gliedstaaten umfassen.

Abkommen mit den Rest-E[...]

Mit den nicht beitretenden EF[...] 22. Juli 1972 Abkommen mit s[...] einer Freihandelszone in gewe[...] schlossen, die zum 1. Januar 1[...] 1. April 1973) in Kraft traten. S[...] nungsvolle und entwicklungsf[...] zwischen den Europäischen G[...] EFTA ein. Bei den Verhandlun[...] Bundesregierung dafür eingese[...] Erweiterung der Gemeinschaft[...] schranken in Europa errichtet [...]

Neuordnung der Beziehung[...] und anderen Staaten des M[...]

Die durch die Erweiterung der [...] lich gewordene Anpassung de[...] zierten und anderen Staaten d[...] bildete den Anlaß, daß die EG [...] ber 1972 erstmalig Vorschläge [...] umfassendes Konzept über die[...] gen zu diesen Staaten erörterte[...] für Vertragsangebote an diese [...] den. Dabei geht es besonders [...] und die Zusammenarbeit in w[...] nischem und finanziellem Geb[...] mandat an die Kommission ert[...] am 25./26. Juni 1973. Die Bu[...] hierdurch in der von ihr vertret[...] tigt, daß die Gemeinschaft der [...] des Mittelmeerraums für Europ[...]

* EFTA (European Free Trade Area) zone. Die Rest-EFTA-Staaten sind[...] Österreich, Portugal, Schweden, S[...] assoziierte Finnland.

---

die Bundesregierung informiert
Verbraucherpolitik

die Bundesregierung informiert
Mietrecht

die Bundesregierung informiert
Renten- und Alterssicherung

Eine der vielen Veränderungen durch die SPD in der heutigen Bundesrepublik ist das erhöhte politische Bewusstsein der Bürger, die sich nach dem Krieg eher unpolitisch und lethargisch verhielten. Es war Willy Brandt, einst ein Flüchtling vor den Nationalsozialisten, der den Deutschen als Erster wieder ihren Stolz gab. 1972, als die SPD die stärkste Partei im Bundestag wurde, war der Wahlspruch: «Deutsche. Ihr könnt stolz sein auf euer Land.»

Politik ist nicht nur für Politiker. Politik ist für Menschen von Menschen. Aber in einem Land, in dem die Medien vorwiegend konservativ ausgerichtet sind, ist es schwer, die Bürger über die Aktivitäten ihrer sozialliberalen Regierung zu informieren. Wie Willy Brandt schrieb: «Die meisten Nachrichten erreichen die Bürger verkürzt, oftmals nur als Andeutung. Im Dialog mit den Bürgern ist es notwendig, dass Zusammenhänge erklärt, Intentionen und Interessen geklärt, Notwendigkeiten interpretiert werden – und dass die Ideen entwickelt werden.»

Um die Kluft zwischen den Medien und der Regierung zu füllen, hat die Regierung ihr eigenes Presse- und Informationsbüro. Dieses bereitet nicht nur Kampagnen in Zeitungen und Magazinen vor, es veröffentlicht auch eine grosse Anzahl von Publikationen als Buch oder Flugblatt. Diese sind entweder direkt vom Pressebüro oder an Präsentationsständen der Partei erhältlich.

Zwischen 1973 und 1976 hat das Pressebüro der Regierung eine Serie von Informationsbroschüren und Anzeigen veröffentlicht, schwarz-weiss und ausschliesslich in typografischer Form. Schwarz-Weiss als die definitive Botschaft. Sie wurden entwickelt von zwei Werbeagenturen in Düsseldorf, ARE und GGK, unter der Aufsicht von Dr. Werner Müller, Leiter des Pressebüros.
(Idea, Nr. 147, 1978)

Booklet and information leaflets
for the German Federal
Government, 1972–1974
A5
100 × 210 mm

Broschüre und Informationsblätter
für die deutsche Bundesregierung,
1972–1974

Leaflets for the campaign
"Politik hoeren" (politics to listen to)
The "talking" symbol derived
from Braille.
SPD PR department, 1974
100 × 210 mm (folded)

Informationsblätter für die Kampagne
«Politik hoeren»
Das Symbol für «Sprechen»
wurde der Brailleschrift entlehnt.
Abteilung für Öffentlichkeitsarbeit
der SPD, 1974

Full-page newspaper ad which appeared in all German newspapers
Press- and Information Center of the Federal Government, 1973

Ganzseitige Anzeige, die in allen deutschen Zeitungen erschien
Presse- und Informationsamt der Bundesregierung, 1973

Cover for political journal
Die Neue Gesellschaft
(The New Society)
Verlag Neue Gesellschaft, 1974
170 × 239 mm

Titel für die Politikzeitschrift
Die Neue Gesellschaft
Verlag Neue Gesellschaft, 1974

Die Neue Gesellschaft is a German political monthly, published by Willy Brandt, Carlo Schmid and others. The covers have a line grid that can take up to seven headlines. If a headline is longer than one unit, it runs into the next one. Black type stands on a solid color base. The color range is always decided for one year in advance.
(*Idea*, No. 156, 1979)

Die Neue Gesellschaft ist ein deutsches Monatsheft, veröffentlicht von Willy Brandt, Carlo Schmid und anderen. Die Titel haben ein Linienraster, das bis zu sieben Überschriften aufnehmen kann. Wenn eine Überschrift länger als eine Einheit ist, läuft sie in die nächste. Schwarze Schrift erscheint auf einer soliden Farbbasis. Die Farbpalette wird immer ein Jahr vorher festgelegt.
(*Idea*, Nr. 156, 1979)

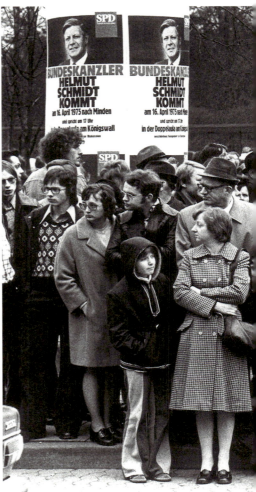

"Bundeskanzler Helmut Schmidt kommt" (Federal Chancellor Helmut Schmidt is coming)
Campaign poster, SPD, 1975
A0

«Bundeskanzler Helmut Schmidt kommt»
Wahlplakat der SPD, 1975

Cover for brochure
Parteiarbeit (Party work)
SPD, 1975
A5

Titel für die Broschüre
Parteiarbeit
SPD, 1975

Cover for brochure
Dokumente (Documents)
SPD, 1975
A5

Titel für die Broschüre
Dokumente
SPD, 1975

Dokumente is a series of important conference papers of the German Social Democratic Party. Programs, guiding principles and laws which are important for work within the political party. The series focuses on a particular target group, on people who want to look more deeply into the political landscape.
The booklets are distributed on the streets or are mailed free of charge. The serial character is achieved by the informative arrangement of the bold sans serif and the small signet-like photo. The political message, as a quote that always accompanies the title, is conveyed directly. Type and photo in black on white. Title of the booklet in red-orange. Special issues are indicated by reversing the colors.
(*TM*, No. 3, 1977)

Cover for *Unkorrigiertes Protokoll* (Unedited Report) of the party conference
SPD, 1975
A5

Titel für das
«Unkorrigierte Protokoll»
des SPD-Parteitags, 1975

Dokumente ist eine Serie wichtiger Konferenztexte der Sozialdemokratischen Partei Deutschlands. Programme, Leitsätze und Gesetze, die für die Arbeit in der Partei wichtig sind. Diese Serie richtet sich an eine bestimmte Zielgruppe, nämlich an Personen, die etwas tiefer in die politische Landschaft hineinblicken möchten. Die Hefte werden auf der Strasse verteilt oder kostenlos zugesandt. Der Seriencharakter wird durch die sachliche Anordnung der fetten Groteskschrift und des kleinen signetartigen Bildes erreicht. Die politische Aussage, zum Titel kommt immer ein Zitat, wird unverschnörkelt vermittelt. Schrift und Foto schwarz auf weiss, Titel des Heftes in Rot-Orange. Sonderhefte werden durch Umkehren der Farbe gekennzeichnet.
(*TM*, Nr. 3, 1977)

Leaflet and letterhead for
Fachkonferenz (symposium)
SPD, 1976
A5, A4

Informationsblatt und
Briefkopf für die
«Sozialdemokratische
Fachkonferenz»
SPD, 1976

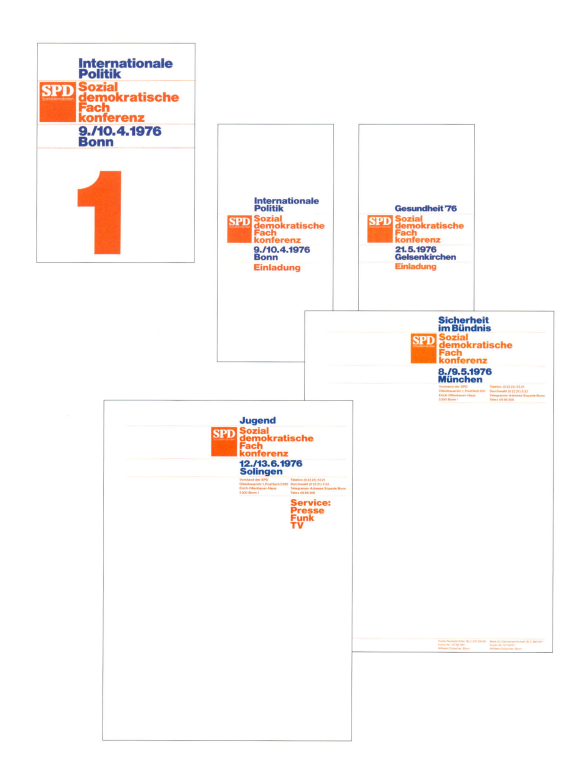

My work for the German Social Democratic Party was inspired
by Nils Johannisson, creative director of the ARE advertising agency.
Our common goal was to present the spirit of the Social Democratic Party as
being trustworthy and contemporary. The enforcement and realization
of my work, of our work, I owe to Nils Johannisson's unwavering support.
(*Helmut Schmid: Design is Attitude*)

Meine Arbeit für die SPD wurde von Nils Johannisson, Creative Director
der ARE-Werbeagentur, inspiriert. Die Gedanken der SPD glaubhaft
und zeitgemäss zu präsentieren, war unser gemeinsames Anliegen.
Aber nur der unerschütterlichen Unterstützung Johannissons verdanke ich
Durchsetzung und Verwirklichung meiner Arbeiten, unserer Arbeiten.
(*Helmut Schmid: Gestaltung ist Haltung*)

Poster
"Responsibility for Germany"
SPD, 1976
A0

Plakat
«Verantwortung für Deutschland»
SPD, 1975

Election campaign poster
Dabeisein (taking part)
SPD, 1976
A0

Wahlplakat «Dabeisein»
SPD, 1976

Election campaign poster
Weiterarbeiten am Modell Deutschland (Continuing work on the German model)
SPD, 1976
A0

Wahlplakat
«Weiterarbeiten am Modell Deutschland»
SPD, 1976

"The trick with the wave" was the title of a *Spiegel* article (No. 39, 1976, pages 28/29) from
which I quote as follows: "For hours the Social Democrats had been discussing the graphic design
of the flag symbol. It should have a certain sweep, the advertising consultants all agreed, but if at all
possible a dip should be avoided. One of the in-house psychologists claimed this would remind voters
of the economic slump. Finally some smart aleck came up with a black-red-gold solution:
the three-color trick with its upwardly rippling waves now to be seen on every SPD poster."

    A party manifesto and party advertising must be created within the party. An advertising agency
can do the visualizing but not the inventing. Only in this way can the truth of a party and
the brains behind it be rendered convincing.
[Letter to the editor of the *Frankfurter Allgemeine Zeitung*, June 8, 2009]
(*AGI Alliance Graphique Internationale Deutsche Mitglieder 1954–2011*)

«Trick mit der Welle» hiess ein Artikel im *Spiegel* (Nr. 39, 1976, Seite 28/29), aus dem ich hier zitiere:
«Bei den Sozialdemokraten hatte die Diskussion über die grafische Gestaltung des Flaggensymbols Stunden
gedauert. Schwung, darüber waren sich die Werbeberater einig, sollte schon drin sein, eine Talkurve
aber möglichst vermieden werden. Denn das, so wollte einer der Baracken-Psychologen wissen,
werde die Wähler an die wirtschaftliche Talsole erinnern. Schliesslich fand dann irgendein Schlauberger
den schwarzrotgoldenen Ausweg: den Dreifarben-Trick mit den Wellen, die nun auf allen SPD-Plakaten
aufwärts schwappen.»

    Parteiprogramm und Parteiwerbung muss in der Partei entstehen. Eine Werbeagentur kann
das visualisieren, aber nicht erfinden. Die Wahrheit einer Partei und ihrer Köpfe kann nur so überzeugen.
[Leserbrief an die *Frankfurter Allgemeine Zeitung*, 8. Juni 2009]
(in: *AGI Alliance Graphique Internationale Deutsche Mitglieder 1954–2011*)

Letterhead for the party conference
SPD, 1975
A4

Briefkopf für den Parteitag
SPD, 1975

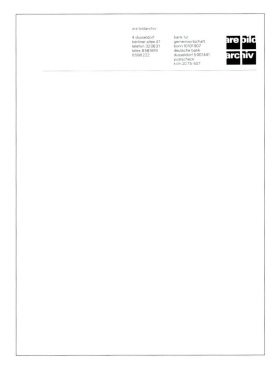

Visual identity for
ARE Bildarchiv (image archive), 1973

Erscheinungsbild für das
ARE-Bildarchiv, 1973

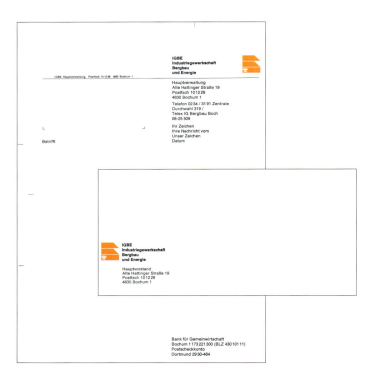

Visual identity for the IGBE
(mining and energy industrial union)
IGBE, 1976

Erscheinungsbild für die IGBE
(Industriegewerkschaft Bergbau und Energie)
IGBE, 1976

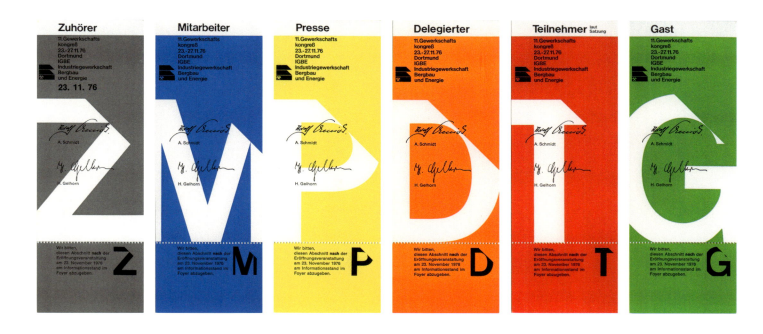

Entrance tickets for the
IGBE congress, 1976
70 × 197 mm

Eintrittskarten für den
IGBE-Kongress, 1976

Booklet for IGBE, 1976
150 × 207 mm

Broschüre für die
IGBE, 1976

das ist der unserer zeit

widerspruch

dass der mensch die urkraft des atoms entfesselte
und sich jetzt vor den folgen fürchtet

dass der mensch die produktivkräfte aufs höchste entwickelte
ungeheuere reichtümer ansammelte
ohne allen einen gerechten anteil
an dieser gemeinsamen leistung zu verschaffen

dass der mensch sich die räume dieser erde unterwarf
die kontinente aneinanderrückte
nun aber in waffen starrende machtblöcke
die völker mehr voneinander trennen als je zuvor
und totalitäre systeme seine freiheit bedrohen

**darum fürchtet der mensch
gewarnt durch die zerstörungskriege und barbareien
seiner jüngsten vergangenheit
die eigene zukunft
weil in jedem augenblick an jedem punkt der welt
durch menschliches versagen
das chaos der selbstvernichtung ausgelöst werden kann**

hoffnung

aber das ist auch die dieser zeit

dass der mensch im atomaren zeitalter sein leben erleichtern
von sorgen befreien
und wohlstand für alle schaffen kann
wenn er seine tägliche wachsende macht über die naturkräfte
nur für friedliche zwecke einsetzt

dass der mensch den weltfrieden sichern kann
wenn er die internationale rechtsordnung stärkt
das misstrauen zwischen den völkern mindert
und das wettrüsten verhindert

dass der mensch dann zum erstenmal in seiner geschichte
jedem die entfaltung seiner persönlichkeit in einer gesicherten demokratie ermöglichen kann
zu einem leben in kultureller vielfalt jenseits von not und furcht

diesen widerspruch aufzulösen
sind wir menschen aufgerufen
in unsere hand ist die verantwortung gelegt
für eine glückliche zukunft
oder für die selbstzerstörung der menschheit

nur durch eine neue und bessere ordnung der gesellschaft
öffnet der mensch den weg in seine freiheit

diese neue und bessere ordnung
erstrebt der demokratische sozialismus

godesberger grundsatzprogramm

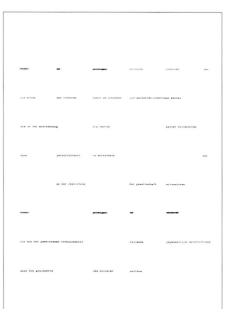
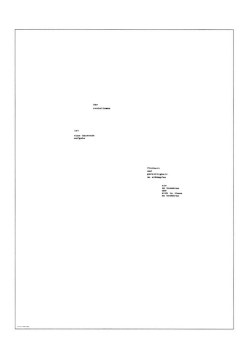
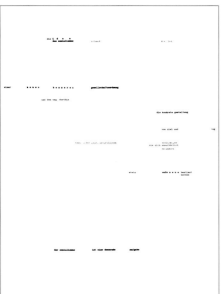
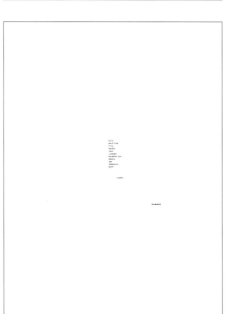
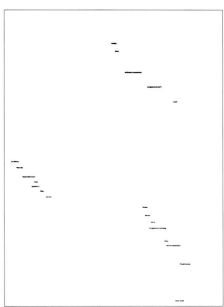
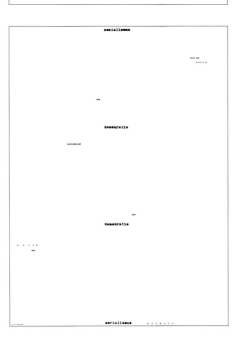
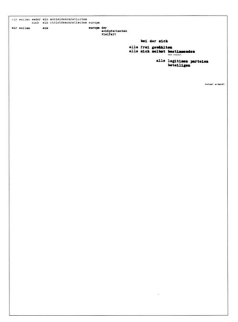

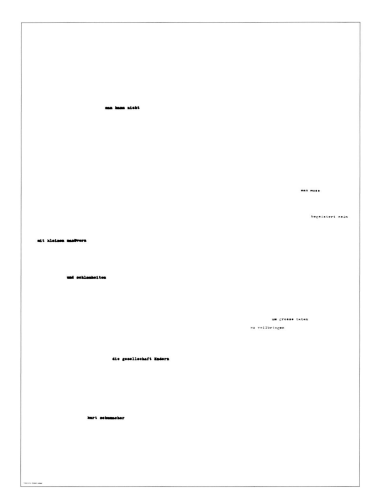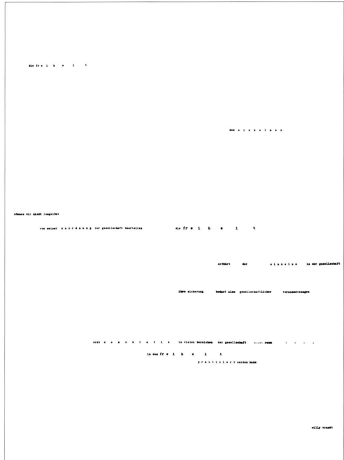

Pages 116–119:
15 Politypographien, 1974–1977
Text: *Godesberger Programm*,
Willy Brandt, Helmut Schmidt et al.
A2

S. 116–119:
15 Politypographien, 1974–1977
Texte aus dem *Godesberger Programm*,
von Willy Brandt, Helmut Schmidt u. a.

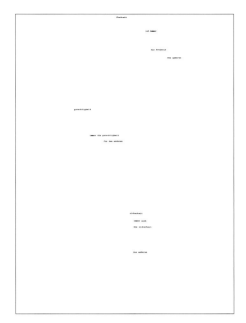  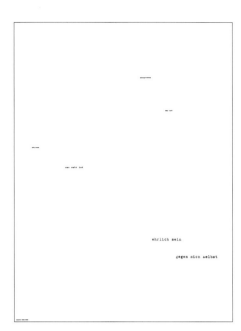

15 Politypographien (Pieter Brattinga coined the title) are my typographic
interpretations of Social Democratic aphorisms, created between 1974 and 1977, at about
the same time that I was taking part in shaping the visual identity of the German
Social Democratic Party. Inspired by Pieter Brattinga's invitation to exhibit at his Print Gallery
in Amsterdam, I decided spontaneously on the message. I probably spent more time
selecting texts than forming them. I still support the content of the texts, but would
probably visualize them today in a different style.
    The unevenness of the typewritten text is intensified by additional deformations,
such as indistinctness, over- and underexposure, typing on different papers. In one word
we can find several thicknesses, which give the word a new meaning.
(*TM*, No. 1, 1980)

    Die *15 Politypographien* (der Titel stammt von Pieter Brattinga) sind meine
typografischen Interpretationen sozialdemokratischer Aphorismen, entstanden zwischen
1974 und 1977, etwa zur selben Zeit, in der ich das visuelle Design der Sozialdemokratischen Partei in der Bundesrepublik Deutschland mitbestimmte. Angeregt
durch Pieter Brattingas Einladung, in seiner ästhetischen Galerie in Amsterdam
auszustellen, entschied ich mich spontan für die Mitteilung. Wahrscheinlich habe ich
mehr Zeit für die Auswahl der Texte als für deren Formung verwendet. Zu den
Texten stehe ich noch, formal würde ich sie heute neu visualisieren.
    Das Zufällige des Schreibmaschinenanschlags ist durch die zusätzlichen Verfor-
mungen wie Unschärfe, Über- und Unterbelichten sowie Schreiben auf verschiedenen
Papieren intensiviert. So sind in einem Wort oft mehrere Dichten, die dem Wort
dann zu einer neuen Bedeutung verhelfen.
(*TM*, Nr. 1, 1980)

6 character and philosophy: corporate and store identity

Charakter und Philosophie:
Corporate und Store Identity

Returning to Japan in 1977, Schmid worked for NIA before going freelance
in 1981 in order to "to concentrate on essential design." In Düsseldorf, he had married
Sumiko Tanaka, a former colleague from his NIA days, and they had a daughter,
Nicole, shortly after returning to Japan.

For Schmid, who was in his mid-30s at the time, it was probably the right time
to settle down. The choice to continue to live and work in Osaka was very natural
for Schmid, who had been to many Western cities, each with its own cultural sphere.
He also had a firm belief that he would never change, regardless of his location.

After becoming a freelancer, Schmid expanded the scope of his work through
the friends and clients he had met at NIA and during his life. In the 1980s,
corporate identity had become a social business trend that transcended the framework of the design industry in Japan.

Schmid, on the other hand, had acquired the basic strategy and know-how of
information design for communicating ideas and ideals to society through his several
years of work for the political party and government in Düsseldorf. Consequently,
from the 1980s onward, identity design became one of Schmid's main fields of work.

The visual identities that Schmid worked on during this time vary in
type and scale, ranging from private offices of acquaintances to major corporations.
However, his way of working was consistent in both cases, and he captured the
essence of the company or product in question, and created simple, elegant details
and basic structures for the logotype.

Schmid's control over words and letters, as well as his ingenuity in creating
each letterform, was made possible by his knowledge of the history of letters and his
understanding of the message to be conveyed. It is not something that can be
created by merely stylizing any given text from a client. Schmid's idea of logotype is
aptly expressed in the following quote:

> "Visually, characters are sound sculptures. The minutest change made to a
> part of a design requires a revamping of the whole. This point becomes
> significant in the design of a logotype, because in a logotype a limited number
> of characters must be united into a new harmony. The smallest detail in the
> thickness of strokes, in form and counterform, in rhythm and space, separates
> a good logotype from a poor logotype.
> A logotype should be an unobtrusive part of the product itself, but it should
> have a certain identification value, a mnemonic device, to stand on its own in an
> advertisement or in a tv commercial. But the logotype should never become
> just an image maker but a signature of quality for a product or company."
> ("Typography derived from content," *Japan Typography Annual 1989*, Robundo, 1989)

In addition, during a roundtable discussion about corporate identity with
designers working in the bubble economy in the 1980s, Schmid stated that it takes time
and trust with a client to create such a logo.

> "It takes years to develop a style. A style is not something that can be created
> in a few months."
> ("Critical discussion about CI," *Graphic Design in Japan*, Vol. 5 Kodansha, 1985)

For Schmid, logos for companies and typography applied to text are both interconnected in terms of conveying messages, regardless of whether the subject is an
individual or a group. Despite the rise and fall of the CI boom, Schmid fostered
trust with his clients in order to create logos with enduring beauty and power.

Nach seiner Rückkehr nach Japan 1977 arbeitete Schmid für die NIA, bevor er sich
1981 selbstständig machte, um «sich auf die Essenz der Gestaltung zu konzentrieren».
In Düsseldorf hatte er Sumiko Tanaka geheiratet, eine ehemalige Kollegin aus seiner früheren
Zeit bei der NIA, und kurz nach ihrer Rückkehr nach Japan bekamen sie eine Tochter, Nicole.

Für Schmid, damals Mitte dreissig, war es wahrscheinlich der richtige Zeitpunkt,
sich niederzulassen. Die Entscheidung, weiterhin in Osaka zu leben und zu arbeiten, war
logisch für ihn, der schon viele westliche Städte mit ihrem eigenen kulturellen Umfeld
kennengelernt hatte. Ausserdem war er der festen Überzeugung, dass er sich nie ändern
würde, unabhängig von seinem Wohnort.

Nachdem Schmid sich als Freiberufler selbstständig gemacht hatte, erweiterte er den
Umfang seiner Tätigkeiten durch die Freundschaften und den Kundenstamm, die er in seinem
Leben und bei der NIA geknüpft und gepflegt hatte. In den 1980er Jahren war der Bereich
Corporate Identity zu einem Geschäftstrend geworden, der den Rahmen der japanischen
Designbranche sprengte.

Die grundlegende Strategie und das Know-how des Informationsdesigns zur Vermittlung von Ideen und Idealen an die Gesellschaft hatte Schmid durch seine mehrjährige
Tätigkeit für die Partei und die Regierung in Düsseldorf erworben. Entsprechend wurde das
Identitätsdesign ab den 1980er Jahren zu einem der Hauptarbeitsfelder von Schmid.

Die visuellen Identitäten, an denen Schmid in dieser Zeit arbeitete, variierten in Art und
Umfang und reichten von privaten Büros von Bekannten bis hin zu grossen Konzernen.
Seine Arbeitsweise war jedoch in beiden Fällen die gleiche: Er erfasste die Essenz des
jeweiligen Unternehmens oder Produkts und schuf einfache, elegante Details und
Grundstrukturen für das Logo.

Schmids Beherrschung von Wörtern und Buchstaben sowie sein Einfallsreichtum
bei der Gestaltung jeder einzelnen Buchstabenform wurden durch sein Wissen über
die Geschichte der Buchstaben und sein Verständnis der zu vermittelnden Botschaft ermöglicht. Das ist etwas, das sich nicht durch die blosse Stilisierung eines beliebigen Kundentexts erreichen lässt. Seine Vorstellung von einem Logo drückt Schmid treffend aus:

> «Visuell sind Schriftzeichen Klangskulpturen. Die kleinste Änderung an einem Teil eines
> Designs erfordert eine Umgestaltung des Ganzen. Dieser Punkt ist beim Entwerfen
> eines Logos von Bedeutung, weil bei einem Logo eine begrenzte Anzahl
> von Zeichen zu einer neuen Harmonie zusammengefügt werden muss. Kleinste
> Details in der Strichstärke, in Form und Gegenform, in Rhythmus und Abstand
> unterscheiden ein gutes von einem schlechten Logo.
> Ein Logo sollte ein unauffälliger Teil des Produkts selbst sein, aber es sollte einen
> gewissen Wiedererkennungswert haben, eine Gedächtnisstütze sein, um in einer
> Werbeanzeige oder in einem TV-Werbespot für sich allein stehen zu können. Das Logo
> sollte jedoch niemals nur ein Imageträger sein, sondern ein Qualitätsmerkmal für
> ein Produkt oder ein Unternehmen.»
> («Typography Derived from Content», in: *Japan Typography Annual 1989*, Roubundo, 1989)

Weiter erklärte Schmid in einer Diskussionsrunde über Corporate Identity mit Designern,
die in der Bubble Economy der 1980er Jahre arbeiteten, dass es Zeit und Vertrauen zu einem
Kunden brauche, um ein solches Logo zu entwerfen.

> «Es braucht Jahre, um einen Stil zu entwickeln. Stil ist nicht etwas, das in ein paar
> Monaten geschaffen werden kann.»
> («Critical discussion about CI», in: *Graphic Design in Japan*, Nr. 5, Kodansha, 1985)

Für Schmid sind Logos für Unternehmen und Typografie für Texte miteinander verbunden,
denn es geht bei beiden darum, Botschaften zu übermitteln, unabhängig davon, ob es sich um
ein Individuum oder eine Gruppe handelt. Ungeachtet des Aufstiegs und Niedergangs des
Bereichs Corporate Identity pflegte Schmid ein Vertrauensverhältnis zu seiner Kundschaft,
um Logos von dauerhafter Wirkung zu schaffen.

Calendar for design agency
and printing company
Yarakasukan / NIA, 1978
364 × 375 mm

Kalender für Designbüro
und Druckerei
Yarakasukan / NIA, 1978

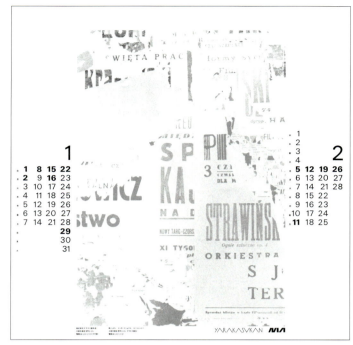

The shapes of letters isolated from their function – readability – become
pure form: straight lines, curved lines, ascending lines, descending lines, dotted
lines. Posters freed from their function – message – have a similar appeal.
Poster walls, with posters beside posters, with lettershapes next to lettershapes,
have a vividness comparable to the modern arts. Street collages of great
vitality can still be seen in poster countries such as Poland and Italy, where
the letters of the posters are still dominant and freely and freshly used.
The poster walls are like multiply exposed pictures, accidental forms
shaped by people, weather, mood and spontaneity.
(*TM*, No. 3, 1978)

Calendar for design agency
and printing company
NIA / Yarakasukan, 1980
364 × 375 mm

Kalender für Designbüro
und Druckerei
NIA / Yarakasukan, 1980

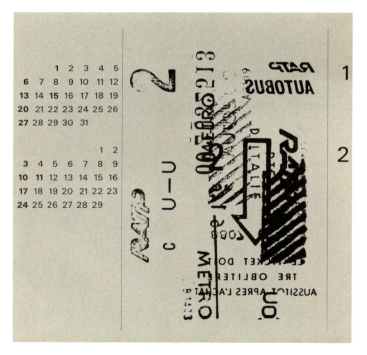

Die Formen der Buchstaben werden zur reinen Form, wenn sie von ihrer Funktion – Lesbarkeit – befreit sind. Gerade Linien, gebogene Linien, anschwellende Linien, abfallende Linien, punktierte Linien. Plakate, von ihrer Funktion – Mitteilung – entbunden, haben einen ähnlichen Appeal.

Plakatwände mit Plakat neben Plakat, mit Buchstabenform neben Buchstabenform haben eine Dynamik, die den Vergleich mit der modernen Kunst erlaubt. Strassencollagen von enormer Lebendigkeit sind immer noch in Plakatländern wie Polen oder Italien anzutreffen, wo Schriften die Plakate dominieren und frei und zwanglos eingesetzt sind. Die Plakatwände sind wie mehrmals belichtete Bilder, sind zufällige Formen, geformt von Passanten, Wetter, Stimmung und Zufall.
(*TM*, Nr. 3, 1978)

 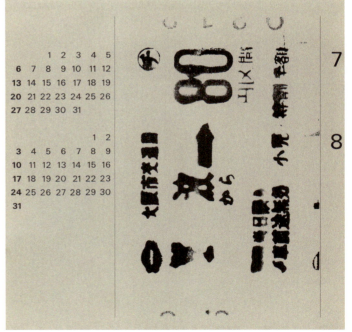

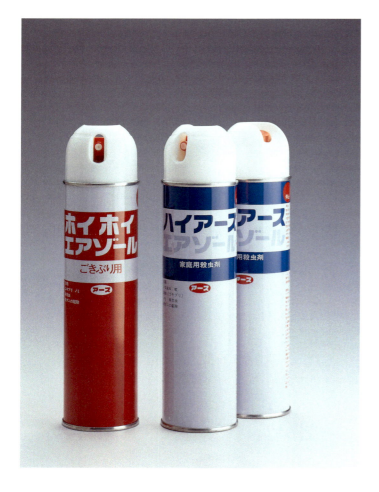

Logo and packaging for
aerosol insecticide
Earth Corporation, 1978

Logo und Verpackung für ein
Aerosol-Insektizid
Earth Corporation, 1978

ハイアースエアゾール
電子アース
　　アースマット ƒ
電子アースコードレス
　　アースレッド
　　アース

Packaging for
Ilford FP4 and Ilford HP4
Ciba Geigy Japan, 1978

Verpackungen für
Ilford FP4 und Ilford HP4
Ciba Geigi Japan, 1978

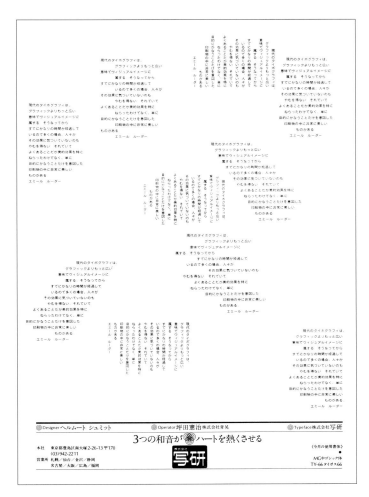

Ads for phototypesetting company
Shaken, 1980
A4

Werbeanzeigen für das
Fotosatz-Unternehmen
Shaken, 1980

Logo for children's care products
manufacturer
Aprica, 1979

Logo für einen Hersteller
von Pflegeprodukten für Kinder
Aprica, 1979

Visual identity for
sales promotion company
Suntory Shopping Club, 1983

Erscheinungsbild für das
Verkaufskaufsförderungs-Unternehmen
Suntory Shopping Club, 1983

Visual identity for clothing company
Sanki Shoji, 1980

Erscheinungsbild für den
Bekleidungshersteller
Sanki Shoji, 1980

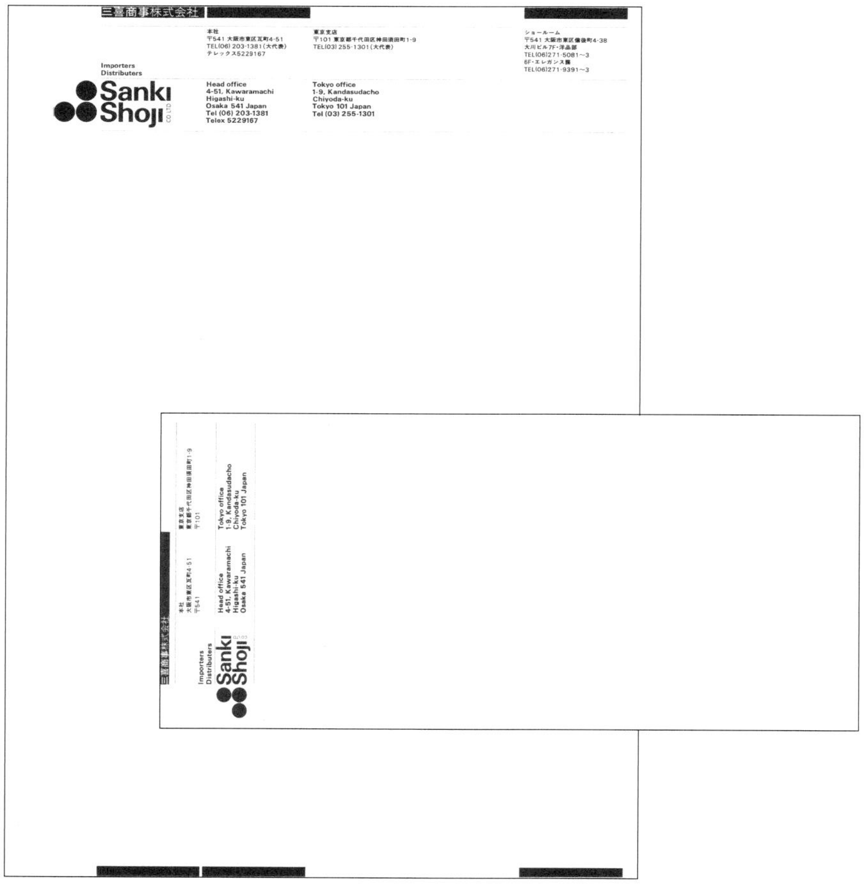

To commemorate the 10th anniversary of the fashion company Itariyard, a new visual identity was introduced. The logo was developed with a drawn Bodoni in lower case. The symbol was inspired by the two *i* dots of the company name and represents East and West, inside and outside, masculine and feminine. It also includes the sign for infinity.
(*Helmut Schmid: Design is Attitude*)

Zum zehnten Jahrestag der Modefirma Itariyard wurde eine neue visuelle Identität eingeführt. Das Logo entstand aus einer gezeichneten Bodoni in Kleinbuchstaben. Das Symbol ging aus den zwei i-Punkten des Firmennamens hervor und repräsentiert Ost und West, innen und aussen, männlich und weiblich. Es beinhaltet gleichzeitig das Zeichen für unendlich.
(*Helmut Schmid: Gestaltung ist Haltung*)

Visual identity for apparel company
Itariyard, 1986
A4

Erscheinungsbild für die Bekleidungsfirma
Itariyard, 1984

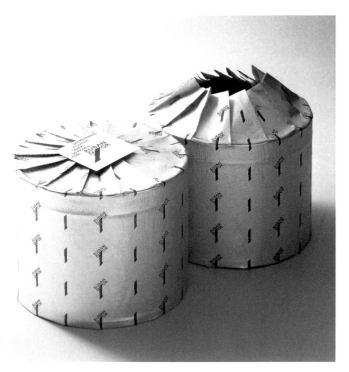

Visual identity for Ruban d'Or,
confectionery brand
Belle, 1981

Erscheinungsbild für die
Konfektmarke Ruban d'Or
Belle, 1981

Visual identity for Kobe Belle
Belle, 1987

Erscheinungsbild für Kobe Belle
Belle, 1987

神戸ベル

Takeo Desk Diary No. 29
Pine Mountain Cloud
Takeo, 1987
180 × 300 mm
Calligraphy and text: Wucius Wong
Painting: Kan Tai-Keung

Takeo-Tischkalender Nr. 29
Kiefer Berg Wolke
Takeo, 1987
Kalligrafie und Text von Wucius Wong
Gemälde von Kan Tai-Keung

Poster for Shino, Japanese typeface
Ryobi, 1987
515 × 728 mm

Plakat für Shino in japanischer Schrift
Ryobi, 1987

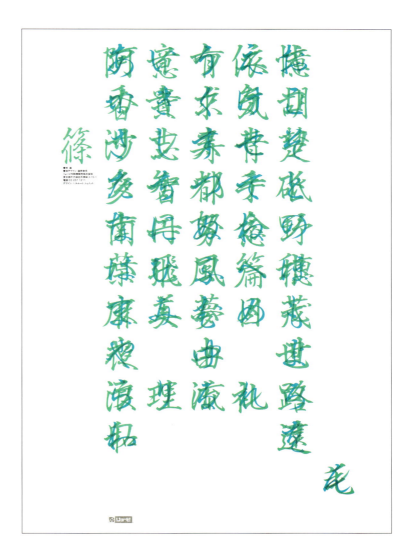

Each year, a different designer is asked to design the desk diary of the paper company Takeo.
When Mr. Kido of Takeo asked me, he had the idea of combining two cultures. He suggested that
the paintings of Hong Kong artist Kan Tai-Keung would make a good contrast with my style of
European grid typography.
   Art in the diary should enrich the dry figures of the calendar and information tables. As a kind
of counterpoint to the delicate paintings, with their Asian flair, I set the paintings' titles in large,
powerful brush strokes. For the cover I used the three Chinese characters of the diary's title –
pine, mountain, cloud, printed in deep blue on a cloud-like high-quality paper.
The actual diary is designed in a clear typography with much attention to the typographic details.
It is great fun to work with different people, who have different ideas, in different countries.
East needs West, West needs East.
(*Cross-Cultural Design*)

Jedes Jahr entwirft ein anderer Grafiker den Tischkalender für die Papierfabrik Takeo.
Als Herr Kido von Takeo mich fragte, hatte er den Gedanken, zwei Kulturen zu vereinen.
Er meinte, die Gemälde des Hongkonger Künstlers Kan Tai-Keung wären ein guter Kontrast zu
meiner europäischen, auf Raster basierenden Typografie.
   Kunst im Kalender sollt die trockenen Zahlen und Informationen bereichern. Als eine Art
Kontrapunkt zu den delikaten Malereien mit ihrem asiatischen Flair setzte ich die Titel der Werke in
grossen, markanten Pinselstrichen. Für den Umschlag benutzte ich drei chinesische Zeichen
für den Titel des Kalenders – Kiefer, Berg, Wolke, gedruckt in tiefem Blau auf einem wolken-
ähnlichen Qualitätspapier. Der Kalender selbst ist mit einer klaren Typografie gestaltet,
mit besonderer Beachtung der typografischen Details. Es macht Spass, mit unterschiedlichen
Leuten mit unterschiedlichen Ideen in unterschiedlichen Ländern zu arbeiten.
Osten braucht Westen, Westen braucht Osten.
(*Cross-Cultural Design*)

Visual identity for
photographer's office
Asai Studio, 1985

Erscheinungsbild für das
Fotostudio
Asai Studio, 1985

Asai is the studio name of the photographers Yasuhiro and Kayoko.
The repetition of the name in the logo, in positive and negative forms,
symbolizes the principles of photography: being a product of the positive
and the negative. It also symbolizes yin and yang, male and female.
(www.hsdesign.jp)

Asai ist der Name des Studios der Fotografen Yasuhiro und Kayoko.
Der Schriftzug wiederholt die Namen in negativer und positiver Form als
Symbolisierung der fotografischen Prinzipien: ein Produkt des Negativen und
Positiven. Es symbolisiert auch Yin und Yang, weiblich und männlich.
(www.hsdesign.jp)

Book design for *Revelation*,
portfolio of Yasuhiro Asai
Asai Studio, 1988
245 × 285 mm

Buchgestaltung für *Revelation*,
eine Mappe von Yasuhiro Asai
Asai Studio, 1988

Visual identity for Masiyak,
flower couture
Hiromi Saito, 1988

Erscheinungsbild für Masiyak,
Gestaltungskunst mit Blumen
Hiromi Saito, 1988

Opening announcement of Masiyak
Hiromi Saito, 1989
250 × 250 mm
Photo: Yasuhiro Asai

Ankündigung der Eröffnung von Masiyak
Hiromi Saito, 1989
Foto: Yasuhiro Asai

Logo for human resource
development company
Face, 1990

Logo für das
Personalentwicklungs-
Unternehmen
Face, 1990

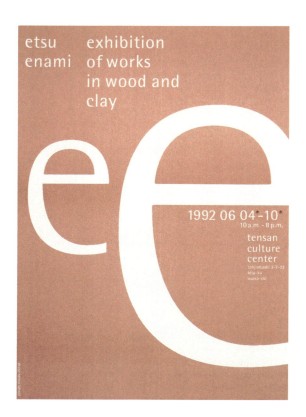

Poster for *Works in Wood and Clay*
Exhibition by Etsu Enami
1992
A2

Plakat für *Works in wood and clay*,
eine Ausstellung von Etsu Enami
1992

Book design
*Tomoko Sugiyama: Heart-Washing Day.
Works, Paintings, Memos 1982–95*
Gallery Shimada Yamaguchi, 1995
250 × 268 mm

Buchgestaltung
*Tomoko Sugiyama: Heart-Washing Day.
Works, Paintings, Memos 1982–95*
Arbeiten von Tomoko Sugiyama
Galerie Shimada Yamaguchi, 1955

Book design
Atashi to issyo no haka ni hairou
(Join me in my grave),
The Collected Poems of
Kyoko Amino
Sougenshisha, 2004
115 × 210 mm

Buchgestaltung
Atashi to issyo no haka ni hairou
(Leg dich zu mir ins Grab):
Die gesammelten Gedichte von
Kyoko Amino
Sougenshisha, 2004

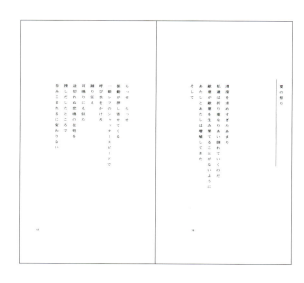

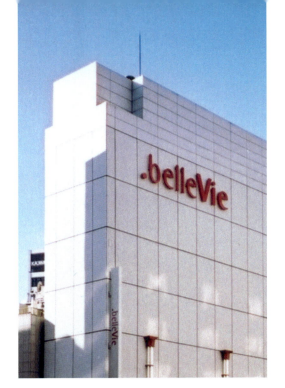

In 2000, Belle Vie Akasaka renovated its building and took this chance to brush up their logo. *Belle vie*, which means "beautiful life" in French, is a good name with an unusually good letter combination of rounded and straight letters. The new logo separates the two words in light and bold, which makes a wordspace unnecessary. *Belle* (beautiful) is set in lower case to give prominence to the words *vie* (life). The point in front of the logo wants to separate Belle Vie from its competitors. It also signifies the beginning of something new (new century, new millennium, refreshment of the enterprise). The new logomark expresses the enterprise as trustful, vivid and forward-striving with a design that is simple and elegant and with a flair of innovation.
(www.hsdesign.jp)

Im Jahr 2000 renovierte Belle Vie Akasaka sein Gebäude und erneuerte bei der Gelegheit auch den Schriftzug. «Belle vie», französisch für «schönes Leben», ist ein guter Name mit einer ungewöhnlichen Kombination von runden und geraden Buchstaben. Der neue Schriftzug trennt die beiden Wörter in mager und fett, somit ist der Zwischenraum nicht nötig. «Belle» (schön) erscheint in Kleinbuchstaben und betont somit das Wort «vie» (Leben). Der Punkt vor dem Schriftzug soll Belle Vie von der Konkurrenz trennen. Er signalisiert auch den Anfang von etwas Neuem (neues Jahrtausend, neues Jahrhundert, Erneuerung des Unternehmens). Der neue Schriftzug visualisiert das Unternehmen als vertrauensvoll, lebendig und in die Zukunft blickend mithilfe einer einfachen und eleganten Gestaltung mit einem Hauch von Innovation.
(www.hsdesign.jp)

Company logo
Belle Vie Akasaka
Tokyo Metro Urban Development,
2000

Logo für das Geschäftsgebäude
Belle Vie Akasaka
Tokyo Metro Urban Development,
2000

Two words are just not enough to capture the mood of grandeur of Kieler Woche: water, sport, culture, play... The corporate design for Kieler Woche 2003 is based on a flexible word-symbol, a typographic wordplay, inviting visitors and spectators to join in creating together, writing together and enjoying together.
A clear, a friendly orange is suggested as the identity color, on which the information rests in white and black. The corporate design lives by the flexibility of the symbols, intended for variable applications.
(www.hsdesign.jp)

Zwei Worte reichen nicht aus, um die grandiose Stimmung der Kieler Woche zu beschreiben: Wasser, Sport, Kultur, Spiel ... Die Gestaltung der Kieler Woche 2003 basiert auf einem flexiblen Wort-Symbol, einem typografischen Wortspiel, das die Besucher und Zuschauer dazu animiert, gemeinsam zu kreieren, zu schreiben und Spass miteinander zu haben. Ein klares, freundliches Orange gilt als Identitätsfarbe, auf dem die Information in Schwarz-Weiss erscheint. Die Identitätsgestaltung lebt durch die Flexibilität der Symbole, vorgesehen für variable Einsätze.
(www.hsdesign.jp)

Proposal for identity program of
Kieler Woche 2003
(awarded but not used)
Kieler Woche, 2001
A1

Plakatvorschlag im Rahmen der
Entwicklung des Erscheinungsbilds
der Kieler Woche 2003
(beauftragt, aber nicht verwendet)
Kieler Woche, 2001

7
linking function and strategy:
packaging
for
otsuka

Funktion und Strategie verbinden:
Verpackungen für Otsuka

Since the 1980s, one of Schmid's most important clients had been Otsuka Pharmaceutical. Schmid used to work for Otsuka Pharmaceutical and its affiliates during his time at NIA on his first visit to Japan. Schmid's return to Japan coincided with the appointment of the company's new president, Akihiko Otsuka, who was beginning to work on further business innovations.

Akihiko was responsible for the planning and development of such epoch-making products as the retort-packed Bon Curry, the health drink Pocari Sweat and the nutritional food Calorie Mate, as well as for strengthening the research and development of the pharmaceutical business and establishing a new era for the Otsuka Group. Akihiko also had a high awareness of design and its importance, and was a good friend of Schmid and liked his work.

"I was also fortunate that the president of Otsuka was very knowledgeable and understanding of the world of design. He immediately decided on the current design out of the three that I had proposed at the presentation. I think he actually wanted to be a designer himself [laughs]. At the time, we were very lucky because Otsuka Pharmaceutical was already profitable with its long-selling product, Oronamin C, and our strategy for the new Pocari Sweat product was to develop the market with a long-term vision of a 10-year cycle. It was unthinkable in the Japanese market, where products are usually replaced at a rapid pace in short cycles."
("What's Next? Chapter 3: Letter, Interview with Helmut Schmid,"
News and Report 90, No. 179, Japan Package Design Association, 2005)

The package for Pocari Sweat, a health drink that launched in 1980 and became a huge hit in Japan, is one of the most well-known among Schmid's works. His relationship with the Otsuka Group continued after he started freelancing in 1981, and he continued to design many logos and packages for the company's beverages, foods and pharmaceutical products.

These designs had an impact on consumers; their modern look was completely different from the pop American food and beverage packaging of the 1970s. Schmid also designed the company's corporate brochures, calendars and even Akihiko Otsuka's personal New Year's greeting cards, giving the company an international flair as it pursued its global expansion.

New Year's greeting of Akihiko Otsuka
Otsuka Pharmaceutical, 1983
400 × 210 mm
Calligraphy: Shizan Uera

Neujahrsgruss von Akihiko Otsuka
Otsuka Pharmaceutical, 1983
Kalligrafie: Shizan Uera

Ab den 1980er Jahren gehörte Otsuka Pharmaceutical zu Schmids wichtigsten Kunden. Schon während seines ersten Aufenthalts in Japan, als Schmid bei der NIA tätig war, hatte er für das Pharmaunternehmen und dessen verbundene Unternehmen gearbeitet. Parallel zu Schmids Rückkehr nach Japan war ein neuer Präsident für das Unternehmen, Akihiko Otsuka, ernannt worden, der weitere geschäftliche Innovationen verantwortete.

Akihiko war verantwortlich für die Planung und Entwicklung von solch wegweisenden Produkten wie die Bon-Curry-Fertiggerichte, das isotonische Erfrischungsgetränk Pocari Sweat und das Nahrungsergänzungsmittel Calorie Mate sowie für die Stärkung des Bereichs Forschung und Entwicklung des Pharmageschäfts. Damit leitete er eine neue Ära für den Otsuka-Konzern ein. Akihiko hatte zudem ein ausgeprägtes Bewusstsein für Design und dessen Bedeutung und war ein guter Freund von Schmid, dessen Arbeit er schätzte.

«Ich hatte auch das Glück, dass der Präsident von Otsuka sehr sachkundig war und einen Sinn für Design hatte. Von den drei Entwürfen, die ich ihm präsentierte, fiel seine Wahl sofort auf das jetzige Design. Ich glaube, er wäre eigentlich selbst gerne Designer gewesen [lacht]. Wir hatten damals grosses Glück, denn Otsuka Pharmaceutical war mit seinem langjährigen Erfolgsprodukt Oronamin C bereits rentabel, und unsere Strategie für das neue Produkt Pocari Sweat bestand darin, den Markt mit einer langfristigen Vision eines 10-Jahres-Zyklus zu entwickeln. Das war auf dem japanischen Markt, wo Produkte in der Regel in kurzen Zyklen ausgetauscht werden, undenkbar.»

(«What's Next? Chapter 3: Letter, Interview with Helmut Schmid», in: *News and Report 90*, Nr. 179, Japan Package Design Association, 2005)

Die Verpackung für Pocari Sweat, ein isotonisches Erfrischungsgetränk, das 1980 auf den Markt kam und in Japan zu einem Bestseller wurde, gehört zu den bekanntesten Arbeiten von Schmid. Seine Beziehung zum Otsuka-Konzern bestand auch nach seinem Schritt in die Selbstständigkeit 1981 fort, und er entwarf weiterhin zahlreiche Logos und Verpackungen für die Getränke, Nahrungsmittel und pharmazeutischen Produkte des Unternehmens.

Seine Entwürfe hatten eine Wirkung auf die Konsumentinnen und Konsumenten; ihr moderner Look unterschied sich völlig von den poppigen amerikanischen Lebensmittel- und Getränkeverpackungen der 1970er Jahre. Schmid gestaltete auch Broschüren und Kalender für das Unternehmen und selbst die persönlichen Neujahrskarten von Akihiko Otsuka, was dem Unternehmen im Zuge seiner weltweiten Expansion ein internationales Flair verlieh.

Mock-up of Pocari Sweat, 1980

Vorführmodell für Pocari Sweat, 1980

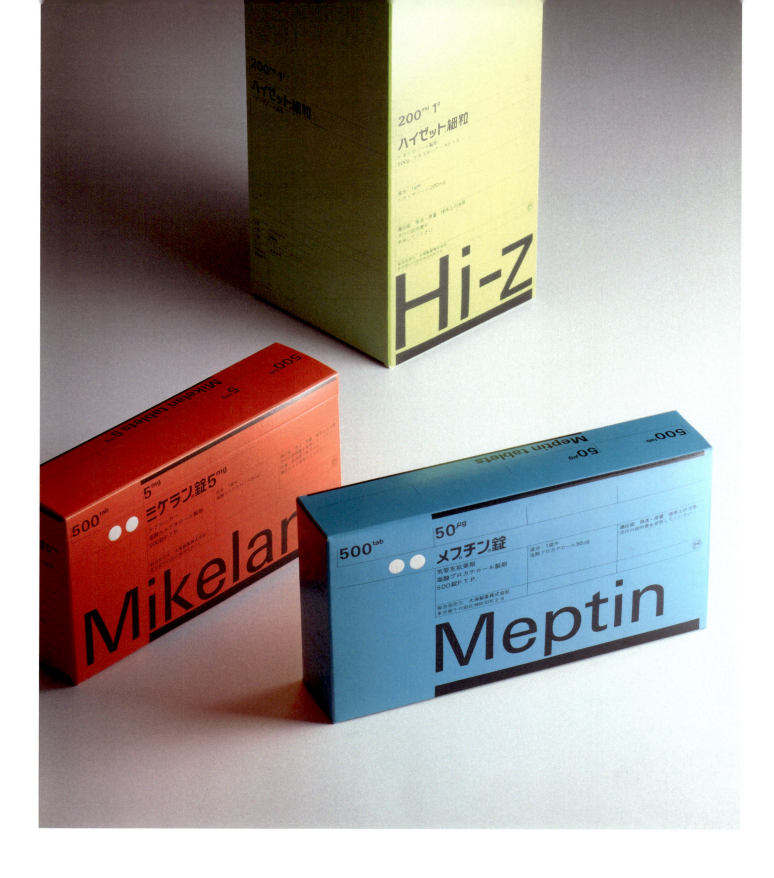

Medical packaging series
Otsuka Pharmaceutical,
1980

Syllable typeface for the
medical packaging series,
Otsuka Pharmaceutical, 1980

Serie von Arzneiverpackungen
Otsuka Pharmaceutical,
1980

Silbenschrift für die Serie
von Arzneiverpackungen
Otsuka Pharmaceutical, 1980

A requirement for packaging in the pharmaceutical industry is that the information be presented in a clear and unambiguous way that permits rapid identification by the physician. The concept of this series is the consistent structuring of product information in horizontal or vertical information areas: amount, contents, product name, classification, composition, dosage, precautions, manufacturer. Each product group has its own color code. The visual characteristic lies in the use of the product groups' symbol-like names in Univers, which coin the image of this purely typographical series.
(*TM*, No. 1, 1989)

Eine Voraussetzung für medizinische Packungen ist die klare und schnelle Information, eine Information, die jeden möglichen Irrtum ausschliesst, wenn das Produkt benötigt wird. Das Konzept dieser Serie besteht aus der konsequenten Gliederung von Produktinformation in horizontal oder vertikal ausgerichteten Informationsfeldern: Menge, Gehalt, Produktname, Klassifizierung, Zusammensetzung, Gebrauchsanleitung, Vorsichtsmassnahmen, Hersteller.
　　Jede Produktgruppe ist durch einen Farbcode unterscheidbar. Die visuelle Charakteristik aber liegt in den signalartig eingesetzten Produktgruppennamen in Univers, die der Serie ihr rein typografisches Gepräge geben.
(*TM*, Nr. 1, 1989)

アイウエオ
ガギグゲゴ
サシスセソ
タチツテト
ナニヌネノ
パピプペポ
マミムメモ
ヤユヨー
ラリルレロ
ワヲァィゥェォ
ンッャュョヮ

This syllable typeface is based in principle on my Katakana Eru, published in 1971. It is designed for horizontal use and to harmonize with the alphabet in bilingual use. With the exception of the straight lines, the characters were drawn without implements in order to retain the characteristics of writing. To counterbalance unevenness in certain combinations, I added alternative signs at a later stage.
(*TM*, No. 1, 1989)

Diese Silbenschrift basiert im Prinzip auf der von mir 1971 veröffentlichten Katakana (Eru). Sie ist konzipiert für die horizontale Verwendung, um sie in zweisprachigem Gebrauch mit dem Alphabet zu harmonieren. Mit Ausnahme der Geraden sind die Zeichen ohne technische Hilfsmittel gezeichnet, um das Charakteristische des Geschriebenen zu bewahren. Um Kombinationsunebenheiten auszugleichen, habe ich später Alternativzeichen hinzugefügt.
(*TM*, Nr. 1, 1989)

Taking advantage of the 1980s health and sports boom, Otsuka Pharmaceutical developed an ion supply drink that met the demand for a mild taste. They requested a design that had to be fresh, informative and reliable; a design that would bring the company one step ahead of the competition. To make an immediate association with the color of the sea, a deep blue was chosen. The waves, originally intended to be information graphs, became a graphic shorthand. The product name in English was divided into two lines to space it differently – to produce a graphic effect. The can is designed in a kinetic flow with no front or back.

In the first year, the Japanese side of the can was used as the advertising side. Since then, the English side has been the A-side. The brand is pronounced Pokari Suetto in Japanese. The word sweat has no offensive connotation; in Japan we all love to work.
(*Cross-Cultural Design*)

Den Vorteil des Aufschwungs von Gesundheit und Sport in den 1980er Jahren nutzend, hat Otsuka Pharmaceutical ein Getränk zur Ionenversorgung entwickelt, das die Nachfrage nach einem milden Geschmack erfüllte. Es wurde eine frische, informative und zuverlässige Gestaltung verlangt; eine Gestaltung, die die Firma im Wettbewerb mit der Konkurrenz einen Schritt vorwärtsbrachte. Ein tiefes Blau wurde gewählt, um sofort eine Assoziation mit der Farbe des Meeres zu schaffen. Die Wellen, ursprünglich durch Informationsdiagramme symbolisiert, wurden zur grafischen Kurzschrift. Der englische Produktname wurde in zwei Zeilen mit unterschiedlicher Spationierung geteilt, um einen grafischen Effekt zu erzielen. Die Dose ist in einem kinetischen Fluss gestaltet, ohne Vorder- oder Rückseite.

Im ersten Jahr wurde die japanische Seite der Dose für Werbezwecke genutzt. Danach war die englische Seite die A-Seite. Im Japanischen wird die Marke *Pokari Suetto* ausgesprochen. Das Wort Schweiss (sweat = *suetto*) hat keine negative Bewertung; in Japan lieben wir alle das Arbeiten.
(*Cross-Cultural Design*)

Visual identity for Pocari Sweat
Otsuka Pharmaceutical, 1980

Erscheinungsbild für Pocari Sweat
Otsuka Pharmaceutical, 1980

Visual identity for Hinex-V
Otsuka Pharmaceutical, 1981

Erscheinungsbild für Hinex-V
Otsuka Pharmaceutical, 1981

Visual identity for Fibe Mini
Otsuka Pharmaceutical, 1988

Erscheinungsbild für Fibe Mini
Otsuka Pharmaceutical, 1988

Visual identity for Fibe Mini Plus
Otsuka Pharmaceutical, 1992

Erscheinungsbild für Fibe Mini Plus
Otsuka Pharmaceutical, 1992

Otsuka Pharmaceutical developed a fiber drink to be sold in small handy
100 ml bottles. The brand name, Fibe Mini, is derived from *fiber,* and *mini* was
added to describe its convenient size. The liquid's color is a delicious salmon pink.
To enhance the appetizing drink, I selected a color for the small label that matched the
contents. As a counterpoint to the feminine color, a dynamic logotype, divided
into two lines, became the solution. The catch phrase "enjoy your day" can be interpreted
as "do not let any problems bother you." All Japanese information was banned
from the face-side, and this gave the product its international look.
(*Cross-Cultural Design*)

Otsuka Pharmaceutical entwickelte ein Ballaststoffgetränk, das in handlichen
100-Milliliter-Fläschchen verkauft werden sollte. Der Markenname Fibe Mini kommt von
fiber (Ballaststoff), und mini wurde hinzugefügt, um die praktische Grösse zu beschreiben.
Die Farbe der Flüssigkeit ist ein köstliches Lachsrosa. Um das appetitliche Getränk
noch attraktiver zu machen, wählte ich für das kleine Etikett eine Farbe, die der des Inhalts
entsprach. Zur femininen Farbe wurde ein Gegengewicht benötigt, die Lösung war
schliesslich ein dynamisches, auf zwei Zeilen verteiltes Schriftlogo. Der Slogan «Enjoy your day»
(Geniesse deinen Tag) kann als «Lass dich von keinem Problem stören» interpretiert werden.
Alle japanischen Informationen wurden von der Vorderseite verbannt, und das gab
dem Produkt sein internationales Erscheinungsbild.
(*Cross-Cultural Design*)

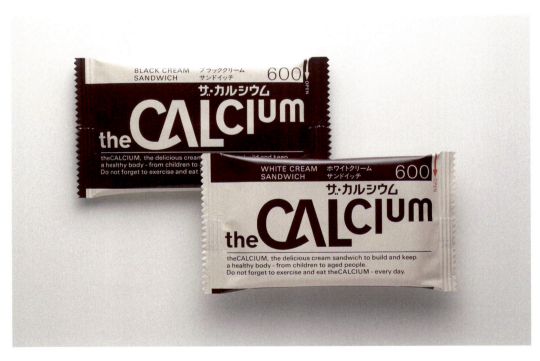

Visual identity for The Calcium
Otsuka Pharmaceutical, 1991

Erscheinungsbild für Energen
Otsuka Pharmaceutical, 1993

Visual identity for Energen
Otsuka Pharmaceutical, 1993

Erscheinungsbild für Energen
Otsuka Pharmaceutical, 1993

The design of the energy supply drink Energen was inspired by the name. When I was asked to design the new drink of internationally oriented Otsuka Pharmaceutical, I was briefed on the features and advantages of the product. I was briefed on the meaning of the name, Energen. And I got the freedom to make a design which can stand on the international scene using Japanese and English.

After a period of meditating on a sheet of white paper, I started with analyzing the letter compositions of the English name in upper case, lower case, mixed, stressing word meanings. Energen with seven letters is on the edge of a comfortable name. There is a double meaning in the word Energen: it means energy but it means also support energy. I wanted to express this double meaning in my design. The logotype for Energen visualizes the important supporting role of the energy drink for active people, it expresses something like arriving at the desired destination with vigor. In this two-line-logo-solution, the logo not only becomes definitive and memorable but also a self-defining brand. Gen (= source) supports ener(gy). Gen gives energy a lift. To stress this idea, I added the catchphrase "reach your summit."

The two-line asymmetric English logotype of straight and italic lowercase letters could be transformed naturally into the Japanese logo. This very rare case boosted also the selection of the design. While working on both logotypes I started with the design of the can, testing different ideas in different directions at the same time. A can is like a never-ending screen, where half of it can be seen at one time. A can should look identical from whatever side it is looked at. Even the smallest information text should harmonize with the design and should be typeset accordingly. Otsuka's products are treated as informative and serious and it is often a struggle with the available space and the necessary information.

The design of Energen was inspired by the name, and the color was inspired by the tasteful color of the drink. In the first presentation, I made variations with different colors for the purpose of comparison. The Energen orange proved its advantages as a brand identity color. The bold logo in definitive black on the clear Energen orange presents the drink as reliable, memorizable and identical in the complete range of products: 1.5 L PET bottle, 500 ml can, 350 ml can, and most recently on the 75 g pouch.
(*Creativity in Graphic Design*)

Die nunmehr international ausgerichtete Otsuka Pharmaceutical bat mich, eine Gestaltung für das Energiegetränk Energen zu entwickeln. Ich wurde über die Vorteile und Wesenszüge des Produkts unterrichtet, und die Bedeutung des Namens Energen war meine Inspiration. Und ich hatte die Freiheit, eine Gestaltung zu schaffen, die die japanische und englische Sprache enthält und sich international behaupten kann.

Nachdem ich eine Weile über einem weissen Blatt Papier meditiert hatte, begann ich mit der Analyse der Buchstabenkompositionen des englischen Namens in Grossbuchstaben, Kleinbuchstaben, gemischt, Wortbedeutungen ausdehnend. Energen mit sieben Buchstaben ist an der Grenze einer komfortablen Bezeichnung. Energen hat auch zwei Auslegungen: einmal als Kraft, zum anderen als Energie. Diese beiden Auslegungen wollte ich mit meiner Gestaltung sichtbar machen. Der Schriftzug für Energen visualisiert die wichtige unterstützende Rolle des Energiegetränks für aktive Menschen, es drückt so etwas aus wie an einem angestrebten Ziel mit Vitalität anzukommen. Durch diese zweiteilige Lösung wird der Schriftzug nicht nur klar und einprägsam, er wird auch zur selbsterklärenden Marke. Gen (= Quelle) unterstützt Ener(gie). Gen erhöht die Energie. Um diese Idee zu betonen, habe ich die Aussage «Erreiche deinen Gipfel» hinzugefügt.

Der zweizeilige asymmetrische englische Schriftzug aus geraden und kursiven Kleinbuchstaben konnte ganz natürlich in den japanischen Schriftzug transformiert werden. Dieser seltene Fall half auch bei der Auswahl der Gestaltung. Während der Arbeit an den beiden Schriftzügen begann ich mit der Gestaltung der Dose, habe gleichzeitig unterschiedliche Ideen in unterschiedlichen Richtungen ausprobiert. Eine Dose ist wie eine unendliche Leinwand. Eine Dose sollte von jeder Seite aus identisch wirken. Selbst der kleinste Informationstext sollte mit der Gestaltung harmonieren und entsprechend gesetzt werden. Otsukas Produkte werden informativ und ernsthaft behandelt, was oftmals ein Kampf mit dem vorhandenen Raum und der nötigen Information bedeutet.

Die Gestaltung von Energen wurde durch den Namen inspiriert, und die Farbe durch die geschmackvolle Färbung des Getränkes. In der ersten Präsentation habe ich Variationen mit unterschiedlichen Farben zum Vergleich gezeigt. Das Energen Orange hat seine Vorteile als Identitätsfarbe für die Marke bewiesen. Der fette Schriftzug in entschlossenem Schwarz auf dem klaren Energen Orange visualisiert das Getränk als zuverlässig, unvergesslich und identisch in der gesamten Produktreihe: 1.5 l-Plastikflasche, 500 ml-Dose, 350 ml-Dose und jüngst als 75 g-Beutel.
(*Creativity in Graphic Design*)

Brand identity for an unsweetened tea in cans by Otsuka Beverage.
The two-line logo is a blend of lowercase letters and capitals. The geometric
shapes of the capitals refer to the geometric patterns on Java.
(*World Trademarks and Logotypes III*)

Die Markenidentität für einen ungesüssten Tee in Dosen von Otsuka Beverage.
Die zweizeilige Wortmarke ist eine Mischung aus Minuskeln und Majuskeln. Die geome-
trischen Formen der Majuskeln nehmen Bezug auf die geometrischen Formen auf Java.
(*World Trademarks and Logotypes III*)

Visual identity for Java Tea
Otsuka Beverage, 1989

Erscheinungsbild für Java Tea
Otsuka Beverage, 1989

Visual identity for Tejava
Dong-A Otsuka, 1997
Otsuka Beverage, 1998

Erscheinungsbild für Tejava
Dong-A Otsuka, 1997
Otsuka Beverage, 1998

A cup of tea was one of the first things when meeting someone in Asia.
Tea in cans is more recent. The product identity for the can drink Tejava for Korea (1997)
and Japan (1998) required the brand name logo to look identical in the three scripts:
Alphabet, hangul (Korea), and katakana (Japan). By differentiating the brand name
in italic and straight letters, TeJava obtained its unobtrusive characteristic.
The logos are integrated with the intertwined rectangles in different line thicknesses.
The organic lines of the tea leaf suggest the taste of the drink.
(*Helmut Schmid: Design is Attitude*)

Eine Tasse Tee zählte zu den ersten Begegnungen in Asien.
Tee in Dosen ist neueren Datums. Die Produktidentität für das Getränk TeJava für
Korea (1997) und Japan (1998) verlangte ein identisch wirkendes Logo in drei
verschiedenen Schriften: Alphabet, Hangul (Korea), Katakana (Japan). Durch die
Differenzierung des Produktnamens in kursiven und geraden Buchstaben
erhielt Te Java eine unaufdringliche Charakteristik. Die Logos sind in miteinander
verwobene Rechtecke in unterschiedlichen Linienstärken integriert. Die organischen
Linien des Teeblattes suggerieren den Geschmack des Getränkes.
(*Helmut Schmid: Gestaltung ist Haltung*)

Visual identity for Demi Soda
Dong-A Otsuka, 1995, 2007

Erscheinungsbild für Demi Soda
Dong-A Otsuka, 1995, 2007

Visual identity and bottle design
for Urepearl Plus Lotion
Otsuka Pharmaceutical, 1992

Erscheinungsbild und
Flaschengestaltung für
Urepearl Plus Lotion
Otsuka Pharmaceutical, 1992

Packaging for Mucosta
Otsuka Pharmaceutical, 1990

Verpackung für Mucosta
Otsuka Pharmaceutical, 1990

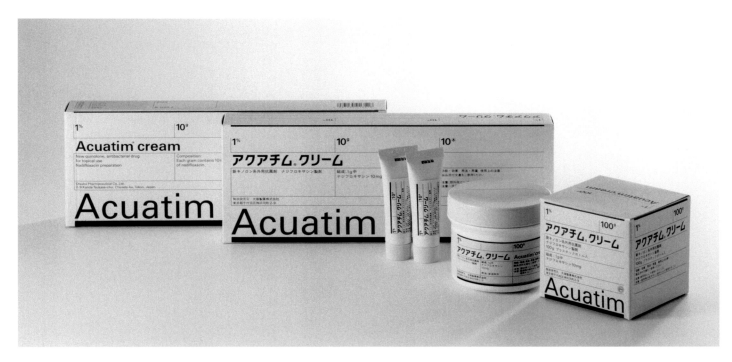

Packaging for Acuatim
Otsuka Pharmaceutical, 1993

Verpackung für Acuatim
Otsuka Pharmaceutical, 1993

Logo and packaging for
Jog Mate Protein
Otsuka Pharmaceutical, 1995

Logo und Verpackung für
Jog Mate Protein
Otsuka Pharmaceutical, 1995

Visual identity for
Ion Water
Otsuka Pharmaceutical, 2013

Erscheinungsbild für
Ion Water
Otsuka Pharmaceutical, 2013

Visual identity for
Pocari Sweat Jelly
Otsuka Pharmaceutical, 2016

Erscheinungsbild für
Pocari Sweat Jelly
Otsuka Pharmaceutical, 2016

Visual identity for
Pocari Sweat Ice Slurry
Otsuka Pharmaceutical, 2018

Erscheinungsbild für
Pocari Sweat Ice Slurry
Otsuka Pharmaceutical, 2018

MERRY CHRISTMAS
AND A HAPPY NEW YEAR 1990

AKIHIKO OTSUKA OTSUKA PHARMACEUTICAL CO LTD
PRESIDENT 3-2-27, OTEDORI, CHUO-KU, OSAKA, JAPAN

MERRY CHRISTMAS
AND A HAPPY NEW YEAR

Christmas and New Year's greeting
of Akihiko Otsuka, 1989, 1990
400 × 210 mm
Suibokuga: Hozan Matsumoto

Weihnachts- und Neujahrsgrüsse
von Akihiko Otsuka, 1989, 1990
Suibokuga: Hozan Matsumoto

Suibokuga is explained by its three ideograms: water, black ink, drawing.
It is the art of describing something with water and ink, to accept the accidental and
at the same time to control the accident. For Hozan Matsumoto, one of the real
artists in today's Japan, *Suibokuga* means when the object, the artist and
the technique are fused in a momentary brush stroke and emerge
as a powerful brush work. Even her smallest works radiate honesty,
simplicity and elegance, radiate clarity and boldness.
(*TM*, No. 1, 2000)

Suibokuga wird mit drei Ideogrammen geschrieben und erklärt: Wasser, schwarze
Tusche, Zeichnung. Es ist die Kunst, mit Wasser und Tusche einen Gegenstand zu beschreiben,
das Zufällige zu akzeptieren und gleichzeitig nichts dem Zufall zu überlassen. Für Hozan Matsumoto,
eine wahre Künstlerin im heutigen Japan, bedeutet *Suibokuga* wenn sich das Objekt, der
Künstler und die Technik zu einem spontanen Pinselstrich vereinen und als ein kraftvolles Werk
hervorgehen. Sogar ihre kleinsten Werke strahlen Echtheit, Einfachheit und Eleganz;
strahlen Klarheit und Ausdruckskraft aus.
(*TM*, Nr. 1, 2000)

MERRY CHRISTMAS
AND A HAPPY NEW YEAR 1989

AKIHIKO OTSUKA
PRESIDENT

OTSUKA PHARMACEUTICAL CO LTD
2-31, OTEDORI, HIGASHI-KU, OSAKA, JAPAN

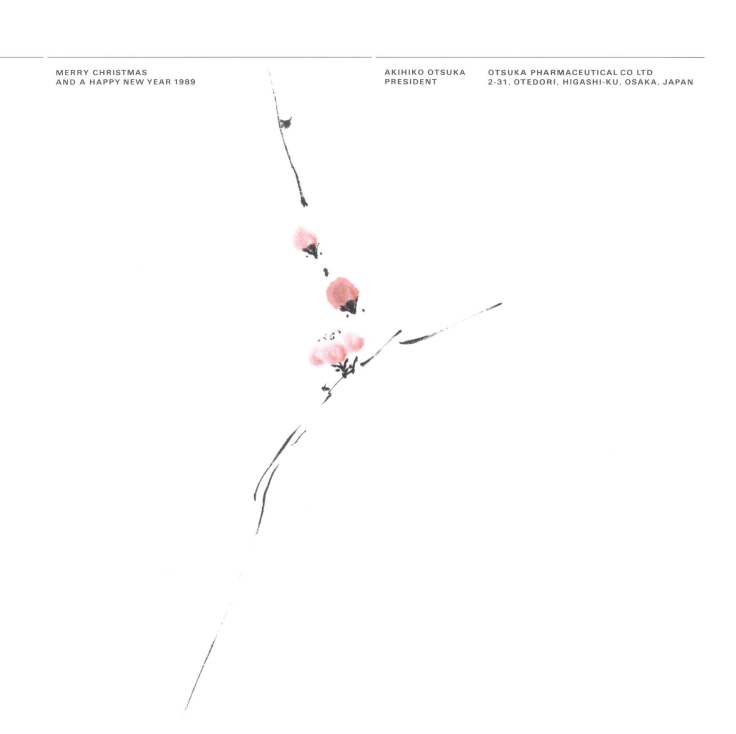

Dark black is not always bold; light black is not always weak. *Sho* is the Japanese word for calligraphy. *Shodo* means the way of writing. In contrast to Western calligraphy, which strives for pleasing writing, *Shodo* is a spiritual, philosophical attitude which strongly influenced the way of life and the arts of Japan. *Sho* is first of all the art of the line. The seemingly accidental brush strokes in black are well-thought-out lines, already in the mind of the writer, before the brush touches the paper.

In collaboration with Shizan Uera, a master of modern calligraphy, I designed New Year greetings for Akihiko Otsuka, president of Otsuka Pharmaceutical. *Ichi, ni, san* (one, two, three) – a saying taken from the *Zenrin-Kushu* [a collection of writings used in the Rinzai school of Zen] and there interpreted as obvious truth – began the series in 1983. Later I selected individual ideograms and gave Shizan Uera a free hand to interpret them. His form variations of one and the same ideogram were astonishing. He explained his suggestions, explained the way of the brush, explained the shades of black ink. But the final selection he left to the designer, since it is the interplay of calligraphy and typography which made the New Year's greetings. Modern Japanese calligraphy and classic modern typography make the utmost contrast: non-repeatable organic form in *sho*; constant repetitive form in typography.

The ideogram 明 *mei* (light), is composed of the left-hand radical sun (日) and the right-hand radical moon (月). In the calligraphy of Shizan Uera this ideogram is intensified since he brings it back to its origin. Emil Ruder wrote it so clearly in his book *Typography*: "In the art of Eastern Asia, script and picture make a single entity, for writing is drawing and drawing is writing."

Shizan Uera, born 1926 in Hyogo prefecture, studied calligraphy from 1949 under Sokyu Ueda and Sesson Uno. He became an active member of associations like Chofukai and Hiunkai. Aspiring to diversity, he polished his calligraphy in the abstract and in the classical style. In 1952 his work received a prize in New York and was included in the collection of the Museum of Modern Art. He took part in exhibitions and gave demonstrations of his expressive art in North and South America, Europe and in Asia. In the midst of vigorous activity, Shizan Uera passed away on the last day of 1995.
(*TM*, No. 1, 2000)

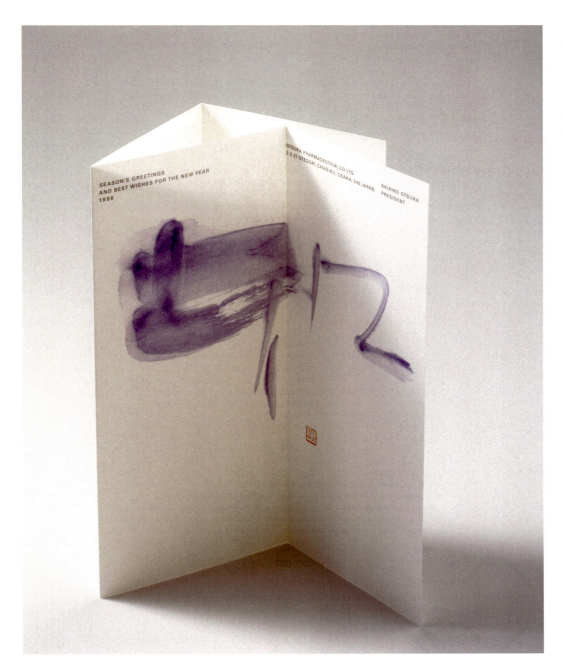

New Year's greeting of
Akihiko Otsuka, 1994, 1996, 1998
400 × 210 mm
Calligraphy: Shizan Uera
Photo: Yasuhiro Asai

Neujahrsgrüsse von
Akihiko Otsuka, 1994, 1996, 1998
Kalligrafie: Shizan Uera
Photo: Yasuhiro Asai

Dunkles Schwarz ist nicht immer kräftig; helles Schwarz ist nicht immer schwach. *Sho* ist das japanische Wort für Kalligrafie. *Shodo* bedeutet der Weg des Schreibens. Im Gegensatz zur westlichen Kalligrafie, die eher das Schönschreiben anstrebt, ist *Shodo* eine geistige, philosophische Haltung, die Lebensweise und Kunst in Japan stark beeinflusst hat. *Sho* ist die Kunst der Linie. Die wie zufällig anmutenden schwarzen Pinselstriche sind in Wahrheit wohlüberlegte Linien, die im Gedanken des Schreibenden feststehen, noch ehe der Pinsel das Papier berührt.

 In Zusammenarbeit mit Shizan Uera, einem Meister der modernen Kalligrafie, gestaltete ich Neujahrsgrüsse für Akihiko Otsuka, Präsident von Otsuka Pharmaceutical. *Ichi, ni, san* (eins, zwei, drei) – ein Zitat aus *Zenrin Kushu* und dort mit offenkundige Wahrheit interpretiert – begann 1983 die Serie. Später wählte ich einzelne Ideogramme (Wortzeichen) und gab Shizan Vera freie Hand, diese zu interpretieren. Seine Formabwandlungen von ein und demselben Ideogramm waren überwältigend. Er erklärte seine Vorschläge, erklärte die Bedeutung der Pinsellinien, erklärte die Töne im Schwarz. Die endgültige Auswahl aber überliess er dem Gestalter, denn erst das Zusammenspiel von Kalligrafie und Typografie ergab den Neujahrsgruss. Die moderne japanische Kalligrafie und die klassisch moderne Typografie geben den stärksten Kontrast: organische, nicht wiederholbare Formen in *Sho*; gleichbleibende, repetitive Formen in der Typografie.

 Das Ideogramm 明 *mei* (hell) ist zusammengesetzt aus den Ideogrammen Sonne (日) und Mond (月). In der Kalligrafie von Shizan Uera wird das Wortzeichen intensiviert indem er es auf den Ursprung des Zeichens zurückführt. Emil Ruder beschrieb das in seinem Buch *Typographie* so klar: «In der ostasiatischen Kunst fügen sich Schrift und Bild zu einer Einheit zusammen, denn Schrift ist Bild und Bild ist Schrift.»

 Shizan Uera, geboren 1926 in Hyogo-ken, studierte Kalligrafie seit 1949 unter Sokyu Ueda und Sesson Uno. Er wurde ein aktives Mitglied von Vereinigungen wie Chofukai oder Hiunkai. Vielfalt anstrebend verfeinerte er seine Kalligrafie im klassischen und im modernen Stil. 1952 erhielt eine Arbeit von ihm einen Preis in New York und wurde in die Sammlung des Museum of Modern Art aufgenommen. Er beteiligte er sich an Ausstellungen und gab Demonstrationen seiner expressiven Kunst in Nord- und Südamerika, Europa und in Asien. Inmitten einer vigorosen Aktivität verstarb Shizan Uera am letzten Tag des Jahres 1995.
(*TM*, Nr. 1, 2000)

Calendar 1998
"The development of the
modern pharmaceutical industry"
Otsuka Pharmaceutical, 1997

Kalender für das Jahr 1998
«Die Entwicklung der modernen
Pharmaindustrie»
Otsuka Pharmaceutical

Calendar 1999
"The development of cell biology –
from the discovery of cells to cloning…"
Otsuka Pharmaceutical, 1998

Kalender für das Jahr 1999
«Die Entwicklung der Zellbiologie –
von der Entdeckung der Zelle
bis zum Klonen …»
Otsuka Pharmaceutical

Calendar 2000
"Folk customs in Medicine as shown
in Nishikie prints"
Otsuka Pharmaceutical, 1999

Kalender für das Jahr 2000
«Volkstümliche Medizinpraktiken
in Nishikie-Drucken»
Otsuka Pharmaceutical

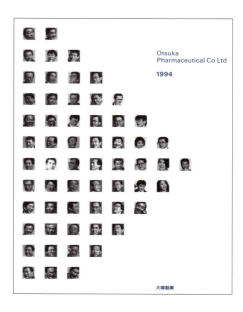

Company brochures of
Otsuka Pharmaceutical,
1990, 1992, 1993, 1994, 1995

Firmenbroschüren von
Otsuka Pharmaceutical,
1990, 1992, 1993, 1994, 1995

Calendar 2002
"Title Pages of Books by
Pioneers of Modern Medicine"
Otsuka Pharmaceutical, 2001

Kalender für das Jahr 2002
«Titelseiten von Büchern von
Pionieren der modernen Medizin»
Otsuka Pharmaceutical

Calendar 2018
"Honzozu ‹Medical Plant Drawings›
in the Edo period"
Otsuka Pharmaceutical, 2017

Kalender für das Jahr 2018
«Honzozu, ‹Zeichnungen von Arzneipflanzen›
der Edo-Periode»
Otsuka Pharmaceutical

8 the essence of elegance: shiseido's brand logotypes

Die Essenz der Eleganz:
Markenlogos für Shiseido

Shiseido is a leading manufacturer of cosmetics in Japan. Since the Meiji and Taisho periods, the company has been a source of modern urban culture and has been involved in activities that go beyond merely manufacturing. It is also known for having established an in-house design department early on, and for having led the Japanese advertising design world with the diverse talent that gathered there. The connection between Schmid and Shiseido began with the logo design for the cosmetics brand Elixir in 1982. Shunsaku Sugiura, the company's art director at the time, made an inquiry to his brother, designer Kohei Sugiura, regarding a logotype designer – previously, logos had been created in-house. This led to a meeting between Shunsaku and Schmid.

Schmid would go on to work for a number of Shiseido brands, including Because, Integrate, UV White, Ayura and Maquillage. In addition to the typographic treatment, at the root of these logotypes is the sense and lettering skill that Schmid honed in Basel.

> "Today's designers seem to be using contemporary tools to make designing typefaces easier. In Basel, I spent three months drawing eight or nine letters of the alphabet under the guidance of Kurt Hauert. What I learned during this experience of discovering forms in black and white is still very useful to me today."
> ("The Great 13: An Interview with Helmut Schmid on Emil Ruder,"
> *JAGDA Report*, No. 160, JAGDA, 2000)

These logotypes are the result of an integration of an Eastern aesthetic sense that he cultivated in Japan and the communication skills that he acquired through client work both in Japan and abroad. Kohei Sugiura describes Schmid's logotype design for Shiseido as follows:

> "In a logotype design for Shiseido, for example, an oriental breath was added to a Western arrangement. What was created was a fruitful crystallization of reason and emotion, of music and plastic art, and of the geometry and physicality of West and East…"
> (Kohei Sugiura, "Order, Dignity, White Space, Yin and Yang, West and East, Chaos, Essence of Empty Space…," *Helmut Schmid: Design is Attitude*, Birkhäuser, 2007)

Even when Schmid was asked to create a logo for another cosmetic company, he refused, saying that he did not accept any clients from the same field as existing ones.

Shiseido ist ein führender Kosmetikhersteller in Japan. Seit 1872 ist das Unternehmen eine Quelle moderner urbaner Kultur, seine Aktivitäten gehen weit über die reine Produktion von Kosmetika hinaus. Shiseido ist auch dafür bekannt, schon früh eine eigene Designabteilung eingerichtet und mit den dort versammelten Talenten eine Vorreiterrolle in der Welt des japanischen Werbedesigns übernommen zu haben. Die Verbindung zwischen Schmid und Shiseido begann mit der Gestaltung des Logos für die Kosmetikmarke Elixir im Jahr 1982. Shunsaku Sugiura, der damalige Art Director des Unternehmens, fragte bei seinem Bruder, dem Designer Kohei Sugiura, nach einem Logodesigner – bis dahin waren Logos intern kreiert worden. So kam es zu einem Treffen zwischen Shunsaku und Schmid.

Schmid arbeitete später für eine Reihe von Shiseido-Marken, darunter Because, Integrate, UV White, Ayura und Maquillage. Neben der typografischen Bearbeitung liegt diesen Logos auch das Gespür und die Schriftkunst zugrunde, die Schmid in Basel verfeinert hatte.

«Die heutigen Designer scheinen moderne Werkzeuge zu benutzen, um die Gestaltung von Schriften einfacher zu machen. In Basel verbrachte ich drei Monate nur damit, unter der Anleitung von Kurt Hauert acht oder neun Buchstaben des Alphabets zu zeichnen. Noch heute profitiere ich von dem, was ich bei der Entdeckung der Formen in Schwarz und Weiss gelernt habe.»
(«The Great 13: An Interview with Helmut Schmid on Emil Ruder», in: *JAGDA Report*, Nr. 160, JAGDA, 2000)

Diese Logos sind das Ergebnis der Verschmelzung des östlichen Sinns für Ästhetik, den er in Japan kultivierte, und der Kommunikationsfähigkeiten, die er durch seine Arbeit für Kunden in Japan und im Ausland erwarb. Über Schmids Logogestaltung für Shiseido schreibt Kohei Sugiura:

«Bei einem Schriftzug für Shiseido, zum Beispiel, wurde der westlichen Ordnung ein orientalischer Hauch hinzugefügt. Eine fruchtbare Kristallisation aus Vernunft und Emotion, aus Musik und Skulptur und aus der Geometrie und der Physikalität von West und Ost wurde geschaffen.»
(Kohei Sugiura, «Ordnung, Würde, weisser Raum, Yin und Yang, West und Ost, Chaos, Wesenheit des leeren Raumes ...», in: *Helmut Schmid: Gestaltung ist Haltung*, Birkhäuser, 2007)

Als Schmid gebeten wurde, ein Logo für eine andere Kosmetikfirma zu entwerfen, lehnte er dies mit der Begründung ab, dass er keine Kunden aus dem gleichen Bereich annehmen würde, in dem er bereits für einen anderen Kunden arbeitete.

Drawing a logo for D Program (Osaka, 1997)

Beim Zeichnen eines Logos für D Program (Osaka, 1997)

ELIXR

A product name should be an unobtrusive part of the product itself, but should also have a certain recognizability, to be able to stand on its own in an advertisement or TV commercial. By opening the joints of the dominating letter *X*, a memorable logotype was created, the design being already inside the word itself.
(*TM*, No. 1, 1989)

Ein Produktname muss sich unaufdringlich in das Produkt einfügen, er benötigt aber doch den gewissen Erkennungswert, um sich auch selbständig in einer Anzeige oder in einem Fernsehspot behaupten zu können. Indem das Zentrum des dominierenden Buchstabens «X» geöffnet wurde, ist eine einprägsame Wortmarke entstanden, deren Gestaltung praktisch im Wort selbst lag.
(*TM*, Nr. 1, 1989)

**Logotype for Elixir
Shiseido, 1983**

Schriftlogo für Elixir
Shiseido, 1983

Open-drawn characters, wide letter spacing and accentuation
of the symmetrically positioned *A* characterize the logotype Because.
The product name blends unobtrusively with the organically shaped
glass bottle of the product, without losing its sales appeal.
(*TM*, No. 1, 1989)

Offen gezeichnete Buchstaben, offener Buchstabenabstand und Betonung
des symmetrisch gelegenen «A» charakterisieren die prägnante Wortmarke Because.
Der Produktname fügt sich unaufdringlich in den organisch geformten
Glasbehälter des Produktes ein, ohne den werblichen Charakter zu verlieren.
(*TM*, Nr. 1, 1989)

Logotype for Because
Shiseido, 1984

Schriftlogo für Because
Shiseido, 1984

Symbol and logotype for UV White
Shiseido, 1985

Schriftlogo für UV White
Shiseido, 1985

The product name Ultra Violet White is formed by the ultra-narrow *U* and by the ultra-wide and fine *V*. Despite the symbol's simplicity a clear product identity is achieved, distinct from those of its competitors.
(*TM*, No. 1, 1989)

Der Name des Produktes, Ultra Violett Weiss, ist durch das ultraschmale «U» und durch das ultraweite und feine «V» visualisiert. Trotz einfacher Gestaltung des Schriftsymboles ist eine klare Produktidentität erreicht, die sich von Konkurrenzprodukten abhebt.
(*TM*, Nr. 1, 1989)

The open letter forms and the intensified vowel *I* convey the feeling of the product's freshness. (*TM*, No. 1, 1989)

Die offenen Buchstabenformen und der intensivierte vokal «I» visualisieren die Frische des Produktes. (*TM*, Nr. 1, 1989)

Logotype and packaging for Ripple
Shiseido, 1987

Schriftlogo und Verpackung für Ripple
Shiseido, 1987

Ipsa is a newly established cosmetics company with sales outlets in department stores in Tokyo, Osaka and Kyoto.
Under the motto "each person is an exception," the customer takes part in the formation of the product.
The name Ipsa is taken from the Latin, where it stands for self, in person, excluding others, alone. This "I am I,"
this "self-assurance," is expressed by the duplication or accentuation of the *I*. The Ipsa identity program was realized
with Shunsaku Sugiura as creative director. Art director Tetsuo Hiro was responsible for the packaging.
(*TM*, No. 1, 1989)

Ipsa ist eine neugegründete Kosmetikfirma mit Verkaufsnischen in Warenhäusern in Tokyo, Osaka
und Kyoto. Unter dem Motto «jeder Mensch ist eine Ausnahme» nimmt der Kunde an der Zusammenstellung
des Produktes teil. Der Name Ipsa ist dem Lateinischen entnommen und bedeutet selbst, in Person,
andere ausschliessend, alleine. In der Wortmarke ist dieses «ich bin ich», dieses Selbstbewusstsein durch
Verdopplung oder Akzentuierung des «I» illustriert. Das Ipsa-Identitätsprogramm wurde von Creative Director
Shunsaku Sugiura geleitet. Art Director Tetsuo Hiro war verantwortlich für die Packungen.
(*TM*, Nr. 1, 1989)

Logotype and original font
Ipsa, 1987

Schriftlogo und eigens
entwickelte Schrift
Ipsa, 1987

**METABOLIZER
CLEANSING OIL
CREAMY CAKE
MILD SHAMPOO
COLOGNE
WHITENING
ESSENCE
EMULSION**

**NAIL COLOR
REMUVER
CLEAR CAKE
REFRESHING
SOFTENING RINSE
ASTRINGENT
FOR
EXTRA DRY HAIR**

Logotype for Savon d'Or
Shiseido, 1990

Schriftlogo für Savon d'Or
Shiseido, 1990

Logotype for HG series
Shiseido, 1990

Schriftlogo für die Serie HG
Shiseido, 1990

Logotype for Cellaid
Shiseido, 1991

Schriftlogo für Cellaid
Shiseido, 1991

uvwhite

New logotype for UV White
Shiseido, 1994

Neues Schriftlogo für UV White
Shiseido, 1994

The point of the design is to emphasize the white, not the *UV*.
The accent on the *I* suggests the shade. A hand held above the head
for protection from the sun. The hand that Yuko Asano puts over
her head to shade her charming face.
(Faxed copy to Shiseido's Advertising Department, dated May 15, 1992)

Der Punkt der Gestaltung ist die Hervorhebung von «Weiss»,
nicht «UV». Der Akzent auf dem «I» suggeriert den Schatten. Eine Hand
über dem Kopf als Schutz vor der Sonne. Die Hand, die Yuko Asano
zum Schutz über ihr charmantes Gesicht hält.
(Kopie des Faxes an Shiseidos Werbeabteilung, 15. Mai 1992)

Logotype for Ayura
Shiseido, 1995

Schriftlogo für Ayura
Shiseido, 1995

The shaping of the logotype for Ayura cosmetics
When we talk about cosmetics, we usually mean Western concepts. Ayura is a new cosmetic concept, which emphasizes the specificity of the Asian origin, emphasizes Asian values and traditions, emphasizes naturalness. The name Ayura comes from the Sanskrit word *ayus* which means "life."

When Mr. Shunsaku Sugiura, chief planner of the Ayura project, asked me to design the logotype to stand as the company name as well as the product name, I was briefed on the unique concept. I was shown first sketches of the impressive organic bottle shapes by Mr. Hiro and I was shown sketches of the symbol by Mr. Shibuya. It all looked and sounded fresh and Asian and exciting.

My logotype should harmonize with the products and with the symbol. It should stand on its own and convince in its simplicity and memorability. Cosmetic is feeling, smelling, beautifying. A cosmetic logomark should reflect just that.

I started as always, with a white sheet of paper on my desk. Keeping it white for quite some time. In the Ayura logotype I searched for openness, elegance, naturalness, transparency and the necessary memorability. I analyzed the letters from the point of their shapes; *U* and *R* are organic shapes, *A* and *Y* are inorganic shapes. I worked on the spacing. I tried different angles, with the help of the computer to save time and I redrew it each time by hand.

When I got the idea with the natural flow of the ending *Y* stroke, giving an inorganic letter an organic accent, I was sure I had found the logotype. With this softly ending *Y* stroke I expressed not only a young branch of a tree, I expressed life, I expressed Ayura. There is no other secret to design than passion. The schedule was extremely tight and I had to send my first designs by express mail. I indicated my favorite logo and included several supporting ideas for the purpose of comparison.

My first proposals were met with mixed opinions. I was asked to try different directions, to bring in more originality (whatever that means). But I worked mainly on my first suggestion, trying different thicknesses and variations in the letter *A* toward a more common shape. I worked intensively to prove that my suggestion was the most suitable one, and with this I went to Tokyo to meet the designers of the project. It is important to get an immediate first-hand reaction; sometimes a spark of an idea comes just by chance. We came to no conclusion but I got additional days to work on the logotype.

Ayura took its name from Sanskrit but I had never considered it a thought to get an idea from that script. As soon as I returned I checked the letterforms of Sanskrit and here it was – the final characteristic to my logotype, the extended left stroke of the *A*! With this additional element in the letter *A*, I incorporated a hint of Sanskrit, and, quite unintentionally, a hint of the Japanese character for "person."

Ayura was inaugurated in the spring of 1995 and the first shops opened in department stores in Tokyo and Yokohama. Intensive communication helped in the shaping of the Ayura logotype. I am grateful and delighted.
(*Creativity in Graphic Design*)

Die Formgebung des Schriftzugs für die Ayura Kosmetik
Wenn wir über Kosmetik sprechen, meinen wir normalerweise westliche Konzepte. Ayura ist ein neues kosmetisches Konzept, das die asiatische Herkunft, die asiatischen Werte und Traditionen und die Natürlichkeit betont. Der Name Ayura kommt von dem Sanskrit-Wort *ayus* und bedeutet Leben.

Als Herr Shunsaku Sugiura, der Leiter des Ayura-Projekts, mich bat, den Schriftzug als Firmen- und Produktnamen zu gestalten, wurde ich über das einzigartige Konzept informiert. Mir wurden erste Skizzen der beeindruckenden organischen Flaschenformen des Herrn Hiro und des Symbolzeichens von Herrn Shibuya gezeigt. Das erschien und klang alles frisch und asiatisch und spannend.

Mein Schriftzug sollte mit den Produkten und dem Symbol harmonieren. Er sollte für sich stehen können und durch seine Einfachheit und Einprägsamkeit überzeugen. Kosmetik ist fühlen, riechen und verschönern. Ein Schriftzug für Kosmetik sollte all das ausdrücken.

Wie immer begann ich mit einem kleinen Stück weissem Papier auf meinem Schreibtisch. Es blieb für eine lange Weile weiss. Für den Ayura-Schriftzug suchte ich nach Offenheit, Eleganz, Natürlichkeit, Transparenz und der nötigen Einprägsamkeit. Ich analysierte die Buchstaben aufgrund ihrer Form; «U» und «R» sind organische Formen, «A» und «Y» sind anorganische Formen. Ich arbeitete an der Spationierung. Ich probierte unterschiedliche Winkel mithilfe des Computers, um Zeit zu sparen, und habe dann alles von Hand neu gezeichnet.

Mit der Idee des natürlich fliessenden Endes des Y-Strichs, wodurch ein anorganischer Buchstabe einen organischen Akzent erhielt, war ich sicher, den Schriftzug gefunden zu haben. Mit diesem weich endenden Y-Strich brachte ich nicht nur den jungen Ast eines Baums zum Ausdruck, ich brachte auch Leben zum Ausdruck, ich brachte Ayura zum Ausdruck. Es gibt kein anderes Geheimnis einer Gestaltung als Leidenschaft. Der Zeitrahmen war sehr eng, und meine ersten Entwürfe musste ich per Eilpost schicken. Ich kennzeichnete meinen favorisierten Schriftzug, und mit enthalten waren mehrere unterstützende Ideen als Vergleichsmaterial.

Meine ersten Vorschläge wurden gemischt beurteilt. Ich wurde gebeten, andere Richtungen auszuprobieren, mehr Originalität zu entwickeln (was immer das bedeutet). Ich arbeitete jedoch hauptsächlich an meinem ersten Vorschlag, versuchte unterschiedliche Strichstärken und Variationen des Buchstaben «A» in Richtung einer üblicheren Form. Ich arbeitete intensiv, um zu beweisen, dass mein Vorschlag die beste mögliche Lösung war, und mit der reiste ich für ein Treffen mit den Gestaltern des Projekts nach Tokio. Es ist wichtig, eine sofortige, unmittelbare Reaktion zu erhalten; manchmal entsteht der Funke einer Idee rein zufällig. Wir konnten uns nicht einigen, aber zumindest bekam ich einige zusätzliche Tage für meine Arbeit am Schriftzug.

Ayura entnahm seinen Namen der Sanskrit-Sprache, aber mir kam nie der Gedanke, eine Idee aus dieser Sprache heraus zu entwickeln. Nach meiner Rückkehr überprüfte ich Buchstabenformen des Sanskrit, und da war sie – die endgültige Charakteristik meines Schriftzugs, der erweiterte linke Strich des «A»! Mit diesem zusätzlichen Element des Buchstabens «A» habe ich einen Hauch von Sanskrit und, rein zufällig, einen Hauch des japanischen Charakters, der japanischen Persönlichkeit, mit eingearbeitet.

Ayura wurde im Frühjahr 1995 eingeführt, und die ersten Geschäfte öffneten in Kaufhäusern in Tokio und Yokohama. Eine intensive Kommunikation unterstützte die Formgebung des Ayura-Schriftzugs. Ich bin dankbar und freue mich.
(*Creativity in Graphic Design*)

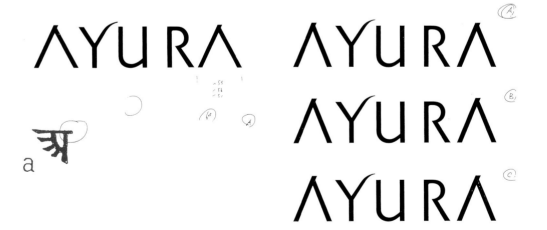

The first presentation with the proposed logotype in different spacings and different angles. The accentuation in the letter *Y* suggests a young tree branch, suggests life, visualizes the Sanskrit word *ayura*.
July 1, 1994

Second presentation in different weights. The aim of the logotype: openness, elegance, naturalness, transparency, memorability.
July 20, 1994

Third presentation with the logotype inspired by the Sanskrit letter *A*. Different widths are tested for the final decision.
September 12, 1994

Die erste Präsentation mit dem vorgeschlagenen Schriftlogo in unterschiedlichen Spationierungen und Neigungswinkeln. Die Akzentuierung des Buchstabens «Y» erinnert an den jungen Zweig eines Baums, verweist auf das Leben und visualisiert das Sankrit-Wort *ayura*.
1. Juli 1994

Die zweite Präsentation mit unterschiedlichen Strichstärken. Das Ziel des Schriftlogos: Eleganz, Natürlichkeit, Transparenz, Einprägsamkeit.
20. Juli 1994

Die dritte Präsentation mit einem vom Sanskrit-Buchstaben «A» inspirierten Schriftlogo. Für die endgültige Entscheidung werden verschiedene Buchstabenbreiten ausprobiert.
12. September 1994

EVENESE DR

Logotype for D Program
Shiseido, 1997

Schriftlogo für D Program
Shiseido, 1997

Logotype for Evenese DR
Shiseido, 1998

Schriftlogo für Evenese DR
Shiseido, 1998

Logotype for Recipist
Shiseido, 2017

Schriftlogo für Recipist
Shiseido, 2017

IN&ON

Logotype for In & On
Shiseido, 2010

Schriftlogo für In & On
Shiseido, 2010

MAQuillAGE

Logotype for Maquillage
Shiseido, 2005

Schriftlogo für Maquillage
Shiseido, 2005

9
a statement of attitude: publications and posters

Eine Stellungnahme:
Veröffentlichungen
und Plakate

Along with his activities in typography and graphic design, Helmut Schmid's activities as a writer, editor and publisher were of great importance to him. Even before he was officially admitted to the AGS Basel, Schmid had begun to publish articles on contemporary typography and Basel trends in Swedish and Austrian journals. Schmid's articles served as an introduction to Basel typography and, after his arrival in Japan, as a valuable point of contact between the Western and Japanese design worlds.

It's possible to say that Schmid's home ground for writing was the Swiss journal *Typografische Monatsblätter (TM)*, which was distributed to industry professionals in Switzerland and featured developments in Swiss typography during the 1950s and 1960s. As already mentioned in Chapter three, Schmid began writing for *TM* with the Japan japanisch series and continued to publish articles on typography in East and West.

Another important medium was Japan's *Idea* magazine. Founded in 1953, *Idea* is a magazine that showcases design from around the world, and also connected Schmid with Japan. After his arrival in Japan, Schmid became a contributor to the journal, introducing his own projects and Basel typographers, such as Emil Ruder and Wolfgang Weingart.

Of particular importance in relation to the journal was a special issue entitled *Typography Today* published in 1980. It was a full-scale introduction to modern typography from its pioneering days in the early twentieth century to its postwar development in Europe and the United States, and had a major impact on designers not only in Japan but also all over the world. This book, which Schmid planned, edited and designed himself, was republished as a new edition in 2003, and is now one of the world's design classics, having been translated into Korean and Chinese editions.

In addition to these contributions, Schmid began publishing the *Typographic Reflections* series in the 1990s. Each issue of the booklet, nearly square in format and basically printed with a single color, focuses on a single theme and was distributed to Schmid's acquaintances and friends. The contents of the leaflets ranged from experiments in typography to the introduction of artists" works, records of workshops, expressions of Schmid's personal philosophy of creation, his love for friends and his opinions on our society. Books such as *The Road to Basel* (1997), documenting his passionate period in Basel, and *Nippon no Nippon* (2012), a collection of articles on Japanese culture featured in *TM*, were published based on this attitude of "reflection."

For Schmid, writing and publishing were not just a single area of design, but projects to share and present his ideas to others. His eyes were always directed toward his predecessors who had paved the way for him, to his contemporaries he talked with, and to the future, upcoming generations. His posters are also characterized by the same mentality.

Since the 2000s, Schmid's projects have grown beyond the surface of paper, becoming three-dimensional and forming new networks between designers, in addition. The spirit of Schmid has been passed on to young people in East Asia and Europe through his design education at Kobe Design University in Japan and Hongik University in Korea, the research and exhibition project *Schmid Today* organized by the students of the Design Department at the University of Applied Technology in Düsseldorf, and the exhibition projects at Tokyo's Print Gallery run by Hirofumi Abe.

Through writings, publications and exhibitions, Schmid has connected many people across the West and the East, the past and the future. Even after his death in 2018, the Japanese edition of Emil Ruder's legendary book *Typography*, put together by Schmid before he passed, was published as a continuation of his legacy. As contemporary designers continue to be marginalized and divided in the face of technological progress, Schmid's achievements will most certainly continue to be referred to as a clue into independent thought.

Cassette tapes with original J-card, 1978

Audiokassetten mit den originalen J-Cards, 1978

Neben seiner typografischen und grafischen Tätigkeit war für Helmut Schmid auch die Arbeit als Autor, Redakteur und Herausgeber von grosser Bedeutung. Noch bevor er offiziell in die AGS Basel aufgenommen wurde, hatte er damit begonnen, in schwedischen und österreichischen Zeitschriften Artikel über zeitgenössische Typografie und Trends der Basler Schule zu veröffentlichen. Schmids Artikel dienten als Einführung in die Basler Typografie und seit seiner Ankunft in Japan als wertvoller Anknüpfungspunkt zwischen der westlichen und der japanischen Designwelt.

Man kann sagen, dass Schmids Heimat als Autor die Schweizer Zeitschrift *Typografische Monatsblätter (TM)* war, die sich mit den Entwicklungen der Schweizer Typografie in den 1950er und 1960er Jahren befasste und an Fachleute in der Schweiz verteilt wurde. Wie bereits in Kapitel 3 erwähnt, begann Schmid mit der Serie «Japan japanisch» für die *TM* zu schreiben und veröffentlichte weiterhin Artikel über Typografie in Ost und West.

Ein weiteres wichtiges Medium war die japanische Zeitschrift *Idea*. Das 1953 gegründete Fachmagazin, das Design aus aller Welt präsentiert, verband Schmid ebenfalls mit Japan. Nach seiner Ankunft in Japan wurde Schmid als Autor für die Zeitschrift verpflichtet, in der er seine eigenen Projekte und Basler Typografen wie Emil Ruder und Wolfgang Weingart vorstellte.

Von besonderer Bedeutung im Zusammenhang mit der Zeitschrift war eine 1980 veröffentlichte Sonderausgabe mit dem Titel *Typography Today*. Dabei handelte es sich um eine umfassende Einführung in die moderne Typografie von ihren Anfängen zu Beginn des 20. Jahrhunderts bis zu ihrer Entwicklung in der Nachkriegszeit in Europa und den USA. Diese Publikation hatte einen grossen Einfluss auf Gestalterinnen und Gestalter nicht nur in Japan, sondern auf der ganzen Welt. Dieses Buch, das Schmid selbst geplant, gestaltet und herausgegeben hatte, wurde 2003 in einer Neuauflage wiederveröffentlicht, ins Koreanische und Chinesische übersetzt und gehört heute zu den Designklassikern der Welt.

Neben diesen Beiträgen begann Schmid in den 1990er Jahren mit der Veröffentlichung der Reihe *Typographische Reflexionen*. Jede Ausgabe der fast quadratischen und grundsätzlich einfarbig gedruckten Broschüre behandelte ein eigenes Thema und wurde an Schmids Bekannte und Freunde verteilt. Inhaltlich reichten die Broschüren von typografischen Experimenten über die Vorstellung der Werke von Künstlern, Aufzeichnungen zu Workshops, Äusserungen über Schmids persönliche Gestaltungsphilosophie und seine Liebe zu Freunden bis hin zu seinen Ansichten über unsere Gesellschaft. Bücher wie *Der Weg nach Basel* (1997), das seine leidenschaftliche Zeit in Basel dokumentiert, und *Japan japanisch* (2012), eine Sammlung von Artikeln über die japanische Kultur, die in *TM* erschienen sind, wurden auf der Grundlage dieser «Reflexionen» publiziert.

Für Schmid waren Schreiben und Publizieren nicht nur ein eigener Gestaltungsbereich, sondern Projekte, über die er seine Ideen mit anderen teilen und präsentieren konnte. Sein Blick war stets auf seine Vorgänger gerichtet, die ihm den Weg geebnet hatten, auf die Mitmenschen, mit denen er sich austauschte, und auf die nachfolgenden Generationen. Auch seine Plakate sind von dieser Mentalität geprägt.

Seit den 2000er Jahren sind Schmids Projekte über die Oberfläche von Papier hinausgewachsen, sind dreidimensional geworden und knüpfen neue Netzwerke zwischen Gestalterinnen und Gestaltern. Der Geist von Schmid wird an junge Menschen in Ostasien und Europa weitergegeben – durch gestalterische Ausbildungen an der Kobe Design University in Japan und der Hongik University in Korea, durch das Forschungs- und Ausstellungsprojekt *Schmid Today* von Studierenden des Fachbereichs Design der Fachhochschule Düsseldorf und die Ausstellungsprojekte der Print Gallery in Tokio unter der Leitung von Hirofumi Abe.

Durch seine Schriften, Publikationen und Ausstellungen hat Schmid viele Menschen im Westen und Osten, in der Vergangenheit und in der Zukunft, miteinander verbunden. Selbst nach seinem Tod im Jahr 2018 wurde die japanische Ausgabe von Emil Ruders legendärem Buch *Typography*, das Schmid vor seinem Tod zusammengestellt hatte, als Fortsetzung seines Vermächtnisses veröffentlicht. Während zeitgenössische Gestalterinnen und Gestalter angesichts des technologischen Fortschritts zunehmend an den Rand gedrängt und gespalten werden, fungieren Schmids Errungenschaften mit Sicherheit weiterhin als Anleitung zu unabhängigem Denken.

With Wolfgang Weingart at
Basel School of Design (Basel, 1982)

Mit Wolfgang Weingart an der
Allgemeinen Gewerbeschule
(Basel, 1982)

タイポグラフィトゥデイは1920年代のパイオニアたちから、最近の発展と傾向までを総括した最初のモダンタイポグラフィ刊行物であり、12ヶ国、65人のデザイナーの作品を網羅している。
コンセプトとデザイン ヘルムート シュミット、寄稿者 ウォルフガング ワインガルト、ウィム クロウエル、杉浦康平、ジョン ケージ、フランコ グリニヤーニ、エミール ルーダー（転載）。

typography today, the first comprehensive publication on modern typography, from the pioneers of the twenties to recent developments and tendencies, illustrated with the work of 65 designers from 12 countries.
Concept and design by Helmut Schmid, with contributions by Wolfgang Weingart, Wim Crouwel, Kohei Sugiura, John Cage, Franco Grignani and a reprint by Emil Ruder.

アイデア別冊
タイポグラフィ トゥデイ
160ページうちカラー45
収録作品 約400点
本文 日英二ヶ国語
発行 誠文堂新光社
定価 3800円

IDEA special issue
typography today
160 pages 45 in color
ca 400 illustrations
text Japanese/English
price US$ 30.-
postage US$ 3.-

今日のタイポグラフィだけでなく、昨日のそして明日のタイポグラフィの集大成としてたいへん貴重なドキュメントだと私は思う。ここに選定された作品は非常に秀れたものばかりで、われわれタイポグラファは、史書あるいは教科書として参考にすべきである。
ピーター ブラティンガ、アムステルダム

I think that the compiling of the documents which do not only show typography today but also typography yesterday and tomorrow is a very worthwhile document. The chosen pieces and work are so outstanding, that we, typographers, have to refer to them like our history books or text books.
Pieter Brattinga, Amsterdam

私を考えこませたのは、リスィツキーやツヴァルトの見解ではない。むしろタイポグラフィとはたとして最高峰の作品のみを崇めたたえてればよいといったものであろうか、という疑問である。
フィリップ ルイドル、フォルム誌、西ドイツ

...Es sind nicht die Meinungen von El Lissitzky oder Piet Zwart, die mich nachdenklich stimmen.
Vielmehr ist es die Frage, darf Typografie überhaupt, was hier als das non plus ultra gefeiert wird.
Philipp Luidl in FORM, Zeitschrift für Gestaltung

すばらしい特集号。ありがとう！
カール ゲルストナー、バーゼル

Eine herrliche Nummer. Merci!
Karl Gerstner, Basel

Seibundo Shinkosha Publishing Co Ltd
5 Nishikicho 1-chome
Kanda, Chiyoda-ku, 101 Tokyo, Japan

Typography Today
Seibundo Shinkosha, 1980
225 × 297 mm

Typography Today
Seibundo Shinkosha, 1980

Advertisement for Typography Today, published in Idea, with comments from reviewers
Seibundo Shinkosha, 1980
225 × 297 mm

Werbeanzeige für Typography Today, veröffentlicht in Idea, mit Kommentaren von Rezensierenden
Seibundo Shinkosha, 1980

Not only did I compile and edit *Typography Today* but I also did all
the artwork. Text and images were pasted on a pre-printed grid.
For the typesetting I had to combine phototype for Japanese text, Monotype for
English body text and metal type hand-setting for larger size English text.
("The demands of the visual presentation are already embodied in the content,"
lecture at MEME Design School, December 1, 2012)

Nicht nur kompilierte und bearbeitete ich die Publikation *Typography Today*,
sondern ich erstellte auch die Reinzeichnungen. Texte und Bilder wurden
auf ein gedrucktes Raster geklebt. Für den Schriftsatz musste ich Fotosatz für den
japanischen Text, Monotype für den englischen Lauftext und handgesetzten
Bleisatz für den grösseren englischen Text kombinieren.
(«Die Anforderungen der visuellen Präsentation sind schon im Inhalt enthalten»,
Vortrag an der MEME Design Schule, 1. Dezember 2012)

Typography Today New Edition*
Seibundo Shinkosha, 2003
225 × 297 mm

* Further enlarged hard cover edition was published in 2015

Typography Today New Edition*
Seibundo Shinkosha, 2003

* 2015 als weiter vergrösserte Hardcover Ausgabe publiziert

The Japanese design magazine *Idea* has existed since 1953. Hiroshi Ohchi, the first editor
and art director, helped me not only to land a job in Japan, he also introduced my work,
created at the Basel school, in *Idea*, No. 78, 1966: Helmut Schmid, young designer of typography.
Idea introduced a wide range of design and it became for me a window to look at the doings
of the graphic design world. Yoshihisa Ishihara, the editor after Hiroshi Ohchi, gave me
the freedom to introduce my world of typography, which resulted in a 160-page publication.
　Typography Today was published in Japanese and English in November 1980 as
a special issue of *Idea*; in 1981 with a dust jacket. The cover uses a quote by Kurt Schwitters,
a memo scribble by Wolfgang Weingart, Katakana Eru designed by Helmut Schmid,
and Univers 55 by Adrian Frutiger.
(*Newwork Magazine*, No. 6, 2010)

Das japanische Design Magazin *Idea* erscheint seit 1953. Hiroshi Ohchi, der erste
Redakteur und Art Director, verhalf mir nicht nur zu meiner ersten Arbeitsstelle in Japan,
er stellte auch meine Arbeiten aus der Basler Studienzeit in *Idea*, Nr. 78, 1966 vor:
Helmut Schmid, junger Gestalter von Typografie.
Idea stellte eine grosse Bandbreite von Gestaltung vor, für mich ein Fenster zum Geschehen
in der gestalterischen Welt. Yoshihisa Ishihara, der Redakteur nach Hiroshi Ohchi, gab mir
die Freiheit, meine Welt der Typografie in einer 160-seitigen Publikation vorzustellen.
　Typography Today, veröffentlicht auf Japanisch und Englisch im November 1980 als
eine Sonderausgabe von *Idea*. Veröffentlicht 1981 mit einem Schutzumschlag. Der Umschlag
benutzt ein Zitat von Kurt Schwitters, eine Notiz von Wolfgang Weingart, die von Helmut
Schmid gestaltete Schrift Katakana Eru und die Schrift Univers 55 von Adrian Frutiger.
(*Newwork Magazin*, Nr. 6, 2010)

All art publications (exhibitions) are subjected to the terror of an
international codified layout (disciplined printed matter).

With this statement by van der Heyden Jan van Toorn opened his critical article on the situation of visual communication in this bulletin on constructive and systematic art.

Art publications are responsible for our internationally rather identical manner of working, for presenting design codes, to an audience en masse. Art publications, including so called design manuals, are responsible for freezing in creativity, for impeding differentiated design approaches to problems which must be different from work to work.

Design codes are usually created by innovators and do, only in the application of innovators, look fresh, even after decades. Thus, not the design codes themselves annoy, but the applications which make the codes worn out and indigestible. Design codes are, to borrow freely from Kandinsky, like a glue that the careless ones fall prey to, like a comfortable chair inviting lassitude.

Kurt Schwitters:
Typographie kann unter
Umständen Kunst sein.

Emil Ruder:
Sometimes form has been accentuated, sometimes function, and in particular blessed periods form and function have been felicitously balanced.

Visual information will always have two alternatives: a meditative one as practiced by Max Bill, Emil Ruder, Karl Gerstner, Wim Crouwel, and an **exploitative** one as practiced by Piet Zwart, El Lissitzky, Wolfgang Weingart, Kohei Sugiura...
Visual information consists of information and interpretation. Interpretation on the other hand can become information itself.

Hans-Rudolf Lutz:
Gestaltung ist auch Information.

It is true that often misleading, irritating and even unnecessary messages are imposed on the public. But designers living in so called free countries, are free to choose what kind of messages they want to shape; they do not have to send **black** signals when they think themselves in red ones. Designers should identify themselves with the work they are doing. Designers should examine a message before they are going to shape it in order to be imposed on the public.

Markus Kutter:
Erspart bleibt uns Werbeleuten die Scham, mit der ein Architekt sein vor 20 Jahren konzipiertes Haus noch immer die Strassenflut verunzieren sieht...

We can not negate advertising completely. Not all advertising is unnecessary and the best of it is not only informative and educational but even **enJOYable**.
In the times of the pioneers, art and information were not separate. Piet Zwart's advertisings were designed without formal boundaries, were practically awaited by the public, were taken for granted by the sponsor.

Something original never imposes itself.

Kohei Sugiura:
Bring letters back to their original powerful figures.

Wim Crouwel's catalogues, designed with an ice-cold grid, show perceptible beauty. Some of GGK's advertisements are even inventive. And in Japan, Kohei Sugiura has created a typography to be enjoyed, to be discovered. His **information** needs the strong will of the reader **to decode** images, colours, messages. Like John Cage has written of modern music that the listener must be part of the music, so the information designer should shape the message to let the receiver take part in the game.

Grey blocks of text do not invite the eyes for a stroll.
Boulevard press and newspapers, even though not made in polished typography, are easier to read.
Sequences of thought units not only help the reading speed but even the learn effect.

Pablo Neruda:
A small black statue on the whiteness.

Letters are soundsculptures, are the tools of the visual designer.
The performance of the visual designer make the letter whisper, make the letter **SHOUT**. If we accept existing typefaces as a given tool for information performance, then there is still an immense field to do detail work.
Design codes are here frozen in lead. And Jan van Toorn also makes no exception in his **text**presentation:
evenlygreytonesettingwithunjustifiedlines
areexistingtypesettingmannerism.

Wolfgang Weingart once crossed out a printed line with the intention of actually underlining it. A pragmatic intellectual statement of the possibilities of visual information.

Wim Crouwel:
Designers should be skilled professionals; aware of their possibilities and the effects of their work.

Professionalism should not be identical with frozen ideologies. Rules should be guidelines to be broken when necessary.
Like a living language is changing, so design must live and change.
There is no fear on the other hand of systematic coding when applied by the professional heart. **Visual information** will always be **ruled by** a visible or invisible **Ordnung**.
Even the most common fly-sheet will have a system or it can only be used as a puzzle.
Systematic coding on the other hand demands a functioning concept and not just applications of existing codes.

More work on the edge will be necessary.

Helmut Schmid
August 1981

"All art publications are subjected to the terror of an international codified layout,"
Spread in *Quad*, No. 4
Frits Bless & Cor Rosbeek, 1981
297 × 420 mm

«Alle Kunstpublikationen sind dem Terror eines international kodifizierten Layouts unterworfen»
Doppelseite in: *Quad*, Nr. 4,
Frits Bless & Cor Rosbeek, 1981

Alle Kunstpublikationen (Ausstellungen) sind dem Terror einer internationalen kodifizierten Anordnung ausgesetzt (disziplinierte Drucksachen).

Mit dieser Aussage von van der Heyden begann Jan van Toorn seinen kritischen Artikel über die Situation der visuellen Kommunikation in dieser Veröffentlichung über konstruktive und systematische Kunst.

Kunstpublikationen für die Masse sind verantwortlich für unsere international ziemlich identische Arbeitsweise, für die Kodifikation der Gestaltung. Kunstpublikationen, einschliesslich der sogenannten Gestaltungshandbücher, sind verantwortlich für das Einfrieren der Kreativität, für die Behinderung differenzierter Gestaltungsansätze zu Problemen, die von Aufgabe zu Aufgabe unterschiedlich sein müssen.

Gestaltungsnormen werden normalerweise von Innovatoren kreiert und erscheinen, aber nur durch die Anwendung von Innovatoren, frisch, selbst nach Jahrzehnten. Insofern verärgern nicht die Gestaltungsnormen selbst, sondern die Anwendungen, die die Normen abgenutzt und unverdaulich erscheinen lassen. Gestaltungsnormen sind, lose ausgeliehen von Kandinsky, wie ein Klebstoff, der die Ahnungslosen zum Opfer macht; ähnlich einem komfortablen Stuhl, der zur Trägheit einlädt.

Visuelle Informationen haben immer zwei Alternativen: eine vermittelnde wie von Max Bill, Emil Ruder, Karl Gerstner, Wim Crouwel praktiziert, und eine ausbeuterische wie von Piet Zwart, El Lissitzky, Wolfgang Weingart, Kohei Sugiura praktiziert ...
Visuelle Information besteht aus Information und Interpretation. Andererseits kann die Interpretation selbst zur Information werden.

Es stimmt, dass irreführende, irritierende und sogar unnötige Botschaften oft der Öffentlichkeit aufgezwungen werden. Aber Gestalter der sogenannten freien Welt haben die Möglichkeit, die Art und Form der Botschaft zu wählen; sie müssen keine schwarzen Signale senden, wenn sie selbst in roten denken. Gestalter sollten sich mit ihrer Arbeit identifizieren. Gestalter sollten die Botschaft prüfen, bevor sie sie gestalten, um sie dann der Öffentlichkeit aufzuerlegen. Wir können Werbung nicht völlig negieren. Nicht alle Werbung ist unnötig, und die beste ist nicht nur informativ und lehrreich, sie ist sogar erfreulich. Zu Zeiten der Pioniere waren Kunst und Information nicht getrennt. Piet Zwarts Werbung war ohne formale Grenzen gestaltet, war praktisch erwartet von der Öffentlichkeit, war von den Sponsoren als selbstverständlich angesehen.

Etwas Originales drängt sich niemals auf.

Wim Crouwels Kataloge, gestaltet mit einem eiskalten Raster, zeigen eine wahrnehmbare Schönheit. Einige der GGK-Anzeigen sind sogar erfinderisch. Und in Japan hat Kohei Sugiura eine Typografie zum Geniessen, zum Entdecken kreiert. Seine Informationen erfordern die grosse Bereitschaft des Lesers, Bilder, Farben, Botschaften zu entschlüsseln. Wie John Cage von moderner Musik schrieb, dass der Zuhörer Teil der Musik sein muss, so muss der Gestalter der Information die Botschaft so formen, dass der Empfänger am Spiel teilnehmen kann.

Graue Textblöcke laden die Augen nicht zum Herumspazieren ein. Boulevardpresse und Zeitungen, obwohl nicht in polierter Typografie präsentiert, sind leichter zu lesen. Die Reihenfolge von Gedankeneinheiten fördern nicht nur ein zügiges Lesen, sondern auch das Lernen.

Buchstaben sind Klangskulpturen, sind das Werkzeug des visuellen Gestalters. Die Aufführung des visuellen Gestalters lässt die Buchstaben flüstern, lässt die Buchstaben schreien. Wenn wir die vorhandenen Schrifttypen als Werkzeug für die Informationsaufführung akzeptieren, dann bleibt uns immer noch ein immenses Feld für die Arbeit am Detail. Designnormen sind hier in Blei eingefroren. Und Jan van Toorn macht auch keine Ausnahme in seiner Textpräsentation:
gleichmässiggrauertextmitungerechtfertigtenlinienist einexistierendersatzmanierismus.

Wolfgang Weingart hat einmal eine gedruckte Linie durchgestrichen, um sie so zu unterstreichen. Eine pragmatisch intellektuelle Darlegung der Möglichkeiten einer visuellen Information.

Professionalität sollte nicht gleichgesetzt werden mit eingefrorenen Ideologien. Regeln sollten Richtlinien sein, die notfalls gebrochen werden. Gestaltung muss leben und sich verändern, genau wie eine lebende Sprache sich auch ändert. Auf der anderen Seite besteht keine Gefahr durch systematische Normen, wenn das professionelle Herz sie anwendet. Visuelle Information wird immer geleitet von einer sichtbaren oder unsichtbaren Ordnung. Selbst das gebräuchlichste Flugblatt hat eine Ordnung, oder aber es kann nur als ein Rätsel benutzt werden.
Andererseits verlangt systematisches Kodieren ein funktionierendes Konzept, nicht nur die Anwendung existierender Normen.

Mehr Arbeit am Rande ist nötig.

Helmut Schmid
August 1981

Kurt Schwitters:
Typography can be art under certain circumstances.

Emil Ruder:
Manchmal wurde die Form betont, manchmal die Funktion, und zu besonders gesegneten Zeiten wurden Form und Funktion angenehm ausgewogen.

Hans-Rudolf Lutz:
Design is also information.

Markus Kutter:
We advertisers are spared the shame with which an architect sees his house, conceived 20 years ago, still marring the streetscape ...

Kohei Sugiura:
Bringe die Buchstaben zu ihrer ursprünglichen, mächtigen Gestalt zurück.

Pablo Neruda:
Eine kleine schwarze Statue auf strahlendem Weiss.

Wim Crouwel:
Gestalter sollten qualifizierte Profis sein; sich ihren Möglichkeiten und dem Effekt ihrer Arbeit bewusst.

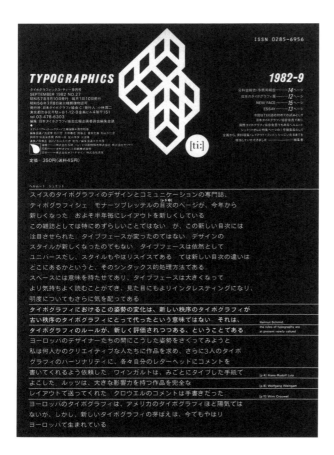

"The rules of typography are
at present newly valued"
contribution for *Typographics ti:*, No. 27
Japan Typography Association, 1982
A4

«Die Regeln der Typografie werden
zur Zeit neu bewertet»,
Beitrag für *Typographics ti:*, Nr. 27
Japan Typography Association, 1982

Wim Crouwel   Lomanstraat 82 hs   1075 RG Amsterdam z

I love the everlasting discussion
on typography in the knowledge
that it will surely go on and on;
for many of us it is a pure religion.

タイポグラフィは、与えられたテキストをタイプフェースの仮装舞踏会よろしく飾りたてることではなく、テキストをヴィジュアライズすることである。山城隆一の森のポスターが広く賞賛を得たのは、それが国際的に「読める」ものであったからだ。すなわち、優れしかもエキサイティングなタイポグラフィはその言語や文字を知らない人にも理解されうるものである。左ページのタイポグラフィック ヴィジュアライゼーションもまた、「読める」ものである。
ウィム クロウエルのジャクソン❶ポロック展のカタログは、ユニバースのタイプフェースのサイズにリズムをもたせるだけで、このアメリカのアーティストの持つ自然さを、ほうふつとさせている。
グラピューは、伝統的なタイポグラフィのルールを無視することで知られている。フランスのグループであるが、ただ現実を主張するだけでなく、グラフィックの点でも、実に鮮やかなポスターを創った。NO❷の大きな文字は、同時に、2行目のNeutrOnsの1部をも構成している。NO NeutrOns Mr reagan（核はごめんだ　レーガンさん）。
時には、メッセージのアイデアがすでに、ことば自身に含まれていることがある。ドイツに本拠を持つ広告代理店GGKが、IBMのポスター制作にあたって、デザイナーがやったことといえば、クライエントの名前を大文字にしただけである。IBMの3文字が、すでにドイツ語の❸schreibmaschinen（タイプライター）の綴りに含まれている。この単語が装飾的な手書きでもなく、流行のタイプフェースでもなく、タイプライター自身の文字で書かれていて、メッセージはさらに強められている。
すばらしいデザイナーであり、芸術家であるカール ゲルスナーは、タイポグラフィに関して多くを著わしているが、デザインに関してはおそらく最後の本になるであろう「アルファベット概要」の中で、ことばのヴィジュアライゼーションを多くあげている。IBMポスターと同類の効果を持つものに、ドイツ語のゼーレーニンジニアがある。この精神の技師を意味する単語の中に、正しくその人ともいうべき❹レーニンが含まれている。
ロンドン／ニューヨークに本拠を持つデザイングループ、ペンタグラムは、本のタイトルON DESIGNと作者名GEORGE NELSONに重複する部分を見つけ、それを重ねてデザインとした。❺
最終的な詩の表現❻としてのコンクリートポエトリー。エルンスト ブッフワルダーによる展覧会の招待状。
スイスの鉄道100年記念のヴィジュアライゼーションは、スペースの変化とレールを暗示する白ヌキで、遠近画法の効果をあげている。❼デザインは、ゲオルク シュテヘリン。
タイポグラフィは、日々これに直面している人々、すなわち読み手の多くにとって、なじみのないことがらである。タイポグラフィはまた実際タイポグラフィを正しく評価すべき立場にある人たち、すなわちデザインスクールにとっても、なじみのうすいことがらである。タイポグラフィは、まず、脚光を浴びることはない。にもかかわらず、私たちはどんな仕事においても、エキサイトメントを見出すことができるし、またそれは、読み手にも伝わりうるだろう。その時、仕事は成功したといえよう。「私は、タイポグラフィについて際限なくディスカッションすることが好きだ。それは必ずし、いつまでも、いつまでも、続くであろうことを知っているから。それというのも、これは私たちの多くにとって、宗教なのである」。これは、ウィム クロウエルがこの特集号に寄せてくれたメッセージである。私たちも、このディスカッションに加わろうではありませんか。そして語り合うだけでなく、実行に移そうではありませんか。

ヘルムート シュミット
翻訳 山田 清美／スミ シュミット

タイポグラフィのルールが今新しく評価されつつある

"Klötzchen"
work for *A Gallery in Type Cases*
at the request of Arno Stolz, 1984
40 × 50 × 30 mm
Photo: Yasuhiro Asai

«Klötzchen»
Arbeit für *Die Galerie im Setzkasten*
auf Einladung von Arno Stolz, 1984
Foto: Yasuhiro Asai

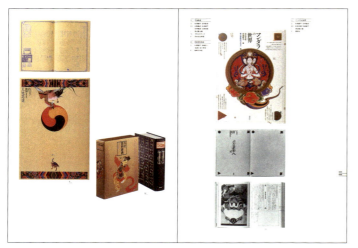
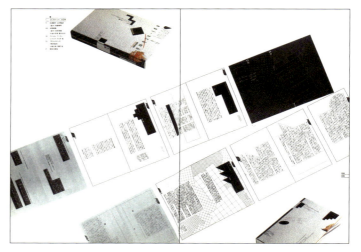

Book design for
Japan Typography Annual 1985
Robundo, 1985
A4

Buchgestaltung für
Japan Typography Annual 1985
Robundo, 1985

Wolfgang,
to work on the annual was exciting. Especially the texts on typography and designing
with the works of Kohei Sugiura. Fundamentally, however, an annual is a bit like a supermarket.
I find your essay in the annual very thoughtful, except for the paean to Japanese design.
But from afar, things always tend to look rosy. Here, we stick to the everyday, like you do in
Switzerland. Swiss design may at present be anemic. But I consider it basically honest.
Here in Japan, design is artificial.
(Letter to Wolfgang Weingart dated 10 June, 1985)

Wolfgang,
die Arbeit hat Spass gemacht. Besonders die Textbeiträge zur Typografie und das Arbeiten
mit den Werken von Kohei Sugiura. Aber irgendwie ist ein Jahrbuch ein wenig wie ein Supermarkt.
Ich finde deinen Beitrag im Jahrbuch sehr nachdenklich, mit Ausnahme des Lobliedes auf
japanisches Design. Aber aus der Ferne sieht alles rosig aus. Wir stehen im Alltag hier.
So wie du in der Schweiz. Schweizer Design mag zur Zeit fantasielos sein, aber im Grunde
finde ich es ehrlich. Hier in Japan ist Design künstlich.
(Briefe an Wolfgang Weingart, 10. Juni 1985)

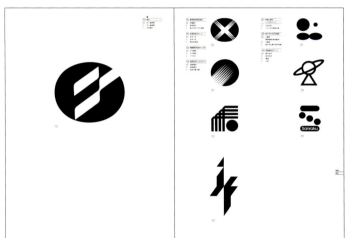

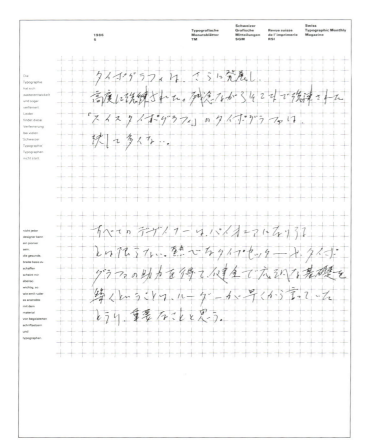
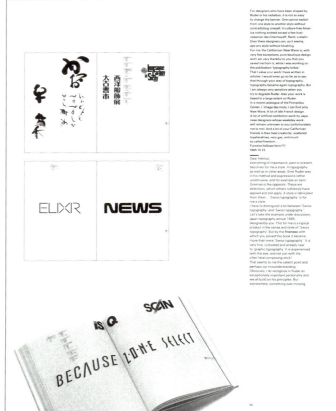

"Helmut Schmid and
Wolfgang Weingart:
a correspondence promped by
the *Japan Typography Annual*"
TM, No. 5, 1986
230 × 297 mm

«Helmut Schmid und
Wolfgang Weingart:
eine Korrespondenz entstanden
durch das *Japanische
Typografie Jahrbuch*»
TM, Nr. 5, 1986

"Typography by Helmut Schmid"
TM, No. 1, 1989
230 × 297 mm

«Typographie von Helmut Schmid»
TM, Nr. 1, 1989

Somewhere the composing stick and the galley came too much to the foreground, at least for me. His freedom, his experimental joyousness was restricted in lead (surely because of the technically limited possibilities). It surely was an experimental joyousness on a high typesetters' level and at a time, during which the symmetric style slowly lost in meaning (to understand this symbolically).
This typography has been developed and even refined. Unfortunately this refinement does not happen with many Swiss typography 'typographers'.
As for your comments on 'New Wave': I am of the same opinion. A chaos, a persistant misunderstanding. What we at the Basle school instructed more than 15 years ago did have a background. To explore Swiss typography. Counter react, letter-spacing, underline, get rid of the right angle and let typography finally become graphic.
Since the middle of the 70's, our teaching has changed and I have recognized the mistakes which I sometimes made and have learned from them. Nevertheless we did, through our ideas, release degeneration, internationally. This was not our intention, we did not want to give a style to the world, we wanted to alter and to renew. Unfortunately it came out differently.
But we must not spend too much thought on the 'Wave' designers'. It is like it is and will pass by like all styles of this world. What we must do – as you write – is to keep the house clean. So your new work is very refreshing, in contrast to the stream of kitsch and New Wave in our time.
1985 10 30

Wolfgang,
Emil Ruder's typography developed by continuous purification. That this purification does not happen with every designer is not Ruder's fault. To try the unexploited is not everyone's desire, and anyhow the design crowd just hold out on frozen typographic rules.
What I want to say is: I accept now your criticism of people who, after their design education lay themselves in the armchair, repeat proven design results and make money. I accept your criticism with the reservation that not every designer can be a pioneer. To establish a healthy, broad basis seems to me as important, as Ruder anticipated, with openminded typesetters and typographers.
What I cannot accept is your criticism of the composing stick typography of Ruder. Of course, Ruder was a lead-typographer, but the first one who, with these lead-conditions, created a functional, graceful and honest typography. Developments happen when the time is ripe. I suppose you do not criticize the Bauhaus typography from today's view and knowledge. The work of Piet Zwart, which still interests us, was done during 10 creative years. Josef Müller-Brockmann shows again and again only his well known posters of the late fifties and early sixties. All designers in Western countries have short creative periods – then they fall silent. We lost Ruder at his zenith.
When looking through his design manual, Typography, it feels like meditation surrounded by today's confused design.
I can today understand your counter-reacting Swiss typography, but I can still not understand your 'let typography finally become graphic'. Maybe I do not understand your thought, but I reject the idea of a typography as the servant of graphic design. I believe that typography very well can have her own independent life and beauty.
To come again to the difficulties of accepting or rejecting typographic expressions. I would like to quote from a letter from the Swedish designer Åke Nilsson, who reacted very sensitively to the Japan typography annual 1985: 'Circlepoint of the letter j did disturb me at first. Later I discovered its own signcharacter and I did have a certain relief. The spaced lowercase letters on the cover however, especially in the line 'graphy' will tantalize me to my last gasp'.
1985 11 08

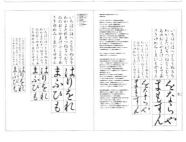

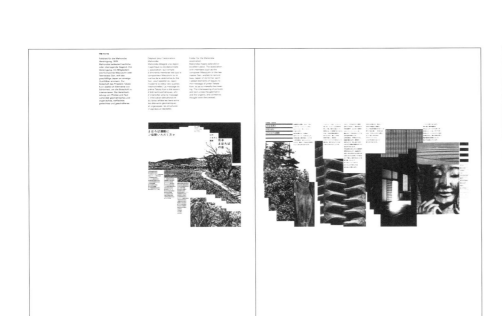

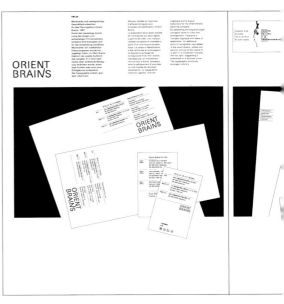

"Hats for Jizo" is a popular Japanese folktale, found in many regions with slightly changed elements. The basic motif is similar: an old, poor, but happy couple, trying to make just enough money to buy rice cakes for the new year; their tenderness toward six unsheltered stone Jizo statues in deep snow; and their wishes being miraculously granted by these Jizo statues. It is a beautiful story of the East, illustrated here as only a child could.
   Nicole encountered this story in her second grade at primary school and made a paper-cut print of her favorite scene. She continued to illustrate the story, because she wanted to tell it to her grandparents in Germany. The drawing, paper-cutting, pasting, and printing were done over the course of a year. The expressive and honest lines of the child's drawings convey the beauty and simplicity of the story.
(www.hsdesign.jp)

Hats for Jizo (Hüte für Jizo) ist ein populäres japanisches Volksmärchen, das man leicht variiert in vielen Regionen findet. Das Basismotiv ist ähnlich: Ein altes, armes, aber glückliches Paar versucht, genügend Geld für den Kauf von Reiskuchen für das neue Jahr zu verdienen; seine Zärtlichkeit gegenüber den sechs im tiefen Schnee ungeschützten Jizo-Statuen; und die Wünsche des Paares werden von diesen Jizo-Statuen auf wundersame Weise erfüllt. Es ist eine schöne Geschichte aus dem Osten, illustriert, wie es nur ein Kind kann.
   Nicole begegnete der Geschichte in der zweiten Klasse in der Grundschule und machte einen Papierschnittdruck ihrer Lieblingsszene. Sie fuhr mit der Illustration der Geschichte fort, denn sie wollte sie den Grosseltern in Deutschland erzählen. Das Zeichnen, Papierschneiden, Kleben und Drucken geschah im Laufe eines Jahres.
   Die ausdruckstarken und ehrlichen Linien der Zeichnung eines Kindes vermitteln die Schönheit und die Schlichtheit der Geschichte.
(www.hsdesign.jp)

Hats for Jizo
Robundo, 1988
259 × 264 mm
Text: Kyoko Iwasaki
Paper-cut-prints: Nicole Schmid

Hats for Jizo
Robundo, 1988
Text: Kyoko Iwasaki
Papierschnittdrucke: Nicole Schmid

freedom **comes** **from inside** **oneself**	**but** **walls can** **stand** **in the way**
freiheit kommt aus dem inneren selbst	aber mauern können im weg stehen
liberté vient de l'interieur de nous-même	mais murs peuvent se dresser sur son chemin

"Freedom comes from inside oneself
but walls can stand in the way"
Poster, 1990
1030 × 728 mm

«Freiheit kommt aus dem Inneren selbst,
aber Mauern können im Weg stehen»
Plakat, 1990

"Deeds. Not words:
The Berlin wall is down, let's down
the many invisible walls"
Poster, 1992
728 × 1030 mm

«Taten. Nicht Worte:
Die Berliner Mauer ist gefallen.
Lasst uns die vielen unsichtbaren
Mauern niederreissen»
Plakat, 1992

On the ninth of October 1989 the Berlin Wall came down. I was very happy about this, as I had worked in Berlin during the Cold War. Four months after the fall, I went to Munich to give a lecture on typography. Of course, I also went to Berlin. There, students and workers were busy in front of the wall with chisels and hammers in their hands. It was a moving experience to watch them at work. They were breaking up the wall and selling it. Thanks to my daughter's request, I was able to take home this unique souvenir.

Design requires constant learning and constant activity, not just when the client gives you a deadline. Just like a violinist or a pianist who practices every day to prepare for the next concert. When I came back to Japan, I felt the need to express the fall of the wall. I had a piece of the wall photographed in a studio. The result was perfect and artificial, controlled by an expert. But I was not satisfied and needed something more honest, and more true. Then, I photocopied this piece of concrete. The output was rough, honest and unadorned, as I had imagined. The next step was to come up with a concise message to go with the image (a designer must be able to think in words as well as images). I decided that the most appropriate words would be "Deeds. Not words." And to make the message even broader: "the Berlin wall is down, let's down the many invisible walls."

I set this message in a number of standard typefaces to find the right one. The form of the letters should be as straightforward as the message, "deeds." It had to be as straightforward as a piece of wall. In the end I decided on Rotis Sans Serif. This is a typeface by the German designer Otl Aicher, released the same year as the fall of the Berlin Wall. Rotis is a little too fashionable, a little too cosmetic for my purposes, but I like the look. The word "deeds" with two *e*'s is very expressive when set with Rotis.

I have designed a series of three posters, printed in three process colors resulting in a soft black. This series was exhibited in Lahti, Brno, Turnava and IDC Bombay and included in the *International Typography Annual* published by Robundo. This "deeds" poster is not only a personal study in design and typography, but also my response and comment to this historical event.
(*Creativity in Graphic Design*)

Am 9. Oktober 1989 fiel die Berliner Mauer. Ich war sehr glücklich darüber, denn ich habe während des Kalten Kriegs in Berlin gearbeitet. Vier Monate nach der Maueröffnung hielt ich in München einen Vortrag über Typografie. Natürlich dann auch in Berlin. Dort waren die Studenten und Arbeiter an der Mauer mit Meissel und Hammer beschäftigt. Sie brachen Stücke von der Mauer und verkauften sie. Auf Wunsch meiner Tochter war ich in der Lage, dieses seltene Souvenir nach Hause zu bringen.

Gestalten verlangt ein ständiges Lernen und eine ständige Aktivität, nicht nur dann, wenn es der Endtermin des Kunden verlangt. Genau wie Violinisten oder Pianisten, die jeden Tag üben und sich auf das nächste Konzert vorbereiten. Als ich nach Japan zurückkehrte, hatte ich das Bedürfnis, den Fall der Mauer auszudrücken. Ich liess ein Stück der Mauer im Studio fotografieren. Das Resultat war perfekt und von einem Experten künstlich beeinflusst. Aber ich war nicht zufrieden und brauchte etwas, das ehrlicher und wahrhaftiger war. Ich fotokopierte das Betonstück. Das Resultat war rau, ehrlich und schmucklos, wie ich es mir vorstellte. Der nächste Schritt war, eine der Abbildung entsprechende prägnante Botschaft zu finden (ein Gestalter muss in der Lage sein, in Worten und Bildern zu denken). Ich habe entschieden, dass die passende Aussage «Taten. Nicht Worte.» war. Und um die Aussage zu stärken: «Die Berlin Mauer ist gefallen. Lasst uns die vielen unsichtbaren Mauern niederreissen.»

Ich habe diese Aussagen in vielen Schrifttypen gesetzt, um die richtige zu finden. Die Form der Buchstaben sollte so aufrichtig sein wie die Aussage, «Taten». So aufrichtig wie das Stück Mauer. Letztendlich entschied ich mich für die serifenlose Rotis. Das ist eine vom deutschen Gestalter Otl Aicher entworfene Schrifttype, herausgebracht im selben Jahr, in dem die Berlin Mauer fiel. Rotis ist für meine Begriffe etwas zu modisch, ein wenig zu kosmetisch, aber ich mochte den Anblick. Das Wort *deed* (Tat) mit seinen zwei «e» ist sehr ausdrucksstark in der Rotis.

Ich habe eine Serie von drei Plakaten entworfen, gedruckt in drei Prozessfarben, um ein weiches Schwarz zu erzielen. Diese Serie wurde in Lahti, Brno, Turnava und IDC Bombay ausgestellt und im von Robundo herausgegebenen *Internationalen Typografie-Jahrbuch* veröffentlicht. Dieses «deeds»-Plakat ist nicht nur eine persönliche Studie in Gestaltung und Typografie, sondern auch meine Reaktion und mein Kommentar zu diesem historischen Ereignis.
(*Creativity in Graphic Design*)

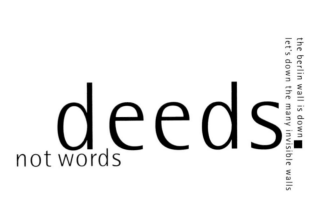

deeds
not words

the berlin wall is down
let's down the many invisible walls

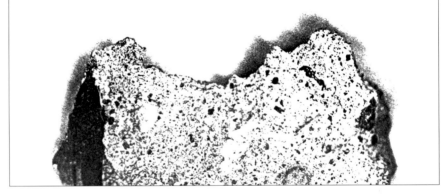

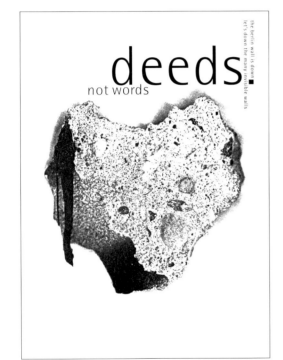

deeds
not words

the berlin wall is down
let's down the many invisible walls

deeds
not words

the berlin wall is down
let's down the many invisible walls

86 04 26: memory of Chernobyl
Poster for The 4th block, international exhibition of graphic art and poster in Ukraine, 1994
728 × 1030 mm

26. 4. 86: Erinnerung an Tschernobyl
Plakat für 4th Block, Internationale Ausstellung Grafischer Kunst und Plakate in der Ukraine, 1994

"Freedom is always the freedom of the other. Justice is always the justice of the other. Safety is always also the safety of the other"
Poster, 1992
602 × 402 mm
Text: Willy Brandt

«Freiheit ist immer die Freiheit des anderen. Recht ist immer das Recht des anderen. Sicherheit ist immer auch die Sicherheit des anderen»
Plakat, 1992
Text: Willy Brandt

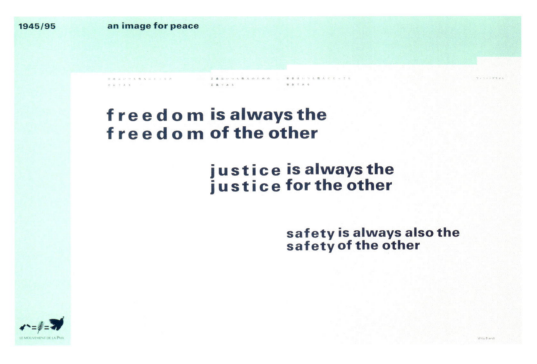

"Live Love"
Poster for campaign against violence worldwide
Edmonton, Canada, 1995
398 × 300 mm

«Live Love»
Plakat für eine Kampagne gegen weltweite Gewalt
Edmonton, Kanada, 1995

"Man made Nature made"
Artwork by fax for *Post office of letters*
Typographics ti:, No. 170, 1995
A4

«Man made Nature made»
(menschgemacht naturgemacht)
Kunst per Fax für die *Post der Buchstaben*
in: *Typographcs ti:,* Nr. 170, 1995

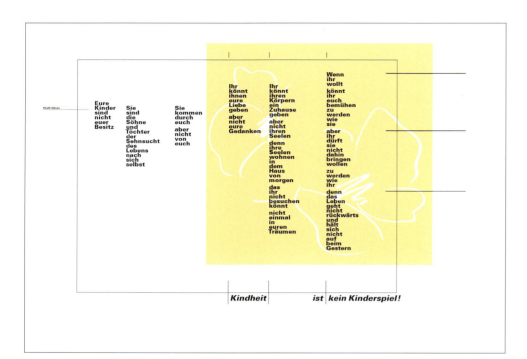

"Childhood is not child's play"
Poster for Plakat Museum Essen
(Museum Folkwang) and
Deutscher Kinderschutzbund
(society for the protection
of children), 1997
A1
Text: Khalil Gibran

«Kindheit ist kein Kinderspiel»
Plakat für Deutsches Plakat Museum
(Museum Folkwang) und
Deutscher Kinderschutzbund, 1997
Text: Khalil Gibran

"Soft water in movement with
time defeats the mighty stone.
You understand, the hard are beaten."
Bertolt Brecht 100 year
anniversary poster
Berliner Ensemble, 1998
A1
Text: Berthold Brecht
Calligraphy: Shizan Uera

«Daß das weiche Wasser in
Bewegung mit der Zeit den
mächtigen Stein besiegt.
Du verstehst, das Harte unterliegt.»
Plakat zum 100. Geburtstag
von Bertolt Brecht
Berliner Ensemble, 1998
Text: Bertolt Brecht
Kalligrafie: Shizan Uera

"To Hans-Rudolf Lutz"
Poster with the last letter from Lutz
and handwritten class schedule
by Ruder, 1999
728 × 1030 mm
Text: T. S. Eliot

«An Hans-Rudolf Lutz»
Plakat mit dem letzten Brief von Lutz
und einem handgeschriebenen
Unterrichtsplan von Ruder, 1999
Text: T. S. Eliot

1998 was the 100th anniversary of the birth of Bertolt Brecht. No reason
for a silent commemoration. The Berliner Ensemble and the association of
graphic designers invite one hundred designers and students...
The poster uses Brecht's poem "Legend of the origin of the book *Tao Te Ching*
on Lao-tzu's road into exile." From the thirteen stanzas the essentials are
highlighted and activated by an abstract, readable calligraphy.
(www.hsdesign.jp)

1998 war der 100. Geburtstag von Bertolt Brecht. Kein Grund für eine stumme
Gedenkfeier. Das Berliner Ensemble und der Verbund der Grafik-Designer laden
einhundert Gestalter und Studenten ein. Das Plakat verwendet Brechts Gedicht
*Legende von der Entstehung des Buches Taoteking auf dem Weg des Laotse
in die Emigration*. Von den 13 Strophen sind die wesentlichen durch eine abstrakte,
lesbare Kalligrafie hervorgehoben und aktiviert.
(www.hsdesign.jp)

The Road to Basel
(*Typographic Reflections 4*)
Robundo, 1997
258 × 262 mm
Photo: Yasuhiro Asai

der Weg nach Basel
(*Typographische Reflexionen 4*)
Robundo, 1997
Foto: Yasuhiro Asai

In the 1950s and 1960s Basel became the meeting place for young typographers and designers from various countries, mainly due to Ruder's work and personality. Ruder awakened an awareness of design on a broad basis: he taught apprentice compositors and printers; he started postgraduate courses for printers; he gave evening classes arranged by the Basel compositors" association, which were open to everyone. The design course for typography (*Typographische Gestaltungsklasse*) between 1956 and 68, however, with two or three students per year, became an ongoing process of education for all those allowed to take part.

To show this meditative period of modern typography unobtrusively beside today's typography, I invited former students to write about their road to Basel and their experience in Basel with such distinguished personalities as Emil Ruder, Robert Büchler, Kurt Hauert and Armin Hofmann, to show their work from that period and to identify work that had an influence on them. [...]

The Road to Basel is a book in an optical square with 96 pages. All texts are in German, English and Japanese. The design of the book tries to visualize the almost invisible transition from the orderly to organic typography. The grid, which gave Swiss typography a bad name, rightly and wrongly, is overplayed by a differentiated, flexible typography. Column widths, type sizes and leading vary. The design, on virgin-white double-page, arose out of the content. The typographic examples portray an epoch. They are as fresh today as when they were made.

Typography has moved in the meantime towards typograffiti, and symmetry or asymmetry is no longer an issue. But Ruder's typography lives because it rejuvenates with each new task, because it evolves through thoughtful refinement.

"I am absolutely sure," writes Fritz Gottschalk, "that Emil Ruder would have welcomed the Mac and that he would have spurred us on to develop something new with this exciting technology. And, as always, he would have set a high standard."

It is time to take the essentials of typography into the new technology and to work on it unwaveringly.
(*TM*, No. 3, 1998)

In den 1950er und 1960er Jahren wurde Basel vor allem durch das Wirken und die Persönlichkeit Emil Ruders zum Treffpunkt für junge Typografen und Grafiker aus verschiedenen Ländern. Ruder erweckte das gewissen für Gestaltung auf der so wichtigen breiten Basis: er unterrichtete die Lehrlingsklassen der Setzer und Drucker und führte junge Grafiker in die Typografie ein; er schuf die Buchdruckfachklasse zur Weiterbildung; er gab Abendkurse, veranstaltet von der Handsetzervereinigung Basel, die jedem offenstanden. Die Gestaltungsklasse für Typografie jedoch wurde, mit zwei oder drei Schülern pro Jahr, zur anhaltenden Ausbildung für die, die zwischen 1956 und 68 an ihr teilnehmen durften.

Um diese meditative Periode der modernen Typografie der heutigen unaufdringlich gegenüberzustellen, lud ich ehemalige Schüler ein, ihren Weg nach Basel und ihr Erlebnis in Basel mit solch herausragenden Persönlichkeiten wie Emil Ruder, Robert Büchler, Kurt Hauert und Armin Hofmann zu beschreiben, eigene Arbeiten von damals zu zeigen und Arbeiten zu nennen, die Einfluss auf sie hatten. [...]

Der Weg nach Basel ist ein Buch im optischen Quadrat mit 96 Seiten. Alle Beiträge sind in Deutsch, Englisch und Japanisch. Die Gestaltung des Buches versucht den Übergang von der strengen zur organischen Typografie aufzuzeigen. Das Raster, das die Schweizer Typografie, zu Recht und zu Unrecht, noch heute in Verruf bringt, wurde durch eine differenzierte, flexible Typografie überspielt. Spaltenbreiten, Schriftgrössen, Durchschuss variieren. Die Gestaltung entstand auf jungfräulich weissen Doppelseiten aus dem Inhalt. Die typografischen Beispiele stehen für eine Epoche. Sie sind heute so frisch wie zur Zeit ihrer Entstehung.

Typografie bewegt sich in der Zwischenzeit in Typograffiti, und Symmetrie oder Asymmetrie ist kein Thema mehr. Emil Ruders Typografie aber lebt, weil sie sich mit jeder Aufgabe erneuert, weil sie sich aus durchdachtem Verfeinern heraus entwickelt.

«Sicher bin ich mir», schreibt Fritz Gottschalk in seinem Beitrag, «Emil Ruder hätte den Mac begrüsst und uns angespornt, mit dieser Technologie etwas Neues zu entwickeln. Die Messlatte hätte er – wie immer – hoch angesetzt.»

Es ist an der Zeit, das Wesentliche der Typografie auf die neue Technologie zu übertragen und unbeirrt daran weiterzuarbeiten.
(*TM*, Nr. 3, 1998)

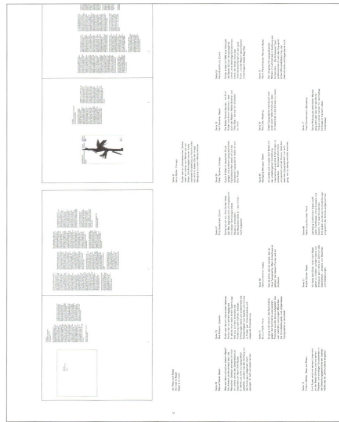

"Emil Ruder will remain an inspiration
and guiding force, especially
in this age of typographic confusion"
TM, No. 3, 1998
230 × 297 mm

«Gerade in unserer Zeit der typographischen
Orientierungslosigkeit bleibt Emil Ruder
Inspiration, bleibt Emil Ruder Orientierung»
TM, Nr. 3, 1998

"Japanese typography and
Swiss typography"
TM, No. 1, 2003
230 × 297 mm

«Japanische Typographie und
Schweizer Typographie»
TM, Nr. 1, 2003

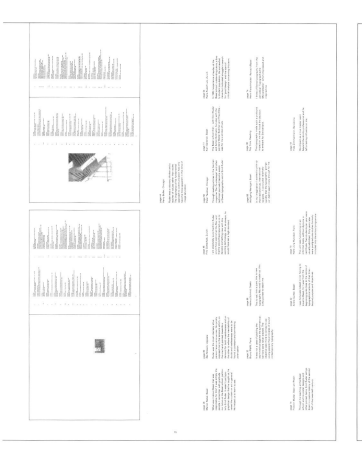

Roy Cole, Reading
the road to Basel

In Britain in the mid 1950s typographic development became synonymous with the aftermath of the Festival of Britain.[1] Slab-serif typefaces revivals from the nineteenth century, along with Mistral script, as perpetrated by Design magazine and Print in Britain and encouraged by the architectural publications, became the norm. Parallel with this Tschichold's influence through his late 1940s work on Penguins was still much in evidence. There was no clear indicator towards future trends and typography receded into a decadent abyss.

It was also in the mid 1950s that I began to notice an alternative typography which had its origins in Switzerland. This was the typography of Akzidenz Grotesk, a sanserif typeface from Berthold peculiarly associated with texts in German and which was complementary with asymmetric composition.[2] This typography made such a profound impact on me that I took the decision to embark for Switzerland.

Arriving in the Jura region I took temporary lodging in a nunnery. Whilst there I was shown some issues of a journal called Typographische Monatsblätter. On the cover of one number was a design comprised of small squares with inter-connecting lines. Another showed squares alone and with rectangles comprised of squares. Three who knew Emil Ruder will be familiar with his enthusiasm for the work of Piet Mondrian. He would explain at length the compositions of line and plane, of opposites and that no two lines were of equal thickness. It is, therefore, interesting to compare Ruder's covers with Mondrian's 'Broadway Boogie Woogie' painting and it was after seeing them that I knew where the centre of typography in Switzerland lay – not in the Solothurn Jura but in Basel. So I headed for Basel.

After the relative tranquility of Solothurn, the city of Basel seemed like a metropolis. The Münster, the Rathaus, the Kunstmuseum, Freie Strasse, Café Atlante, jazz, Birkhäuser, the Gewerbeschule. Here, in this old building, was the true centre of that phenomenon now known as Swiss typography?

I met Ruder for coffee in the Hotel Schweizerhof one Saturday morning. Here he outlined the typography course at the Gewerbeschule, explained what would be expected from me, and said that I should forget everything I ever learned about typography – 'hier fangen wir von vorne an'. At the time, this was hard to digest, but I knew it was the right thing to do.

By any standards the Gewerbeschule had a formidable team of tutors: Büchler, Hauert, Hofmann and Ruder himself. If Swiss typography was a phenomenon, then Ruder was phenomenal. His very presence in the composing room (which he liked to refer to as the laboratory) inspired one. It was here, where I heard him explaining to the then director B. von Grüningen the rhythmical design of his political poster for local elections. Rhythm in typography has remained with me ever since.

He was surely the foremost exponent of contemporary typography of this century and a creator of Swiss typography.[3] In a sense it is unfortunate that he achieved so much, for typographic development has not increased significantly since.

It has to be said that Switzerland's neutrality allowed typographic development to continue during the 1940s, when the rest of Europe was engaged in other activities. Nevertheless, the achievement of a country of only six million inhabitants, in creating a typographic style which attained world recognition, is remarkable.

December 1994

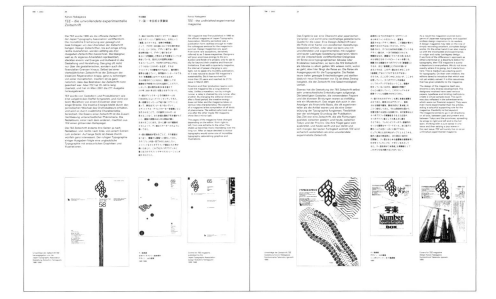

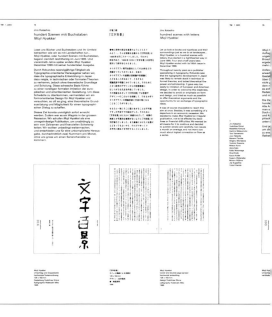

Poster content

place	special lecture	speaker	date
kobe design university ippanto, room 1225	on typography on modern typography	helmut schmid typographer	2000 01 26 14:40

場所
神戸芸術工科大学
一般棟 1225教室

視覚情報デザイン特別講義 C
タイポグラフィ について

講師
ヘルムート シュミット
タイポグラファー

日時
2000年1月26日(水)
14:40

on typography

"On typography"
Poster for a special lecture
Kobe Design University, 2000
728 × 1030 mm

«On typography»
Plakat für einen Vortrag an der
Kobe Design University, 2000

"Democracy Hypocrisy"
Poster at the request of Kai Bernau
using his typeface Neutral, 2005
700 × 1030 mm
Text: James P. Pinkerton

«Democray Hypocrisy»
(Demokratie Heuchelei)
Auf Wunsch von Kai Bernau
gestaltetes Plakat mit
dessen Schrift Neutral, 2005
Text: James P. Pinkerton

Today's digital technology allows us to work with ease in the most precise way, lets us work functionally in the most expressive way. Typography to be read and typography to be seen have never been so close at hand and so convenient. Typograffiti, not typography, is today in the hands of everyone. It is handy, it is trendy, it is cool.
Real typography works and continues its tradition and purpose. It's not a narrow-minded, detail-obsessed, rule-conscious typography I have in mind, but a typography which fuses mathematical precision and organic vitality. A typography in the beauty of the completed incomplete. A typography in the beauty of the perfect imperfect. A typography that lets the message talk.
(*Japan Typography Annual 1998*)

Die heutige digitale Technik ermöglicht uns ein einfaches und sehr präzises Arbeiten, lässt uns auf ausdruckstärkste Weise funktional arbeiten. Typografie zum Lesen und Typografie zum Betrachten waren niemals so dicht beieinander und so bequem zu nutzen.
Typograffiti, nicht Typografie, steht heute jedem zur Verfügung. Es ist handlich, es ist im Trend, es ist immer noch eine reale Typografie, die weiterhin auf ihrer Tradition und ihrem Zweck basiert.
In meiner Vorstellung keine kleingeistige, auf Details und Regeln versessene Typografie, sondern eine Typografie, die mathematische Präzision mit organischer Vitalität fusioniert. Eine Typografie in der Schönheit der vollständigen Unvollständigkeit. Eine Typografie in der Schönheit des perfekten Imperfekten. Eine Typografie, die die Botschaft sprechen lässt.
(*Japan Typography Annual 1998*)

Hongik graduate exhibition poster
Hongik University, 2006
728 × 1030 mm

Plakat für eine Abschlussausstellung
von Hongik-Studierenden
Hongik University, 2006

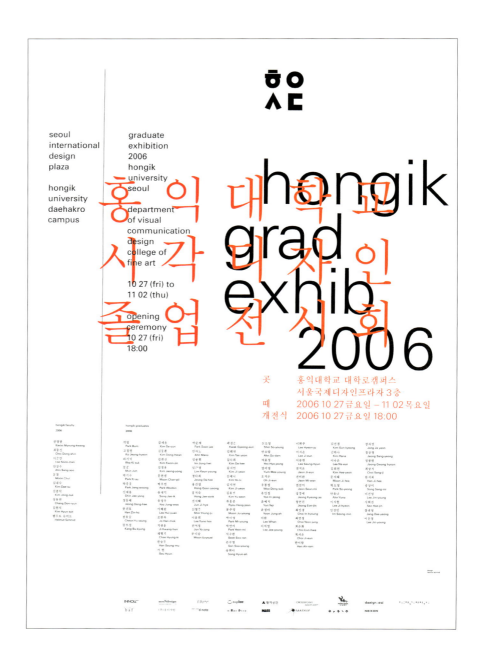

For the last two years I stayed three semesters in Korea, giving typography classes
at Hongik University in Seoul. To see hundreds of passionate students involved
in typography gave me a memorable present.
When asked to design the poster for the graduate exhibition 2006, I wanted to express
my appreciation for the students' effort, and I incorporated all the names of the graduates in
both languages, English and Korean, in Latin alphabet and hangul letters. As a personal
first attempt I blended sans serif (alphabet) and serif type (hangul) into a unity,
trying to bring out a mix of West and East.
(www.hsdesign.jp)

In den letzten zwei Jahren verbrachte ich drei Semester in Korea und unterrichtete Typografie
an der Hongik Universität in Seoul. Hunderte von leidenschaftlichen Studierenden zu sehen,
die sich mit Typografie beschäftigten, wie ein unvergessliches Geschenk für mich.
Als ich den Auftrag bekam, das Plakat für die Absolventen-Ausstellung 2006 zu gestalten,
wollte ich meine Anerkennung für den Einsatz der Studierenden zeigen, indem ich die Namen aller
Absolventen in beiden Sprachen, Englisch und Koreanisch, integrierte, mit lateinischen und
koreanischen (Hangul) Buchstaben. Als einen persönlichen ersten Entwurf vermischte ich
serifenlose Schrift (lateinisch) und Serifenschrift (Hangul) zu einer Einheit,
der Versuch einer Mischung von Westen und Osten.
(www.hsdesign.jp)

The work originated as a proposed advertisement for Shaken phototype in the 1980s, when Japanese baseball hero, Sadaharu Oh, hit three home runs in one game. The headline of the newspaper at that time used the full impact of the Japanese script: The syllables katakana and hiragana and the Chinese ideograph kanji. The kanji is the player's name and means "king." An amazing visualization of an event that can only be made with the mix of the Japanese letters. The work was recreated as a poster for the *design is attitude* exhibition at ddd gallery in Osaka, 2007.
(*Newwork Magazine*, No. 6, 2010)

Die Arbeit war ursprünglich in den 1980er Jahren als eine Anzeige für den Shaken-Fotosatz gedacht, als der japanische Baseballheld Sadaharu Oh in einem Spiel drei Home Runs erzielte. Die Überschrift der Zeitung nutzte damals die volle Wirkung der japanischen Schrift: die Silben Katakana und Hiragana und das chinesische Ideogramm Kanji. Das Kanji ist der Name des Spielers und bedeutet «König». Eine erstaunliche Visualisierung eines Ereignisses, das nur mit der Mischung der japanischen Buchstaben erreicht werden kann. Der Entwurf wurde als Plakat für die Ausstellung *Gestaltung ist Haltung* 2007 in der ddd gallery in Osaka nachgestellt.
(*Newwork Magazin*, Nr. 6, 2010)

"Fountains of Swiss Typography"
Poster for the lecture,
Kobe Design University, 2006
728 × 1030 mm

Plakat für den Vortrag
«Fountains of Swiss Typography»
(Quellen der Schweizer Typografie)
Kobe Design University, 2006

o o ohh: katakana, hiragana, kanji
Poster honoring the triad of
the Japanese script, 2007
728 × 1030 mm

o o ohh: katakana, hiragana, kanji
Plakat-Hommage an die Triade der
japanischen Schrift, 2007

Poster for the exhibition
Design is Attitude
ginza graphic gallery / ddd gallery, 2007
728 × 1030 mm

Plakat für die Ausstellung
Gestaltung ist Haltung
ginza graphic gallery / ddd gallery, 2007

Poster for the exhibition
Danke Emil Ruder
Print Gallery Tokyo, 2014
210 × 715 mm

Plakat für die Ausstellung
Danke Emil Ruder
Print Gallery Tokyo, 2014

Idea, No. 333:
Ruder typography Ruder philosophy *
Seibundo Shinkosha, 2009
225 × 297 mm

* The hardcover edition was published in 2017

Idea, Nr. 333:
Ruder Typografie Ruder Philosophie *
Seibundo Shinkosha, 2009

* Hardcover-Ausgabe aus dem Jahr 2017

The Japanese design magazine *Idea*, published in Japanese and English under the editorship of Kiyonori Muroga, devotes from time to time whole issues to influential designers. After Jan Tschichold (321), Otl Aicher (322), Wim Crouwel (323), *Idea* 333 is devoted to the Swiss typographer, teacher and philosopher Emil Ruder.

Ruder typography Ruder philosophy is a first attempt to capture the personality of this exceptional typographer. Ruder's typography speaks for itself. Wherever possible his comments, taken mainly from his publications in *TM* (*Typographische Monatsblätter*) are included. To show the development, his work is grouped in three sections: serif typography, sans serif typography and Univers typography. The influence of a typeface on typography thus becomes visible.

To round out the image of Ruder, his colleagues from the Basel school, his international students and established designers wrote about the man and his work. Contributors include: Armin Hofmann, Karl Gerstner, Wim Crouwel, Kurt Hauert, Lenz Klotz, Åke Nilsson, Fridolin Müller, Hans Rudolf Bosshard, Adrian Frutiger, André Gürtler, Harri Boller, Taro Yamamoto, Juan Arrausi, Maxim Zhukov, Fjodor Gejko, Helmut Schmid, Susanne Ruder-Schwarz. The introduction to the world of Ruder is by Kiyonori Muroga and Helmut Schmid.
(www.hsdesign.jp)

Das japanische Designmagazin *Idea*, veröffentlicht auf Japanisch und Englisch unter der Redaktion von Kiyonori Muroga, widmet gelegentlich einflussreichen Gestaltern eine ganze Ausgabe. Nach Jan Tschichold (321), Otl Aicher (322) und Wim Crouwel (323) war *Idea* 333 dem Schweizer Typografen, Lehrer und Philosophen Emil Ruder gewidmet.

Ruder Typografie, Ruder Philosophie ist der erste Versuch, die Persönlichkeit dieses aussergewöhnlichen Typografen zu erfassen. Ruders Typografie spricht für sich selbst. Wann immer möglich, sind auch seine Kommentare enthalten, meistens seinen Veröffentlichungen in *TM* (*Typografische Monatsblätter*) entnommen. Um die Entwicklung zu demonstrieren, ist sein Werk in drei Abschnitte unterteilt: Serifen-Typografie, serifenlose Typografie und Univers-Typografie. Auf diese Weise wird der Einfluss einer Schrifttype auf die Typografie deutlich.

Um das Image von Ruder abzurunden, haben seine Kollegen der Basler Schule, seine internationalen Schüler und etablierte Gestalter sich schriftlich über den Mann und sein Werk geäussert. Beiträge unter anderem von: Armin Hofmann, Karl Gerstner, Wim Crouwel, Kurt Hauert, Lenz Klotz, Åke Nilsson, Fridolin Müller, Hans Rudolf Bosshard, Adrian Frutiger, André Gürtler, Harri Boller, Taro Yamamoto, Juan Arrausi, Maxim Zhukov, Fjodor Gejko, Helmut Schmid und Susanne Ruder-Schwarz. Die Einleitung zu der Welt von Ruder ist von Kiyonori Muroga und Helmut Schmid.
(www.hsdesign.jp)

Emil Ruder, *fundamentals:*
four lectures from the 1950s
by the master of timeless typography
Seibundo Shinkosha, 2013
225 × 297 mm

Emil Ruder, *Grundlagen:*
vier Vorträge aus den 1950er Jahren
von dem Meister der zeitlosen Typografie
Seibundo Shinkosha, 2013

山田光

「出会った形に触発されることはある。
創作する時に思案することはない。
私の内部から自ずと生じてくるものを形に
するだけだ」。山田光は私にこのように言って、
彼の陶磁器創作の奥義を語ってくれた。

山田光の日常使う器は機能と使いやすさを
併せ持っている。花瓶は有機的に丸みを帯び、
湯呑み茶碗は持ちやすい形をしている。
徳利は非対称形、杯は繊細で小ぶりである。

山田光が造る日常使いの器には磁土と
呼ばれる、白い土が使われている。艶消しの
釉薬には透明釉に珪石を加えたものを使う。
抽象的な模様や筆で描いた線、切り込み
などを加えて本体を弱めるようなことは
滅多にしない。

Hikaru Yamada

'It is possible that I was inspired
by a form which I once encountered.
I have never thought about how
I create. I form my objects as they
arise within me.'
This was how Hikaru Yamada
explained the secret of his creativity
in clay and in porcelain.

Hikaru Yamada's everyday table-ware
unites usefulness with elegance:
kabin, the organically rounded flower
vase; yunomi chawan, the handily
formed tea bowls; tokkuri, the
asymmetrically formed sake holder
and sakazuki, the delicate tiny
sake cups.

Yamada's everyday utensils are
made from white porcelain clay,
known as jido. For the matt glazing,
transparent glaze mixed with
silica is used. Only occasionally
does he weaken the material with an
abstract ornament, through
a few brush strokes or through
the incision of lines.

畳

金色のイグサを織り込んだ畳表、縦横の配置の仕方、1本と2本の縁が織り成す幾何学模様、これはきっとモンドリアンをも刺激したに違いない。

日本人は、部屋に敷き詰めるマットレスを畳と呼ぶ。厚さ数センチに圧縮された稲わら床は、きれいに織られたイグサ表で覆われている。縦横の割合は1対2、あるいは約1×2メートルである。長い方の辺、又は間と呼ばれる側のヘリは布製の帯で綴じる。その色や模様は様々である。間は日本家屋の建築の際用いられる基準尺度で、17世紀以来畳の大きさの基準になっている。

日本家屋の部屋の簡素さはこの畳に負う。

Tatami

Its texture of plaited, golden rush straw in a configuration of long and short sides with borders positioned singly or doubly next to each other make for a geometric form which might well have provided inspiration for Mondrian.

Tatami is the name given by the Japanese to the mats which they use as room flooring: rice straw compressed to a thickness of a few centimetres, with a covering layer of finely woven rush straw. Its ratio of its sides one to two, or approximately one metre by two. The longer side, girded with a band of cloth which in colour and pattern can vary, is also known as the ken side. Ken is the standard measurement used for building Japanese houses and which since the seventeenth century has dictated the tatami's dimensions.

It was tatami which gave Japanese rooms their characteristic simplicity.

Previous spread:
Exhibition view of *Nippon no Nippon*
(Japan Japanese)
kyoto ddd gallery, 2015
Photo: Nobutada Omote

Vorangehende Doppelseite:
Ausstellungsansicht *Nippon no Nippon*
(Japan japanisch)
kyoto ddd gallery, 2015
Foto: Nobutada Omote

Japan japanisch, Japan Japanese
Robundo, 2012
250 × 255 mm

Japan japanisch, *Japan Japanese*
Robundo, 2012

Poster for the exhibition
Nippon no Nippon (Japan Japanese)
kyoto ddd gallery, 2015
728 × 1030 mm

Ausstellungsplakat für
Nippon no Nippon (Japan japanisch)
kyoto ddd gallery, 2015

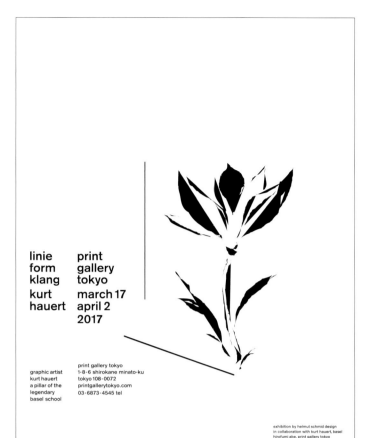

Poster for the exhibition
Linie Form Klang (Line Form Sound)
Kurt Hauert
Print Gallery Tokyo, 2017
728 × 1030 mm

Ausstellungsplakat für
Linie Form Klang Kurt Hauert
Print Gallery Tokyo, 2017

Typographic Reflections 1:
1989 11 09, the Berlin wall falls
(Headline of the Asahi newspaper)
Text: Japanese
1992, 20 pages
250 × 255 mm

"The Berlin wall falls." The heading of the Asahi newspaper of November 10, 1989, announcing the fall of the Berlin wall, inspired the first issue. By applying a kinetic flow, the issue became an explanation of the triad of the Japanese script: kanji, hiragana and katakana.
(*Newwork Magazine*, No. 6, 2010, and hereinafter)

Typographic Reflections 2:
Point line movement, experimental Typographic covers for the Swedish magazine Grafisk Revy
Introduction by Åke Nilsson
Text: Swedish, English, German
1993, 36 pages

Typographic Reflections 3:
Communal harmony,
Typography workshop at
IDC IIT Bombay
Students' comments on their works,
Contributions by Kirti Trivedi,
R. K. Joshi and Sudhahar Nadkarni
Text: English
1995, 32 pages

Communal harmony typography workshop at the industrial design center of IIT Bombay in India. Professor Kirti Trivedi of IDC encouraged me to add a workshop to my lecture, "design is attitude." My hesitating answer: "Will there be students interested in old-fashioned typography?"

Typographic Reflections 5:
Democracy / Hypocrisy,
Interpretation of a Newspaper article
by James. P. Pinkerton
Text: English
2003, 8 pages

Typographische Reflexionen 1:
1989 11 09, the Berlin wall falls
(Schlagzeile der Tageszeitung *Asahi*)
Text: Japanisch
1992, 20 Seiten

«Die Berliner Mauer fällt» – die Schlagzeile der Tageszeitung *Asahi* vom 10. November 1989 – inspirierte die erste Ausgabe. Durch Anwendung eines kinetischen Flusses wurde diese Ausgabe zu einer Erläuterung der Triade der japanischen Schrift: Kanji, Hiragana und Katakana.
(Hier und im Folgenden: *Newwork Magazine*, Nr. 6, 2010)

Typographische Reflexionen 2:
Punkt Linie Bewegung
Umschläge für die schwedische Fachzeitschrift Grafisk Revy
Einführung von Åke Nilsson
Text: Schwedisch, Englisch, Deutsch
1993, 36 Seiten

Typographische Reflexionen 3:
Communal harmony,
Typography workshop at
IDC IIT Bombay
Studierende kommentieren ihre Arbeiten Beiträge von
Kirti Trivedi, R. K. Joshi und
Sudhahar Nadkarni
Texte: Englisch
1995, 32 Seiten

Der Typografie-Workshop «Communal harmony» fand im Industrial Design Center des Indian Institute of Technology Bombay statt. Professor Kirit Trivedi vom IDC ermutigte mich, meinem Vortrag «Gestaltung ist Haltung» einen Workshop hinzuzufügen. Ich antwortete zögerlich: «Wird es dort Studierende geben, die sich für altmodische Typografie interessieren?»

Typographische Reflexionen 5:
Democracy / Hypocrisy,
Interpretation of a Newspaper article
by James. P. Pinkerton
Text: Englisch
2003, 8 Seiten

*Typographic Reflections 6:
Arrange, Select and Explore,
Typography workshop at Hongik
University in Seoul*
Text: English, Korean
2005, 32 pages

"Arrange Select Explore," typography workshop XD 6, at Hongik University in Seoul. Front and back of the CD of *naui dang, naui minjokiyo!* (My land, My people!), by Korean composer Isang Yun, was used as study material to arrange, to select, and to explore.

*Typographic Reflections 7:
Toshiro Mayuzumi's Nirvana
Symphony composed on the
Hand press and*
Text: English, Japanese
2010, 40 pages

In 1969, I recorded a conversation with the internationally active composer Toshiro Mayuzumi on a 60-minute tape. It is printed here for the first time. It also includes my typographic studies of the symphony composed in the hand press and in the darkroom from that period. Printed in black and vermilion.

*Typographic Reflections 8:
project Fukushima,
a Typography project at
Kobe Design University
Work of Mayuko Morimoto*
Text: English, Japanese
2012, 16 pages

*Typographic Reflections 9:
Working with words,
Typography workshop at
Nanyang Technological University
in Singapore*
Text: English
2012, 24 pages

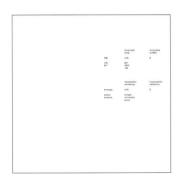

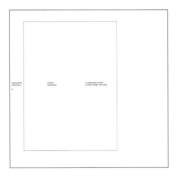

*Typographische Reflexionen 6:
Arrange, Select and Explore,
Typography workshop at
Hongik University in Seoul*
Text: Englisch, Koreanisch
2005, 32 Seiten

Der XD 6-Typografie-Workshop «Arrange Select Explore» fand an der Hongik University in Seoul statt. Die Vorder- und Rückseite der CD «Mein Land, mein Volk!» (naui dang, naui minjokiyo!) des koreanischen Komponisten Isang Yun diente als Studienmaterial, um zu arrangieren, auszuwählen und zu erforschen.

*Typographische Reflexionen 7:
Toshiro Mayuzumi's Nirvana
Symphony composed on
the Hand press and*
Text: Englisch, Japanisch
2010, 40 Seiten

1969 nahm ich auf einem 60-Minuten-Tonband ein Gespräch mit dem international tätigen Komponisten Toshiro Mayuzumi auf. Es ist hier zum ersten Mal abgedruckt. Enthalten sind auch meine typografischen Studien zur Symphonie aus dieser Zeit, die auf der Handpresse und in der Dunkelkammer entstanden. Gedruckt in Schwarz und Zinnoberrot.

*Typographische Reflexionen 8:
project Fukushima,
a Typography project
at Kobe Design University
Work of Mayuko Morimoto*
Text: Englisch, Japanisch
2012, 16 Seiten

*Typographische Reflexionen 9:
working with words
Typography workshop at
Nanyang Technological University
in Singapore*
Text: Englisch
2012, 24 Seiten

Typographic Reflections 10:
Type and Illustration
Text: English, Japanese
2014, 16 pages

Typographic Reflections 11:
Man made Nature made
Text: English, Japanese
2014, 36 pages

Typographic Reflections 12:
A walk through the exhibition
Nippon no Nippon
Text: English, Japanese
2016, 28 pages

Typographic Reflections 13:
Mit freundlichen Grüssen an alle
Kurt Hauert (My best regards
to everyone)
Text: German, English
2017, 28 pages

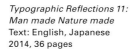

Typographische Reflexionen 10:
Type and Illustration
Text: Englisch, Japanisch
2014, 16 Seiten

Typographische Reflexionen 11:
Man made Nature made
Text: Englisch, Japanisch
2014, 36 Seiten

Typographische Reflexionen 12:
A walk through the exhibition
Nippon no Nnippon
Text: Englisch, Japanisch
2016, 28 Seiten

Typographische Reflexionen 13:
Mit freundlichen Grüssen an alle
Kurt Hauert
Text: Deutsch, Japanisch
2017, 28 Seiten

*Typographic Reflections 14:
2018 04 27*, studies from
the 2018 PaTI typography workshop
Text: English
2018, 28 pages
255 × 215 mm

*Typographische Reflexionen 14:
2018 04 27*, studies from
the 2018 PaTI typography workshop
Text: englisch
2018, 28 Seiten

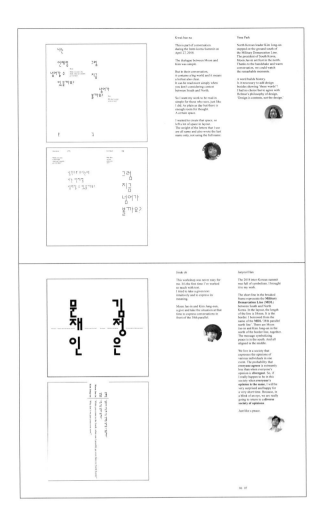

My typography workshop at PaTI Paju Typography Institute was planned months in advance:
a series of book covers for the British author Kazuo Ishiguro, the 2017 Nobel prize winner in literature.
On April 27, the day of the inter-Korean summit, I arrived in Seoul. During dinner with friends,
the discussion was all about the words and deeds of the leaders of the two Koreas. It sounded almost
unbelievable and I remembered the day the Berlin Wall came down, November 9, 1989,
and I felt the need to adjust the theme of my typography workshop at PaTI.
 We found the material for the workshop in the smiling words of the two leaders.
The aim of the workshop: to set the words and make them appear as talking and reporting, without
thinking of design. Design without design. Student Park So-young expressed it beautifully:
"Design that listens to and conveys the message of content, rather than design that
attracts attention only as a decorative element."
(*Typographic Reflections 14*)

Mein Typografie-Workshop im PaTI Paju Institut für Typografie war Monate vorher geplant:
eine Serie von Buchumschlägen für den britischen Autor Kazuo Ishiguro, dem Empfänger des Nobel-
preises im Jahr 2017. Am 27. April kam ich in Seoul an, dem Tag des interkoreanischen Gipfeltreffens.
Während des Abendessens mit Freunden drehte sich das Gespräch um die Worte und Taten der
Präsidenten der beiden Koreas. Es klang fast unglaublich und erinnerte mich an den Fall der Berlin Mauer
am 09.11.1989, und ich hatte das Bedürfnis, das Thema meines PaTI Typografie-Workshop anzupassen.
 Wir fanden das Material für den Kurs in den strahlenden Worten der beiden Präsidenten.
Das Ziel des Kurses: Die Worte zu nehmen und sie als sprechend und berichtend erscheinen zu lassen,
ohne an Gestaltung zu denken. Gestaltung ohne Gestaltung. Der Student Park So-young hat es hervor-
ragend ausgedrückt: «Eine Gestaltung, die hinhört und den Inhalt der Botschaft vermittelt, anstatt
einer Gestaltung, die eine Aufmerksamkeit nur als dekoratives Element erreicht.»
(*Typographische Reflexionen 14*)

am dreaming of a typography where the attitude is attitude
am dreaming of a typography where the space is space
am dreaming of a typography where the encounters are encounters
am dreaming of a typography where the names are names
am dreaming of a typography where the sound is sound
am dreaming of a typography where the content is content
am dreaming of a typography where the elegance is elegance
am dreaming of a typography where the beauty is beauty
am dreaming of a typography where the variations are variations
am dreaming of a typography where the tension is tension
am dreaming of a typography where the rules are rules
am dreaming of a typography where the typefaces are typefaces
am dreaming of a typography where the detail is detail
am dreaming of a typography where the passions are passions
am dreaming of a typography where the experiments are experiments
am dreaming of a typography where the printing is printing
am dreaming of a typography where the paper is paper
am dreaming of a typography where the colour is colour
am dreaming of a typography where the proportions are proportions
am dreaming of a typography where the emotional is emotional
am dreaming of a typography where the imitators are imitators
am dreaming of a typography where the details are details
am dreaming of a typography where the computers are computers
am dreaming of a typography where the television is television
am dreaming of a typography where the lines are lines
am dreaming of a typography where the asymmetry is asymmetry
am dreaming of a typography where the symmetry is symmetry
am dreaming of a typography where the honest is honest
am dreaming of a typography where the numbers are numbers
am dreaming of a typography where the points are points
am dreaming of a typography where the designers are designers
am dreaming of a typography where the artists are artists
am dreaming of a typography where the pioneers are pioneers
am dreaming of a typography where the univers is univers
am dreaming of a typography where the movements are movements
am dreaming of a typography where the study is study
am dreaming of a typography where the poetic is poetic
am dreaming of a typography where the harmony is harmony
am dreaming of a typography where the rhythmical is rhythmical
am dreaming of a typography where the creativity is creativity
am dreaming of a typography where the kinetic is kinetic
am dreaming of a typography where the dynamic is dynamic
am dreaming of a typography where the ideas are ideas
am dreaming of a typography where the form is form
am dreaming of a typography where the counter-form is counter-form
am dreaming of a typography where the thoughts are thoughts
am dreaming of a typography where the mac is mac
am dreaming of a typography where the writing is writing
am dreaming of a typography where the messages are messages
am dreaming of a typography where the graffiti is graffiti
am dreaming of a typography where the dreams are dreams
am dreaming of a typography where the words are words
am dreaming of a typography where the typography is typography

10 lecture: design is attitude

Vortrag:
Gestaltung ist
Haltung

Cover and work on back cover (left)
of the Indian magazine *Motif*, No. 6
Mudra, 1998
204 × 254 mm

Umschlag und Werk auf der
Umschlagsrückseite (links) der
indischen Zeitschrift *Motif*, Nr. 6
Mudra, 1998

design is attitude
helmut schmid, osaka, japan

(lecture at idc, iit bombay, 1992,
from *motif*, no. 6, mudra, 1998)

answers for the future are in the past. and by looking at design works which surrounded us in the past, we try to find the meaning in today's design.

that i work as a designer, to be exact as a typographer, is thanks to pure luck. luck is essential for any profession. of course, also talent, energy and ability, but first of all we need to get the possibility to find and to develop our own personality.

the entrance to the world of typography i found in the radiating personality of emil ruder, teacher of typography at switzerland's allgemeine gewerbeschule basel, today's basel school of design. ruder's work, ruder's teaching, ruder's philosophy, ruder's attitude opened for me a world of commitment. in ruder's typography, form is not made, it is developed. words and lines were not sketched as it was common at that time – words were proofed in the handpress and then cut and placed on a given paper size, then the lines were moved until a clear composition was found. for me it was a most impressive entrance into a world of attitude, and i have tried to work according to these principles ever since.

years before the first of 18 issues of *neue grafik* [fig.1] appeared from the zurich design scene in 1958, with its editors richard lohse, j. müller-brockmann, hans neuburg, carlo vivarelli: before the first of 21 issues of the magazine *ulm* appeared in the same year, (available today as *readings from ulm*, compiled by prof. kirti trivedi of idc bombay): years before modern typography was named swiss typography, there was a typography of order practiced at the basel school which did not care about style and publicity. it was practiced like a mission, and the mission of teachers like emil ruder and robert büchler attracted people in switzerland and abroad through the swiss journal *typographische monatsblätter*, tm, which was designed according to the principles of the basel school.

at the same time as zurich and ulm started their magazines, karl gerstner and markus kutter, the designer/copywriter team, worked in basel on *die neue graphik: its origins, its peculiarities, its task, its problems, its manifestations, and its future* [fig. 2]. the theme of the new graphic, of the new typography was in the air and the difference was of course not only in the use or non-use of lowercase letters, or in writing the german word *graphik* with *ph* (basel) or *grafik* with *f* (zurich), there was a clear difference in the philosophy between basel typography and zurich typography.

the typographic interpretations of the 3 design centers: basel, zurich, ulm, were completely different but they shared one preference – the typeface akzidenz grotesk [fig. 3].

one of the most impressive statements of typography from that period is probably the *tm* special issue "integrale typographie" from the year 1959 [fig. 4]. karl gerstner coined the title and emil ruder designed the cover in the clearest proportion of printed and unprinted. in that issue, ruder counters tschichold's attack on the overuse of sans serif and asymmetry in basel and switzerland.

johannes, ivan, jan tschichold (whose first name depended on the time), started as a traditional calligrapher in germany. after visiting an exhibition at the bauhaus he published *elementare typographie* (1925), a 24-page comment on the movement of modern art, and *die neue typographie* (1928), a 240-page book on the rules of the new typography. in 1933 he emigrated to basel in switzerland and published *typographische gestaltung* (1935) [fig. 5], an elaborate book of 112 pages (with 8-pages of ads) and his last one in asymmetry. he then devoted his attention again to symmetry and denounced all and everybody who did not follow his u-turn.

heated discussions developed about whether symmetry or asymmetry was the proper way of typography; heated discussions followed about whether sans serif or serif were the best readable typefaces. discussion of such small things are out of date today. today, where imitations are brushed aside with the word "quote." today, where the smallest designer boasts of being the creator of the wheel.

it was ruder, and not tschichold, who became teacher of typography at the basel school in 1942. that situation surely influenced tschichold's polemic. that situation probably inspired both typographers to develop their typographic attitudes. there exists one design which unites both: the cover for the *tm* bauhaus issue (1952, no. 2). ruder designed the cover and tschichold designed the *tm* logomark. (the attitudes of ruder and tschichold are only superficially observed like water and oil. both searched for quality in typography.)

while the magazines from ulm and zurich remained on a rigid grid, the *tm* changed its layout practically every 2 years. the basel designers were less dogmatic and so emerged from the basel school a typography which was rhythmical and refined. it did not emerge from a fashionable wave, it originated with a new typeface – univers [fig. 6] – designed by the swiss adrian frutiger at the type foundry deberney & peignot in paris. ruder's influence on univers typography is acknowledged, but ruder's influence on the creation of univers has never been properly stated. it was ruder who introduced the typeface to an international audience in the 2nd issue of *neue grafik*, and when *tm* in 1961 devoted the january issue to the new typeface [figs. 7 and 8], it was the wish of frutiger that ruder, "who is familiar with the typeface like no one else," would design the issue.

ruder designed the univers issue from the inside toward the outside and with it he arrived at a typography of classical beauty. after the cool designs in akzidenz grotesk, the trademark of the swiss-influenced designers, ruder's univers typography looked virtuous, light, elegant, graceful. the typeface had its share in that look: the subtlety of the letterforms, the optical corrections in the details, the openness of the form and counterform.

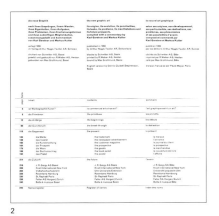

1
Neue Grafik, New Graphic Design
Magazine cover
Carlo Vivarelli, Zurich 1958

2
Die Neue Graphik,
The New Graphic Art
Table of contents
Karl Gerstner, Basel 1958

3
Typeface Akzidenz Grotesk
H. Berthold AG., 1898

4
Typographische Monatsblätter
Magazine cover
Emil Ruder, Basel 1959

5
Typographische Gestaltung
Cover
Jan Tschichold, Basel 1935

6
Typeface Univers
Adrian Frutiger, Paris 1957

gestaltung ist haltung
helmut schmid, osaka, japan

(vortrag am idc, iit bombay, 1992,
aus *motif*, nr. 6, mudra, 1998)

antworten für die zukunft findet man in der vergangenheit. und wenn wir die arbeiten betrachten, die uns in der vergangenheit umgaben, versuchen wir, die bedeutung des heutigen designs zu verstehen.

dass ich als designer arbeite, als typograph, um genau zu sein, verdanke ich reinem glück. glück ist für jeden beruf entscheidend. selbstverständlich auch talent, energie und fähigkeit. aber zuerst müssen wir die möglichkeit bekommen, unsere eigene persönlichkeit zu entwickeln.

den zugang zur welt der typographie fand ich in der strahlenden persönlichkeit von emil ruder, typographielehrer an der gewerbeschule basel (heute bekannt als schule für gestaltung). ruders werk, ruders unterricht, ruders philosophie, ruders haltung eröffneten mir die welt der verpflichtung. in ruders typographie wird form nicht gemacht, sondern entwickelt. texte und linien werden nicht skizziert, wie es damals üblich war. texte wurden abgesetzt, in der handpresse abgezogen, ausgeschnitten und dann auf einem papierformat plaziert. die textzeilen wurden so lange geschoben, bis sich eine klare komposition einstellte. für mich war es die eindrucksvollste einführung in die welt der haltung, und seither versuche ich, nach diesen prinzipien zu arbeiten.

jahre bevor 1958 die erste von 18 ausgaben von *neue grafik* [abb. 1] aus der zürcher designszene erschien, herausgegeben von richard lohse, josef müller-brockmann, hans neuburg und carlo vivarelli; bevor die erste von 21 ausgaben der zeitschrift *ulm* im gleichen jahr erschien (verfügbar heute als *readings from ulm*, zusammengestellt von kirti trivedi am idc bombay); jahre bevor moderne typographie «schweizer typographie» genannt wurde, wurde diese typographie der ordnung an der basler schule praktiziert, die sich weder um stil noch um selbstlob kümmerte. sie wurde missionarisch von emil ruder und robert büchler praktiziert und erweckte die aufmerksamkeit von berufsleuten aus der schweiz und dem ausland, bestärkt durch die schweizer zeitschrift *typographische monatsblätter*, die nach den regeln der basler schule gestaltet war.

zur gleichen zeit, als zürich und ulm ihre zeitschriften starteten, arbeiteten in basel karl gerstner und markus kutter am buch die *neue graphik* [abb. 2] (nach ihren ursprüngen, ihrem werden, ihren eigenheiten, ihren aufgaben, ihren problemen, ihren erscheinungsformen und ihren zukünftigen möglichkeiten). das thema der neuen graphik lag in der luft, und der unterschied war natürlich nicht nur in der anwendung oder nichtanwendung von kleinschreibung oder in der schreibung des wortes «graphik» mit «ph» (basel) oder «grafik» mit «f» (zürich). es gab einen deutlichen unterschied zwischen basel typographie und zürich typographie.

die typographischen interpretationen der drei designzentren: basel, zürich und ulm waren verschieden, sie teilten aber eine präferenz, die schrift akzidenz grotesk [abb. 3].

eine der eindruckvollsten aussagen der typographie aus dieser periode ist die *tm*-sondernummer *integrale typographie* aus dem jahr 1959 [abb. 4]. karl gerstner prägte den titel, und emil ruder gestaltete den umschlag in klarster proportion von bedruckt und unbedruckt. in dieser *tm* antwortet ruder im artikel «zur typographie der gegenwart» auf tschicholds polemik zur serifenlosen und asymetrischen typographie in basel und der schweiz.

johannes, ivan, jan tschichold (mit vornamen je nach zeitgeist) begann als traditioneller kalligraph in deutschland. nach einem besuch einer ausstellung am bauhaus veröffentlichte er *elementare typographie* (1925), ein 24-seitiger kommentar zur bewegung der modernen kunst, und die *neue typographie* (1928), ein 240-seitiges buch der regeln der neuen typographie. und nach der emigration 1933 nach basel, schweiz, veröffentlichte er 1935 im verlag benno schwabe *typographische gestaltung* [abb. 5], ein durchdachtes 122-seitiges buch (mit acht inseratseiten) und sein letztes in asymmetrie. danach widmete er sich wieder der symmetrie und beleidigte jeden, der seiner kehrtwende nicht folgte.

es entwickelten sich heisse diskussionen, ob symmetrie oder asymmetrie die korrekte art der typographie sei. ob serifenlose schriften oder serifenschriften die am besten lesbaren schriften seien. diskussionen um solch kleine dinge sind heute nicht gefragt. heute, wo der unbedeutendste designer sich als erfinder des rades rühmt.

es war ruder und nicht max caflisch oder jan tschichold, der 1942 als lehrer für typographie an die basler schule berufen wurde. sicher beeinflusste diese situation tschicholds polemik. diese situation inspirierte vermutlich die beiden typographen, ihre typographische haltung zu entwickeln. es gibt eine arbeit, die sie vereinigt; der umschlag für die *tm*-sondernummer *basler schule* (tm 1952/nr. 2). ruder gestaltete den umschlag und tschichold das *tm*-logo. (die haltung von ruder und tschichold ist nur oberflächlich wie wasser und öl. beide suchten nach qualität in der typographie.)

während die zeitschriften aus ulm und zürich auf einem starren raster ausharrten, änderte die *tm* praktisch alle zwei jahre ihr layout. die gestalter in basel waren weniger dogmatisch, und so entstand an der basler schule eine typographie, die rhythmisch und verfeinert war. sie entstand nicht aus einer neuen modewelle, sie entstand aus einer neuen schrift, univers [abb. 6], entworfen vom schweizer adrian frutiger für deberney & peignot in paris. ruders einfluss auf die univers-typographie ist bekannt, aber ruders einfluss auf die schrift univers kam nie an die öffentlichkeit. es war ruder, der die schrift, in der zweiten nummer von *neue grafik*, einem internationalen publikum vorstellte. und als die *tm* die januarnummer 1961 ganz der neuen schrift widmete [abb. 7 und 8], war es der wunsch frutigers, dass ruder, «der wie kein zweiter mit der schrift vertraut ist», die ausgabe gestaltete.

ruder gestaltete die univers-sondernummer von innen nach aussen und kam dadurch zu einer typographie von klassischer schönheit. nach den kühlen entwürfen in akzidenz grotesk, kennzeichen des von schweizer typographie beeinflussten designs, sah die univers-typographie von ruder virtuos, leicht, elegant und graziös aus. die schrift hatte ihren teil am aussehen: die feinheiten der schriftformen, die optischen korrekturen in den details, die offenheit von form und gegenform.

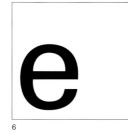

1
Neue Grafik, New Graphic Design
Titel der Zeitschrift
Carlo Vivarelli, Zürich 1958

2
Die Neue Graphik
Inhaltsverzeichnis
Karl Gerstner, Basel 1958

3
Schrift Akzidenz Grotesk
H. Berthold AG, 1898

4
Typographische Monatsblätter
Titel der Zeitschrift
Emil Ruder, Basel 1959

5
Typographische Gestaltung
Titelseite
Jan Tschichold, Basel 1935

6
Schrift Univers
Adrian Frutiger, Paris 1957

a typography of lightness was applied 11 years later in the visual identity for the munich olympics in germany. the typeface used: univers 55. there exist few applications with such a consistent look. otl aicher and rolf müller designed in a pleasant and not invading typography. the official gift of the munich olympics was a book with a collection of german writers, *german mosaic* [fig. 9]. the dust jacket, designed by aicher, in glossy silver, had a rhythmical arrangement, almost ruder style, except for the tight use of the letterspace. (16 years later, aicher accepted the open letterspace of univers – and quite a lot of the characteristics of the lettershapes – and applied it in his own typeface, rotis.)

in 1967, emil ruder published his long-awaited book, *typographie* [fig. 10], a 276-page manual of design. the result of his 25-year typography teaching at the basel school. designed in three sizes of univers medium, based on a simple grid, which is overplayed by a rhythmical application, where one page spread flows kinetically to the next. almost all works by ruder or by his students from the typography classes are reproduced in original size.

typography is devoted to a clear purpose, which is to convey meaning through the use of type. it cannot be exempted from this obligation by any kind of argument or any consideration. the printed product that cannot be read has no meaning whatsoever. (ruder)

when univers typography (on the surface) became available to everybody, there reappeared bold typefaces, extreme indents, letterspacing, underlining of words. the power of advertising crept into everyday typography. texts were not just placed but interpreted. rise and fall [fig. 11] could be expressed just by letting the words rise and fall. aie-eue-öeei is not a sound poem by schwitters but a cover design for an austrian journal [fig. 12], using the vowels of the journal's name (*graphische revue österreichs*) as sound colors.

in that period of changes, wolfgang weingart became in 1964 a student at the basel school, in the same year as i re-entered, after a two-year working journey. typography in swiss style or not was the daily theme then and still is. (swiss typography is loved and hated like any movement of importance. unfortunately, it was never understood in its depth.)

ruder became director of the basel school in 1965 and weingart, three years later, teacher of typography. and as tschichold provoked ruder, so ruder provoked weingart, who opposed swiss typography. weingart bent line material which was straight on the shelves. he used plaster as non-printing material [fig. 13]. he worked undisturbed and unmoved by the swiss surroundings and with never-fading energy he arrived at a typographic style which had a great influence, especially on american designers.

the *tm* covers from the years 1972 to 1973 became a cornerstone of weingart's typography. on each cover he interprets aphorisms of designers like bill, maldonado and ruder. each cover is a challenge in typographic expression [fig. 14]. the roots of his work are from the pioneers of the 1920s and when he made them, they looked heavy. but he refined and reshaped his influence and he arrived at typographic details which had become ignored during the high time of the swiss style.

to break the rules of typography was the destination for many and very few could convince. hans-rudolf lutz, also a student of ruder and an active teacher and publisher in zurich, succeeded with an alternative typography. his *tm* covers, "design is information," 1977, are outstanding. lutz copied famous magazines like the american news magazine *time* and the german *der spiegel* and made *tm* covers out of them. with this he did not propagate imitation, but he wanted to say that the magazine title is read by the design. (while i was working for the german social democratic party, and for the chancellors willy brandt and helmut schmidt, we used the same trick. to spread political ideas of the spd to a public which reads the mass newspaper *bild*, we imitated its looks. instead of *bild* we made *buh*, and we presented the information in *bild* style.)

7
Typographische Monatsblätter
Cover and back cover
Special issue on Univers
Emil Ruder, Basel 1981

8
Typographische Monatsblätter
Page construction
Emil Ruder, Basel 1981

9
Deutsches Mosaik, German Mosaic
Two book jackets
Otl Aicher, Rotis 1972

10
Typographie, Typography
Book jacket
Emil Ruder, Basel 1967

11
Rise and Fall of the City of Mahagonny
(Music by Weill)
Helmut Schmid, Basel 1964

12
Cover for an Austrian magazine
Helmut Schmid, Basel 1965

13
Letter combination without meaning
Morphologic type-case 9
Wolfgang Weingart, Basel 1971

14
Typographische Monatsblätter
The Learning covers
Wolfgang Weingart, Basel 1973

eine typographie der leichtigkeit wurde elf jahre später für das erscheinungsbild der münchner olympiade 1972 in deutschland angewendet. die angewandte schrift: univers 55. es existieren wenige anwendungen von solcher konsequenz. otl aicher und rolf müller entwarfen in einer angenehmen und zurückhaltenden typographie. *deutsches mosaik* [abb. 9], das offizielle geschenk der münchner olympiade, war ein buch mit einer sammlung von texten deutscher schriftsteller. der schutzumschlag, entworfen von aicher, in glänzendem silber, hatte eine rhythmische textanordnung, fast im stil von ruder, mit ausnahme der engen buchstabenabstände. (16 jahre später akzeptierte aicher die offenen buchstabenabstände und ziemlich viele charakteristiken der univers-buchstabenformen und wandte sie in seiner schrift rotis an.)

1967 veröffentlichte der niggli-verlag in teufen emil ruders 274-seitiges gestaltungslehrbuch *typographie* [abb. 10]. die summe 25-jährigen wirkens als typographielehrer an der basler schule. entworfen in drei schriftgraden der univers medium (55), in der eine seite kinetikartig in die nächste fliesst. fast alle arbeiten von ruder oder von seinen schülern aus dem typographie-kurs sind in originalgrösse reproduziert.

«typographie ist einem eindeutigen zweck verpflichtet, und zwar der schriftlichen mitteilung. durch kein argument und durch keine überlegung kann die typographie von dieser verpflichtung entbunden werden. das druckwerk, das nicht gelesen werden kann, wird zu einem sinnlosen produkt.» (emil ruder)

als die univers-typographie (oberflächlich gesehen) für jeden verfügbar schien, kamen wieder fette schriften, extreme kursive, buchstaben-spationierungen und wortunterstreichungen. die energie der werbung kroch in die typographie des alltags. texte wurden nicht nur plaziert, sondern interpretiert. aufstieg und fall wurde visualisiert durch die plazierung der wörter. Aie-eue-öeei ist kein lautgedicht von schwitters, sondern der umschlag für eine österreichische fachzeitschrift, in der die vokale des zeitschriftennamens (*graphische revue österreichs*) [abb. 12] als klangfarben eingesetzt wurden.

in dieser periode der veränderungen trat wolfgang weingart (1964) als schüler in die basler schule ein, im selben jahr, als ich nach einem zweijährigen arbeitsaufenthalt wieder zurückkam. typographie im schweizer stil oder nicht war das tägliche thema und ist es immer noch. (schweizer typographie ist geliebt und gehasst wie jede wichtige bewegung. leider wurde sie nie in ihrer ganzheit erkannt.)

ruder wurde 1965 direktor der basler schule und weingart, drei jahre später, lehrer für typographie. und wie tschichold einen ruder provozierte, so provozierte ruder einen weingart. weingart bog das linienmaterial, das gerade im kasten lag. er verwendete gips als nichtdruckendes material [abb. 13]. er arbeitete unbehelligt und ungebeugt in der schweizer umgebung und erreichte mit nicht nachlassender energie einen typographischen stil, der einen grossen einfluss vor allem auf die amerikanischen gestalter hatte.

die *tm*-umschläge aus dem jahr 1972/73 wurden zum grundstein der weingart-typographie. auf jedem umschlag interpretierte er aphorismen von gestaltern wie bill, maldonado oder ruder. jeder umschlag ist eine herausforderung eines typographischen ausdrucks [abb. 14]. die wurzeln dieser arbeit entstammten den arbeiten der pioniere der 20er jahre, und als weingart sie entwarf, wirkten sie schwer. aber er verfeinerte und verbesserte seinen einfluss und kam zu typographischen details, die sogar während der hohen zeit der schweizer typographie ignoriert wurden.

die typographischen regeln zu brechen war das ziel von vielen, doch wenige konnten überzeugen. hans-rudolf lutz, ein schüler von ruder und ein aktiver lehrer und verleger in zürich, war mit einer alternativen typographie erfolgreich. seine *tm*-umschläge, *design ist information*, 1977, sind herausragend. lutz kopierte bekannte nachrichtenmagazine wie die amerikanische *time* oder den deutschen *spiegel* und schaffte *tm*-umschläge. damit wollte lutz nicht das plagiat propagieren, sondern er wollte sagen, dass magazin-titel durch das design gelesen werden. (während ich für die sozialdemokratische partei deutschlands und für die kanzler willy brandt und helmut schmidt arbeitete, wandten wir 1976 denselben trick an. um die politischen ideen der spd einem publikum näherzubringen, das vorwiegend die *bild*-zeitung liest, imitierten wir deren aussehen. *bild* ersetzten wir durch *buh*, und die information erschien im stil von *bild*.)

10

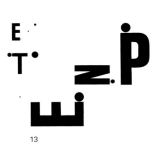
11

12

13

14

7
Typographische Monatsblätter
Titel vorne und Rückseite
Sondernummer zur Schrift Univers
Emil Ruder, Basel 1981

8
Typographische Monatsblätter
Seitenaufbau
Emil Ruder, Basel 1981

9
Deutsches Mosaik German Mosaic
Zwei Buchumschläge
Otl Aicher, Rotis 1972

10
Typographie
Buchumschlag
Emil Ruder, Basel 1967

11
Aufstieg und Fall der Stadt Mahagonny
(Musik von Weill)
Helmut Schmid, Basel 1964

12
Titel für eine österreichische Zeitschrift
Helmut Schmid, Basel 1965

13
Buchstabenkombination ohne Bedeutung
(morphologische Schrift Fall 9)
Wolfgang Weingart, Basel 1971

14
Typographische Monatsblätter
Lehrreiche Titel
Wolfgang Weingart, Basel 1973

i planned and designed in 1980 *typography today* [fig. 15], a bilingual book on modern typography. my cover design has a 2-layered message: the printed message with a quotation by kurt schwitters; the written message with a memo pad of weingart's article. the book is grouped in three parts: the recent, the timeless, the pioneers. i had complete freedom in the selection of the designers, works and authors and i selected 65 designers from 12 countries. kohei sugiura is one of two japanese designers in the book. he created influential typographic works in the editorial field in an asian style. his covers are not just make up of design but interpretations of content. he has invented what i called "talking typography."

two fascinating books are hans-rudolf lutz's: *1979. eine art geschichte* [fig. 16]. this is the story of 1979 told with newspaper pages. each day, one page is taken at random from one of the four zurich newspapers and reduced to book size. in the first book, a 7 × 10 mm part is at random taken out. in the second book, this part is blown up to the book's size (208 × 295 mm). informative pages in the first book. graphic experience in the second book.

typography has always taken fresh impulses from people outside the profession. in the 1920s it was the russian artist el lissitzky and the dutch architect piet zwart [fig. 17]; in the 1940s it was the swiss architect and sculptor max bill, and in the 1960s it could be said it was the american composer john cage. cage, who invented the prepared piano and the music of chance operation, applied this chance operation also in typography. "2 pages, 122 words on music and dance," published in his book *silence* (1961), moved me deeply. incredible! one of the most influential composers of this century showed also an interest in typography! and when i prepared *typography today*, i asked cage to re-arrange this 2-page composition of 122 words to the different size of my book [fig. 18].

m [fig. 19] is another book by cage in typographic chance operation. in his illustrative *62 mesostics re merce cunningham*, each line consists of one word or syllable. the names merce or cunningham can be read from top to bottom in each type sculpture. it takes quite some time to decode the words, but i can imagine the laughing face of cage when he composed it. and compose he really did – with 700 different typefaces and typesizes – from letraset.

at the end of the 1970s began a typography of gravitylessness. letters, lines, squares, circles, triangles float three-dimensionally on a two-dimensional space. typography became free, colorful and open to all. what started in basel in opposition to the standard typographic style, became in california form-formalism of worldwide impact: new wave. the queen of that movement is the american designer april greiman [fig. 20], who studied for 6 months in basel under weingart and armin hofmann. her early works reveal the strictness of the basel typography but she developed her own style in exploring the electronic collaging of computer technology.

what lissitzky [fig. 21] or piet zwart had to finalize with great effort in metal type became a small thing with phototype and offset. lissitzky himself wrote on the process of his book design, *for the voice*, from 1922/23: "usually, our books were prepared at large printing plants. when we made *for the voice*, the editor found us a small printing shop. the typesetter was german. he typeset absolutely mechanically, for each page i made him a sketch. he thought we were crazy." 1991 was lissitzky's 100th birthday. darmstadt, the city where he studied architecture, honored him with an exhibition and with the book *el lissitzky – konstrukteur, denker, pfeifenraucher, kommunist* (architect, thinker, pipe-smoker, communist; designed by victor masly). in other places, the designers preferred just to use his ideas – free of charge of course.

15

16

17

19

15
Typography Today
Dust jacket
Helmut Schmid, Osaka 1980

16
1979, a kind of story
Book 1: with newspaper page
Book 2: with detail blow-up
Hans-Rudolf Lutz, Zurich 1980

17
Advertisement for Dutch N. K. F
Multiple reading in 2 directions
Piet Zwart, Delft 1926

18
John Cage: "2 pages, 122 words on music and dance"
(Third version for *Typography Today*)
John Cage, New York 1979

19
Type Sculpture from the book
M: writings '67–'72
John Cage, New York 1974

20
Advertisement for China Club
April Greiman, Los Angeles 1979

21
Page from the book
About Two Squares
El Lissitzky, Berlin 1922

mehr konzeptionell plante und gestaltete ich *typography today* [abb. 15]. das zweisprachige werk über moderne typographie erschien 1980 als *idea*-sondernummer bei seibundo shinkosha in tokio. der umschlag hatte eine zweischichtige botschaft: eine gedruckte botschaft mit einem zitat von kurt schwitters; eine geschriebene botschaft mit einem memopad von weingarts artikel. das buch hat drei teile: das heute; das zeitlose; die pioniere. ich hatte völlige freiheit in der auswahl der designer, der arbeiten und der autoren, und ich wählte 65 designer aus 12 ländern. kohei sugiura ist einer der zwei japanischen designer im buch. er schuf einen typographischen stil editorialer gestaltung mit asiatischem flair. seine umschläge sind kein make-up von design, sondern sind interpretationen des inhalts. er hat etwas geschaffen, das ich sprechende typographie nennen möchte.

zwei faszinierende bücher sind die beiden bände hans-rudolf lutz: *1979, eine art geschichte*. es ist die geschichte des jahres 1979, erzählt mit zeitungs-seiten. jeden tag ist eine seite aus einer der vier zürcher zeitungen zufällig ausgewählt und zur buch-seite (208 × 295 mm) reduziert worden. im ersten buch ist ein 7 × 10 mm-teil zufällig herausgenommen. im zweiten buch ist dieser ausschnitt zur buchseite aufgeblasen. informative seiten im ersten buch. graphische erlebnisse im zweiten buch.

typographie hat immer neue impulse von leuten ausserhalb der sparte empfangen. in den 20er jahren waren es der russische künstler el lissitzky und der holländische architekt piet zwart [abb. 17]. in den 40er jahren war es der schweizer architekt und bildhauer max bill, und in den 60er jahren, könnte man sagen, war es der amerikanische komponist john cage. cage, der das präparierte klavier und die musik des zufalls erfand, wandte das zufällige auch in der typographie an. «2 seiten, 122 wörter über musik und tanz», veröffentlicht in seinem buch *silence* (wesleyan university press, 1961) berührte mich tief. unglaublich! einer der einflussreichsten komponisten des 20. jahrhunderts zeigte auch ein interesse an typographie! und als ich *typography today* plante, bat ich cage, mir diese zwei seiten komposition von «122 wörtern» auf das format meines buches neu zu komponieren. [abb. 18]

m: writings '67–'72 (wesleyan university press, 1972) [abb. 19] ist ein weiteres buch von cage in typographischer zufälligkeit. in seinen illustrativen «mesostics re merce cunningham», besteht jede zeile aus einem wort oder einer silbe. die namen merce und cunningham können in diesen typographi-schen skulpturen von oben nach unten gelesen werden. es dauert eine weile, bis man die wörter entziffern kann, aber ich kann mir das lachende gesicht von cage vorstellen, als er das komponierte. und er komponierte wirklich – mit 700 verschiedenen schriften und schriftgrössen – in letraset!

ende der 70er jahre begann eine typographie der schwerelosigkeit. buchstaben, linien, quadrate, kreise, dreiecke schwebten dreidimensional auf einer zweidimensionalen fläche. typographie wurde frei, farbig und offen für alle. was in basel als opposition zum typographischen stil begann, wurde in kalifornien form-formalismus mit weltweiter auswirkung: new wave. die königin dieser bewegung war die amerikani-sche designerin april greiman [abb. 20], die sechs monate in basel unter armin hofmann und weingart studierte. ihre frühen arbeiten offenbaren die strenge der basel typographie, aber sie entwickelte ihren eigenen stil, indem sie die elektonischen collagen der computer-technologie erforschte.

was lissitzky [abb. 21] und piet zwart unter grosser mühe in bleisatz verwirklichen liessen, wurde eine mühelose sache in photosatz und offset. lissitzky selbst schrieb über den vorgang seines designs für das buch *für die stimme* (1922/23): «normalerweise wurden unsere bücher in grossen druckereibe-trieben vorbereitet. als wir *für die stimme* schufen, fand uns der redaktor eine kleine druckerei. der setzer war ein deutscher. er setzte absolut mecha-nisch. für jede seite machte ich ihm eine skizze. er dachte, wir seien verrückt.» 1990 war lissitzkys 100. geburtstag. darmstadt, die stadt, in der er architektur studierte, ehrte ihn mit einer ausstellung und mit einem buch: *el lissitzky – konstrukteur, denker, pfeifenraucher, kommunist* (herausgegeben und gestaltet von victor malsy im schmidt-verlag, mainz). andernorts zogen die designer es vor, seine ideen zu verwerten – selbstverständlich kostenlos.

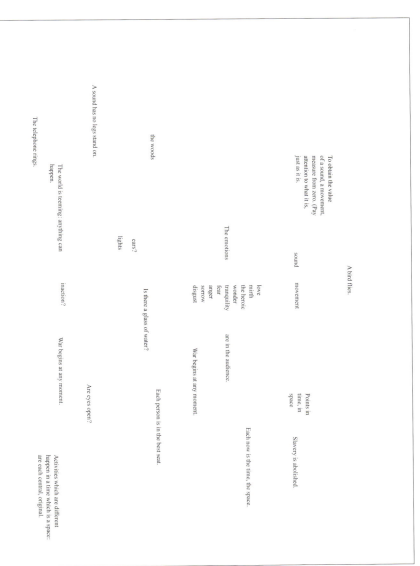

15
Typography Today
Schutzumschlag
Helmut Schmid, Osaka 1980

16
1979, eine Art Geschichte
Band 1: mit Zeitungsseite
Band 2: mit stark vergrössertem Detail
Hans-Rudolf Lutz, Zürich 1980

17
Werbung für die niederländische Firma
N. K. F
Mehrere Lesarten in zwei Richtungen
Piet Zwart, Delft 1926

18
John Cage: 2 Seiten, 122 Wörter über
Musik und Tanz
(3. Fassung für *Typography Today*)
John Cage, New York 1979

19
Typografische Skulptur aus dem Buch
M: writings '67–'72
John Cage, New York 1974

20
Werbung für den China Club
April Greiman, Los Angeles 1979

21
Seite aus dem Buch *Suprematistische Geschichte von zwei Quadraten*, einem Märchen mit Konstruktions-material für eine neue Weltordnung
El Lissitzky, Berlin 1922

stiff and heavy lettershapes, applied carelessly and arrogantly, gave birth to a new designer in england – neville brody. working for a monthly magazine for the young, brody's hard-edged letters became dominating illustrations. for a story on the american rock queen madonna, he made a clumsy *m*. later he designed a story on warhol; he cut the *m* from the madonna article (including some lines and part of the madonna photo) turned it round, and had the *w*.

arrows and stop signs organize texts like traffic roads in brody's layout. for a logo for a belgian rock group [fig. 22]) he did not supply the traffic for reading: one has to be very patient to discover in this logo the name minimal compact, since letters have to be read several times.
"from the very beginning we wanted a reader who is his own editor. when the reader needs half an hour to understand a layout, okay; who says, that one should take the work away from the reader?" (brody)

it is only 15 years since the mac, the computer for everybody, arrived. every mac owner became a designer in the same way as the copy-machine made each user a writer. the design language has freed itself from the bondage of tradition. two young designers, rudy vanderlans and zuzana licko, emigrated from europe to california and founded *emigre* [fig. 23]. this magazine is probably the best example of how to use the mac in an intelligent way. the layout is challenging. the typefaces are out of the everyday. the text is self-centered but casual. *emigre* has become the alternative journal. there is no other magazine at present which can compete with it in typographic innovation.

after new wave, next wave, we arrived at deconstructivism. the message reads: the aim is to promote multiple rather than fixed readings, to provoke the reader into becoming an active participant in the construction of the message.

john cage had said it many years earlier:
we have to arrange music in a way that the people feel, that they do something, and not, that something is done for them.

the american magazine *ray gun* multiple reading is designed. when looking at the magazine spread "mixed messages," two text columns, set in justified setting and in unjustified setting, can be found. these text blocks are not continuous but repetitions. designer david carson, the new superstar of typograffiti narcissism, explained the meaning to me in this way: since the text is written by two authors, i wanted to express this with typographic means. designers must have fun. (in his poster for his own exhibition [fig. 24], david carson is true and believable. his design here is casual and even poetic.)

design should be fun. but over-design can also be uncomfortable. when the design group 8vo published their first of 8 issues of *octavo*, in 1986, they criticized their british surrounding for using text as the gray stuff underneath the photos. in their thin but large-format pamphlet on their work for a dutch museum, typographic treatment degrades to an effect of a well-designed wallpaper. *octavo* was a refreshing publication at a time of extreme over-design.

there are designers who can live without the waves of fad, who work undisturbed and at their own speed. jost hochuli designs books in a typography free from style [fig. 25]. *statements on typography in the 20th century, theses about typography*, (1985, 1986, 1989) edited by friedrich friedl and designed by wolfgang schmidt is a pleasure in content and typography. more typographers and designers see the need to work again with content and concept. even recent works of weingart have a rare simplicity, as if he wanted to shout: "look at the worldwide chaos, let's go back to the basics!" weingart's cover design for an exhibition catalog seems to return to the style which he so bitterly attacked but never really abandoned – swiss typography. he even used symmetry recently, to break away again from the crowd. (i remember a conversation with him in 1978 in basel when he suddenly said, "i do not know where we are going in typography. maybe we come back again to ruder.")

what will be has always been: the words of louis i. kahn, rizzoli 1986 [fig. 26]. this book cover is impressive because it has a meaning. it ignores the fashion and fad. it uses the handwriting of the architect which is more powerful than the thousands of typefaces which we carry along, or which the typeface companies throw at us. ever since i saw this book i wanted to make my own interpretation of the words [fig. 27].

otl aicher has practiced a design of restraint, a kind of instant typography. aicher's work over the years is not as consistent as it looks today. he has now more influence on typography than he had during his ulm days. with his own typeface rotis [fig. 28], created in the late 1980s, and named after the village where he used to live, aicher irritated at first many designers. rotis is a controversial typeface – a typeface that is loved and a typeface that is hated. the typeface applies the open letter space which made univers so different and elegant. rotis has a wonderful and characteristic lowercase e with a clear proportion and with an elegant ending stroke. rotis gives a particular typographic look, when properly applied. but with all my respect for aicher, his own application of the typeface is contrary to his teaching and writing. and it proves again that the designer of a typeface is not necessarily the master of its use. frutiger had emil ruder to bring out the beauty and characteristic of the typeface univers. looking at aicher's oversized and overweight book *typographie* from the year 1988, one is stunned by the fact that content and application are in such a discrepancy. the letter space and the line space are fighting and the letters start to flicker when reading a longer text block. aicher's attitude is in his words. his deeds are different.

23

24

25

22

22
Logomark with multiple reading
for a Belgian rock group
Neville Brody, London ca. 1980

23
Emigre No. 19, Starting from zero,
Rudy VanderLans, Berkeley 1991

24
Poster for the designer's exhibition
David Carson, 1995

25
In Memory of R. H.
(Rudolf Hostettler, editor of the Swiss professional magazine *Typographische Monatsblätter*)
Book cover
Jost Hochuli, St. Gallen 1983

26
*What will be has always been:
the words of Louis I. Kahn*
Book cover
R. S. Wurman, New York 1986

27
New Year's greeting card with a
quotation by Louis Kahn
Helmut Schmid, Osaka 1997

steife und schwere buchstaben, achtlos und arrogant angewandt, brachten einen neuen designer in england hervor – neville brody. für eine monatszeitschrift für die jugend arbeitend, wurden brodys hartkantige buchstaben dominierende illustrationen. für eine story über die rock queen madonna konstruierte er ein plumpes «m». später gestaltete er eine story über warhol. er schnitt das «m» aus dem madonna-artikel aus (einschliesslich einiger linien und fragmente des madonnaphotos), drehte es und hatte das «w».

pfeile und stop-zeichen organisieren texte wie verkehrsstrassen in brodys layout. für ein logo für eine belgische rockgruppe [abb. 22] lieferte er die verkehrszeichen zum lesen nicht mit. man muss schon geduldig sein, um in diesem logo den namen minimal compact zu entdecken, weil einige buchstaben mehrmals gelesen werden müssen. brody: «von anfang an wollten wir einen leser, der sein eigener editor ist. es ist okay, wenn der leser eine halbe stunde zum entziffern braucht. wer sagt, dass wir dem leser die arbeit ersparen sollen?»

1984 erschien der mac, der computer für jedermann. jeder mac-besitzer wurde zum gestalter, genauso wie die kopiermaschine jeden anwender zum verfasser machte. die sprache des design hat sich von den fesseln der tradition befreit. zwei junge designer, rudy vanderlans und zuzana licko, wanderten von europa nach kalifornien aus und gründeten 1984 die zeitschrift emigre [abb. 23], vermutlich das beste beispiel dafür, wie man den mac auf intelligente weise einsetzt. das layout ist herausfordernd. die schriften sind nicht alltäglich. der text ist ichbezogen aber lässig. emigre wurde die alternative zeitschrift. es gibt zur zeit keine andere zeitschrift, die mit deren typographischen innovationen konkurrieren kann.

nach new wave, next wave kommen wir zum dekonstruktivismus. die botschaft heisst: «das ziel ist mehr die mehrfache als die bestimmte leseart, um den leser zu stimulieren, ein aktiver teilnehmer in der konstruktiven botschaft zu werden.»

john cage sagte es wiedermal jahre früher: «wir müssen musik in so einer art arrangieren, dass die leute fühlen, dass sie etwas tun müssen, und nicht, dass etwas für sie getan wird.»

mehrfaches lesen ist in der amerikanischen zeitschrift ray gun angewendet. wenn man auf die doppelseite «mixed messages» schaut, entdeckt man zwei textkolumnen in block und flattersatz. diese textblöcke sind nicht kontinuierlich, sondern sind wiederholungen. designer david carsson, der neue superstar des typograffiti-narzissmus, erklärte mir die bedeutung auf diese weise: «da der text von zwei personen geschrieben war, wollte ich das mit typographischen mitteln ausdrücken. designer sollen spass an der sache haben.» (in seinem plakat für seine ausstellung in venedig [abb. 24] wirkt david carsson echt und glaubwürdig. sein design ist hier lässig und sogar poetisch.)

design soll spass machen. aber overdesign kann auch ungemütlich sein. als die designgruppe octavo 1986 ihre erste nummer von octavo veröffentlichte, kritisierte sie ihre britische umgebung, die text als graufläche unterhalb der photos einsetzte. in ihrem dünnen, aber grossformatigen pamphlet über ihre arbeit für ein holländisches museum degradiert die typographische gestaltung zur effekthaschenden, gut gestalteten tapete. octavo war eine erfrischende publikation in einer zeit von extremem overdesign.

es gibt entwerfer, die ohne trend leben können, die ungestört und in ihrem persönlichen tempo arbeiten. jost hochuli entwirft bücher in einer stilfreien typographie [abb. 25]. thesen über typographie (1985, 86, 89), zusammengestellt von friedrich friedl und gestaltet von wolfgang schmidt, ist ein genuss in inhalt und typographie. mehr typographen und designer sehen die notwendigkeit, wieder mit inhalt und konzept zu arbeiten. sogar neue arbeiten von weingart sind von seltener einfachheit, so als ob er schreien wollte: «schaut euch dieses weltweite chaos an, lasst uns zu den grundlagen zurückkehren!» weingarts umschlagentwurf für einen ausstellungskatalog scheint zu einem stil zurückzukehren, den er so bitter attackierte, aber eigentlich nie richtig verliess – die schweizer typographie. er verwendete neulich sogar symmetrie, um sich von der masse abzuheben. (ich erinnere mich an ein gespräch mit ihm 1978 in basel, als er plötzlich sagte: «ich weiss nicht, wohin wir in der typographie gehen. vielleicht kommen wir wieder zurück zu ruder.»)

«was sein wird, war immer da» sind worte von louis kahn [abb. 26]. der umschlag des buches über den architekten (rizzoli, new york 1986) ist eindrucksvoll, weil er aus dem inhalt kommt. er ignoriert mode und trends. er verwendet die handschrift des architekten, die kraftvoller ist als die tausenden von schriften, die wir mit uns herumschleifen oder die uns die schriftfirmen nachwerfen. seit ich dieses buch (gestaltet von r. s. wurman) traf, wollte ich die aussage interpretieren. [abb. 27]

otl aicher praktizierte eine gestaltung der beschränkung, eine art instant-typographie. aichers werk ist eigentlich nicht so konsequent, wie es heute den anschein hat. er hat heute mehr einfluss auf die typographie, als er das in seiner zeit in ulm hatte. mit seiner schrift rotis [abb. 28], entworfen ende der 80er jahre und benannt nach dem dorf, in dem er tätig war, irritierte aicher zunächst viele designer. rotis ist eine kontroverse schrift eine schrift, die geliebt und gehasst ist. sie bedient sich offener buchstaben-zwischenräume, die die univers so unterschiedlich und elegant machten. rotis hat ein herrliches und charakteristisches kleines «e» in klarer proportion und mit einem elegant auslaufenden endstrich. rotis, richtig eingesetzt, ergibt ein interessantes typographisches aussehen. aber bei allem respekt vor aicher, seine anwendung der schrift steht im gegensatz zu seinen belehrungen und texten. und es zeigt sich wieder einmal, dass der gestalter einer schrift nicht unbedingt der meister der anwendung ist. frutiger hatte emil ruder, um die schönheit und die charakteristik der schrift zur geltung zu bringen. schaut man aichers überdimensionales und übergewichtiges buch typographie aus dem jahr 1988 an, ist man erstaunt, dass inhalt und anwendung von solch krasser unstimmigkeit sind. buchstabenzwischenräume und zeilenzwischenräume bekämpfen sich, und die buchstaben beginnen zu flimmern. aichers haltung ist in seinen worten. seine taten sind anders.

22
Schriftlogo mit mehreren Lesarten
für eine belgische Rockgruppe
Neville Brody, London, um 1980

23
Emigre No. 19: Starting From Zero,
Rudy Vanderlans, Berkeley 1991

24
Plakat für eine Ausstellung des
Designers
David Carson, 1995

25
In Memory of R. H.
(Rudolf Hostettler, Herausgeber der
Schweizer Fachzeitschrift Typographische Monatsblätter)
Bucheinband
Jost Hochuli, St. Gallen 1983

26
What will be has always been: the
words of Louis I. Kahn
Bucheinband
R. S. Wurman, New York 1986

27
Neujahrsgrüsse mit einem Zitat von
Louis Kahn
Helmut Schmid, Osaka 1997

26

27

i have used the typeface rotis (to be exact: rotis sans serif and rotis semi sans) a few times to challenge myself, but also to counter some critics who claim that i use univers only. in memory of the fall of the berlin wall i designed the poster series "deeds. not words" [fig. 29]. i used rotis after having tested typefaces like univers, frutiger, akzidenz grotesk, helvetica. i believe that a typographer should test new typefaces. i have come under attack again, the poster looks too cosmetic.

i do in fact do some work in the field of cosmetics and i make an effort to express logomarks with a touch of character. typefaces just do not meet that purpose.

in my design i still prefer to use univers (even the univers on the mac) not because it is fashionable, was fashionable, or will stay fashionable, but because i find the original shapes elegant [fig. 30]. by using univers constantly i believe that i understand the typeface, since i have an ongoing dialogue with it. one of my more successful designs is the bilingual packaging series for ethical drugs of a japanese pharmaceutical company. this series (developed in 1980 and still in use), has a consistent structuring of product information and is shaped by the use of univers.

i have never felt the need to depart from the clear typography of emil ruder. i have tried and i will try to build on it. i believe that natural is better than semi-skilled, light is better than heavy (i prefer mozart to beethoven), simple is better than complicated, and quiet is better than noisy. i believe that honest design is in the end more valuable than an application of a fad, and that design which serves a purpose is in the end better than a designer's ego trip.

it is not the accidental which makes a designer but his continuity, and continuity means to work and to search, to work and to fight, to work and to find, to find and to see, to see and to communicate, and again to work and to search. designers must challenge the past, must challenge the present, must challenge the future. but first of all, designers must be true to themselves. design is attitude.

"fortunate the man who, at the right moment, meets the right friend; fortunate also the man who, at the right moment meets the right enemy."
(t. s. eliot)

ich habe die schrift (um genau zu sein, rotis sans serif und rotis semi sans) einige male verwendet, um mich selbst herauszufordern, aber auch, um kritikern entgegenzutreten, die meinen, ich verwende nur univers. in erinnerung an den fall der berliner mauer entwarf ich die plakatserie *deeds. not words (taten. nicht worte)* [abb. 29]. ich verwendete rotis, nachdem ich schriften wie univers, frutiger, akzidenz grotesk und helvetica ausprobierte. ich meine, dass ein typograph die neuen schriften prüfen soll. ich wurde wieder attackiert. die plakate seien zu kosmetisch.

ich arbeite tatsächlich im feld der kosmetik, und ich versuche, logos mit einem hauch von charakter zu versehen. schriften genügen dazu nicht.

in meinem design bevorzuge ich immer noch die univers (sogar die univers im mac), nicht weil sie modisch ist, modisch war oder modisch bleiben wird, sondern weil ich die formen elegant finde [abb. 30]. indem ich univers konstant verwende, glaube ich, dass ich einen anhaltenden dialog mit der schrift habe. eine meiner erfolgreichen gestaltungen ist die zweisprachige verpackungsserie für medizinische produkte einer japanischen pharmazeutischen firma. die serie (entstanden 1980 und noch immer im gebrauch) hat eine konstante strukturierung der produkt-information und ist geprägt durch die anwendung der univers.

ich sah nie die notwendigkeit, mich von der klaren typographie von emil ruder zu entfernen. ich habe versucht und ich will weiter versuchen, darauf aufzubauen. ich glaube, dass natürlich besser ist als schwer (ich bevorzuge mozart vor beethoven), einfach besser ist als kompliziert und leise besser ist als laut. ich glaube, dass ehrliches design schlussendlich mehr der sache dient als eine anwendung einer moderichtung und dass design, das einem zweck dient, besser ist als ein ego-trip des designers.

es ist nicht das zufällige, das einen designer ausmacht, sondern seine kontinuität. und kontinuität bedeutet arbeiten und suchen, arbeiten und kämpfen, arbeiten und finden, finden und sehen, sehen und kommunizieren und wieder arbeiten und suchen. gestalter müssen die vergangenheit herausfordern, müssen die gegenwart herausfordern, müssen die zukunft herausfordern. aber zuallererst müssen gestalter sich selbst treu sein.
gestaltung ist haltung.

«glücklich der mensch, der im rechten moment den rechten freund trifft; glücklich auch der mensch, der im rechten moment den rechten feind trifft.»
(t. s. eliot)

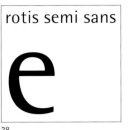

28

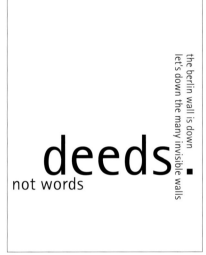

29

28
Typeface Rotis
Rotis Sans Serif, Rotis Semi Sans
Otl Aicher, Rotis 1988

29
"The Berlin wall is down, let's down the many invisible walls"
"Deeds. Not words." poster
Typeface: Rotis Sans Serif
Helmut Schmid, Osaka 1992

30
Poster for an ecology-conscious paper company
Typeface: Univers 75
Helmut Schmid, Osaka 1997

28
Schrift Rotis
Rotis sans serif, Rotis semi sans
Otl Aicher, Rotis 1988

29
«Die Berliner Mauer ist gefallen. Lasst uns die vielen unsichtbaren Mauern niederreissen»
Plakat *Taten. Nicht Worte.*
Schrift: Rotis sans serif
Helmut Schmid, Osaka 1992

30
Plakat für einen umweltbewussten Papierhersteller
Schrift: Univers 75
Helmut Schmid, Osaka 1997

"The dry river-bed finds
no thanks for its past"
Poster
Heiwa Paper, 1998
728 × 1030 mm
Text: Rabindranath Tagore

«Das trockene Flussbett findet
keinen Dank für seine Vergangenheit»
Plakat
Heiwa Paper, 1998
Text: Rabindranath Tagore

afterword from the publisher

my decision in the early 1970s to pursue graphic design came at a time when the world was in upheaval: the vietnam and yom kippur wars, the protests, the hippie movement, the energy crisis. my education, however, was rooted in certain unshakable constants. the precepts of swiss graphic design and its underlying objectivity, developed since the 1950s and respected and applied around the world, asserted a timelessness that only later came under pressure from market-driven opportunism.

at the design schools, first in basel, then in zurich, i encountered both currents of swiss graphic modernism. too young to leave my own mark as a designer, but mature enough to be enthralled by this style, i adopted some of its principles as a foundation for my own lifestyle. in my initial years as a publisher, starting in 1983, i devoted myself, first exclusively and then consistently, to the manifestations of swiss design and the people involved in it since the 1950s. i wanted to understand the principles upon which the protagonists base their attitude, as their headstrong, even aloof, manner is often seen as representative of the whole country.

although i personally felt drawn to the stricter zurich school, my ties to basel remained active, and emil ruder and armin hofmann remained stalwart guides on the more liberal edge of the design spectrum. i became friends with wolfgang weingart early on. he was the rebel who, with a profound knowledge of ruder's guidelines, vigorously attempted to break and refute them. nevertheless, he became ruder's successor as an influential instructor at the allgemeine gewerbeschule basel. i knew helmut schmid from sporadic encounters; he had moved to japan. i was not a particular fan of his work, being fond of the helvetica typeface and not the univers he preferred. however, we became friends when i met up with him in japan on several occasions, and we discovered many shared convictions and interests.

helmut and wolfgang were friends who treated each other with great respect. although they had learned their craft from emil ruder in basel at the same time, their ambitions in design were diametrically opposed. while weingart radically sought a new beginning and caused an international stir with his typography, schmid decided to continue on the path of strict, rule-based typography. this caused a sensation among his colleagues in japan, since the latin alphabet rendered in swiss style offered the greatest possible contrast to the japanese characters. schmid's katakana eru syllabary proved to be a worthy modern typeface.

the concern that helmut's death would relegate his work to being a mere footnote of japanese design was countered by the museum für gestaltung zurich. this institution, with which i have been affiliated for many years, has included helmut schmid's estate in its collection. there he again meets wolfgang weingart, who has entrusted his archive to the museum. both holdings augment the collection with works from the second generation of swiss postwar modernism of basel provenance. they also confirm my favorite observation: that from today's perspective, the basel and zurich schools promote variations of the same belief in achieving modern design according to rational criteria. back then, when these schools were having their greatest impact, their relationship was defined by rivalries and contrasts. at the museum für gestaltung zurich, these currents have come together in a variety of ways, preserving helmut schmid's work for the future.

lars müller

nachwort des verlegers

mein entschluss anfang der 1970er jahre, den beruf des grafikers zu erlernen, fiel in eine zeit, in der die welt in aufruhr war, vietnam und jom-kippur-krieg, proteste, hippie-bewegung, ölschock. meine ausbildung beruhte derweil auf konstanten, die sich durch die wirren nicht erschüttern liessen. die prämissen der schweizer grafik und ihre objektivität und sachlichkeit, entwickelt seit den 1950er-jahren und weltweit beachtet und angewandt, nahm für sich in anspruch, zeitlos zu sein und geriet erst später durch den marktgeleiteten opportunismus in bedrängnis.

an den schulen, erst in basel, dann in zürich, kam ich mit beiden strömungen der schweizer grafik-moderne in berührung. zu jung, um mich selbst als gestalter beizutragen, aber reif genug, um mich vom stil mitreissen zu lassen, machte ich mir einige der prinzipien zu eigen als grundlage für mein eigenes lebenskonzept. in meinen ersten jahren als verleger, ab 1983, widmete ich mich erst ausschliesslich und dann fortwährend den erscheinungen und persönlichkeiten der schweizer gestaltung seit den 1950er jahren. ich wollte verstehen, worauf das selbstverständnis der beteiligten gründet, deren eigensinn, ja sprödheit oft synonym für die mentalität des landes stehen.

obwohl ich mich selbst der strengeren zürcher schule zugezogen fühlte, blieben meine beziehungen zu basel lebhaft und emil ruder und armin hofmann solide leitplanken am freieren rand des gestalterischen spektrums. mit wolfgang weingart verband mich früh eine freundschaft. er war der rebell, der mit profunder kenntnis des ruder'schen regelwerks energisch an dessen brechung und widerlegung arbeitete und trotzdem ruders nachfolger als einflussreicher lehrer an der allgemeinen gewerbeschule basel wurde. helmut schmid kannte ich von sporadischen begegnungen – er lebte schon in japan. ich war ihm nicht hold, war ich doch der schrift helvetica zugetan und nicht seiner bevorzugten univers. wir wurden freunde, als ich ihm öfters in japan begegnete und wir uns über viele gemeinsame überzeugungen und interessen freuen konnten.

helmut und wolfgang waren freunde und begegneten sich mit grossem respekt. hatten sie gleichzeitig in basel von emil ruder gelernt, so lagen ihre gestalterischen ambitionen doch diametral auseinander. während weingart radikal einen neubeginn suchte und mit seiner typografie internationale aufregung verursachte, entschloss sich schmid, den weg einer strengen regelbasierten typografie weiterzugehen. in seinem wirkungsfeld in japan hat das für aufsehen gesorgt, erlaubte doch das lateinische alphabet im schweizer stil den grösstmöglichen kontrast zur den japanischen schriftzeichen. mit seinem silbenalphabet katakana eru hat schmid eine ebenbürtig moderne schrift gestaltet.

der sorge, dass nach helmuts tod sein werk als anekdote des japanischen designs in vergessenheit geraten würde, wirkte das museum für gestaltung zürich entgegen. die institution, mit der ich seit vielen jahren verbunden bin, hat den werknachlass von helmut schmid in seine sammlung aufgenommen. dort begegnet er wieder wolfgang weingart, der dem museum sein archiv anvertraut hat. beide bestände bereichern die sammlung um werke der zweiten generation der schweizer nachkriegsmoderne basler provenienz und weisen nach, was meine liebste feststellung ist: dass die basler und zürcher schulen aus heutiger sicht spielformen derselben überzeugung mit gemeinsamen zielen sind: einer modernen gestaltung nach rationalen kriterien. damals, zur zeit ihrer grössten wirkung haben konkurrenz und gegensätze das verhältnis geprägt. am museum für gestaltung zürich finden die strömungen in vielfältiger form zusammen, und helmut schmids werk ist auf dauer gesichert.

lars müller

Typography as visual poetry

Helmut Schmid's typography brings blank surfaces to life by subtly balancing the printed and the unprinted. Precise down to the smallest detail, it is usually quiet and possesses a simple elegance. This is especially true of his wordmarks for Japanese cosmetic lines and his cultural graphics. Schmid's typography can sometimes be loud, however, as when it is used in political propaganda. Then the bold letters scream as if in a tabloid newspaper. To Schmid, typography meant "freeing the design that's inherent in the project" (*TM*, No. 1, 1989). In his private work, this also meant prioritizing formal expression over legibility.

In his adopted country of Japan, Schmid refined the approach to design taught by Emil Ruder, his mentor in Basel. Impressed by Japanese poster art and the "quiet beauty of Japanese things," he applied Ruder's principles of design to the pure forms of Japanese characters. This was a challenge, because the ideograms and syllables of the three parallel scripts kanji, hiragana and katakana did not reveal themselves to him through their content, but only through formal analysis. After gaining initial experience in designing logos for Japanese companies, he created his own modern syllabic script in the style of Adrian Frutiger's Univers typeface and named it Katakana Eru in honor of Emil Ruder. In an adapted form it found its way into his commercial graphics, especially the lettering for pharmaceutical packaging, and was featured in *TM* in 1973. After a time, his Hiragana Eru followed, which he used in noncommissioned projects.

I first encountered the work of Helmut Schmid in my research on the typography of Wolfgang Weingart, with whom Schmid had hotly debated the sustainability of Ruder's approach to design in *TM* and to whom he had given a platform in his publications *Typography Today* (1980) and *The Road to Basel* (1997). I became more thoroughly acquainted with Schmid's work during a visit to his archive in Osaka in 2020 which had been facilitated by Lars Müller and Chikako Tatsuuma and which followed an appraisal of its contents by Christian Brändle, the director of the Museum für Gestaltung Zürich. It soon became clear that Helmut Schmid's oeuvre would be an important addition to the museum's permanent collection, which also includes the archives of Wolfgang Weingart, Hans-Rudolf Lutz, Adrian Frutiger and Josef Müller-Brockmann, with whom Schmid had been in contact through the years.

This publication offers a view from a Japanese perspective that profits from the knowledge of insiders, Kiyonori Muroga and Schmid's daughter Nicole, who also selected the works and quotations of Helmut Schmid. Nicole Schmid gave this clearly structured compendium its pleasing design. She and her mother, Sumi, have earned the museum's profound gratitude for entrusting the archive of Helmut Schmid's life's work to the museum. In return, the museum will catalog his works, publish them on its online platform eMuseum.ch, and host a solo exhibition dedicated to the internationally renowned typographic designer in 2024, which will tour Europe with the support of the kyoto ddd gallery and DNP Foundation for Cultural Promotion.

Schmid's refined typography has outlived pop, new wave and other design fads. It is high time to appreciate his work in depth and in quiet contemplation.

Barbara Junod
Curator Graphics Collection
Museum für Gestaltung Zürich

Typografie als visuelle Poesie

Die Typografie von Helmut Schmid bringt die weissen Flächen zum Klingen, indem sie Bedrucktes und Unbedrucktes subtil ausbalanciert. Präzis bis ins kleinste Detail ist sie meist leise und besitzt eine schlichte Eleganz. Dies trifft vor allem auf seine Wortmarken für japanische Kosmetiklinien und auf seine Kulturgrafik zu. Schmids Typografie kann jedoch auch laut werden, wenn es beispielsweise um politische Propaganda geht. Dann schreien die fetten Lettern wie in einer Boulevard-Zeitung. Typografie hiess für Schmid, «das bereits in der Aufgabe liegende Design freizustellen» (*TM*, Nr. 1, 1989). Für seine freie Arbeit bedeutete dies auch eine Priorisierung des formalen Ausdrucks gegenüber der Lesbarkeit.

In seiner Wahlheimat Japan verfeinerte Schmid den Gestaltungsansatz seines Basler Lehrmeisters Emil Ruder. Unter Eindruck der japanischen Plakatkunst und der «leisen Schönheit japanischer Dinge» verband er Ruders Gestaltungsprinzipien mit den reinen Formen der japanischen Schriftzeichen. Das war eine Herausforderung, denn die Ideogramme und Silben der drei parallel verwendeten Schriften Kanji, Hiragana und Katakana erschlossen sich ihm nicht durch ihren Inhalt, sondern einzig durch formale Analyse. Nach ersten Erfahrungen im Gestalten japanischer Firmenlogos schuf er in Anlehnung an Adrian Frutigers Schrift Univers eine eigene moderne Silbenschrift und nannte sie zu Ehren von Emil Ruder Katakana Eru. In angepasster Form fand diese Schrift Eingang in seine Gebrauchsgrafik, vor allem in die Beschriftung der Pharma-Verpackungen, und wurde 1973 in den *TM* vorgestellt. Etwas später folgte seine Hiragana Eru, die er für freie Arbeiten verwendete.

Dem Werk von Helmut Schmid begegnete ich erstmals in meiner Forschung über die Typografie von Wolfgang Weingart, mit dem Schmid in den *TM* kontrovers über die Nachhaltigkeit der Ruder-Lehre diskutierte und dem er in seinen Publikationen *Typography Today* (1980) und *Der Weg nach Basel* (1997) eine Bühne gab. Eingehender lernte ich sein Werk bei einer Archivsichtung in Osaka 2020 kennen, die durch die Vermittlung von Lars Müller und Chikako Tatsuuma zustande kam und der eine Besichtigung durch Christian Brändle, dem Direktor des Museum für Gestaltung Zürich, vorausging. Schnell wurde klar, dass der Nachlass von Helmut Schmid eine wichtige Erweiterung der Bestände des Museums darstellt, das auch die Nachlässe von Wolfgang Weingart, Hans-Rudolf Lutz, Adrian Frutiger und Josef Müller-Brockmann beherbergt, mit denen Schmid im Austausch stand.

Die aktuelle Publikation bietet eine Betrachtung aus japanischer Sicht, die durch das Insider-Wissen von Kiyonori Muroga und Schmids Tochter Nicole bereichert wird, welche auch die Werke und Zitate von Helmut Schmid ausgelesen haben. Das schöne Design dieses klar strukturierten Übersichtswerks verantwortet Nicole Schmid. Ihr und ihrer Mutter Sumi gebührt der grosse Dank des Museums, dass sie diesem den Nachlass von Helmut Schmid anvertraut haben. Im Gegenzug arbeitet das Museum den Nachlass auf, veröffentlicht diesen auf seiner Online-Plattform eMuseum.ch und richtet dem international bekannten typografischen Gestalter 2024 eine Einzelausstellung aus, die mit der Unterstützung der kyoto ddd gallery und der DNP Foundation for Cultural Promotion in Europa auf Tournee geht.

Schmids kultivierte Typografie hat den Pop, den New Wave und andere Modeströmungen im Design überdauert. Die Zeit ist reif, das Werk eingehend und in stiller Kontemplation zu würdigen.

Barbara Junod
Kuratorin Grafiksammlung
Museum für Gestaltung Zürich

References

Books

Typographie, Emil Ruder, A. Niggli, 1967
Hats for Jizo: A Japanese folk story, Kyoko Iwasaki, Paper-cut prints by Nicole Schmid,
    Translation by Sumi Schmid, Robundo, 1988
Cross-Cultural Design: Communicating in the Global Marketplace, Henry Steiner (ed.),
    Thames and Hudson, 1995
Swiss Graphic Design: The Origins and Growth of an International Style 1920–1965,
    Richard Hollis, Laurence King Publishing, 2006
Helmut Schmid: Design is Attitude / Gestaltung ist Haltung,
    Fjodor Gejko, Victor Malsy, Philipp Teufel (ed.), Birkhäuser, 2007
AGI Alliance Graphique Internationale Deutsche Mitglieder 1954–2011, Hesign, 2011
30 years of Swiss typographic discourse in the Typografische Monatsblätter*: TM RSI SGM 1960–90*,
    ECAL/École cantonale d'art de Lausanne et al. (ed.), Lars Müller Publishers, 2013

The Third Lettering Exhibition, Catalog for Japan Lettering Designers' Association, 1971
Japan Typography Annual 1985, Japan Typography Association Annual Editing Committee (ed.), Robundo, 1985
Japan Typography Annual 1989, Japan Typography Association (ed.), Robundo, 1989
Logo ON. Package, Sumio Hasegawa (ed.), Graphic-sha, 1990
World Trademarks and Logotypes III, Takenobu Igarashi (ed.), Graphic-sha, 1991
Creativity in Graphic Design, Idea (ed.), Seibundo Shinkosha, 1996
Yarakasukan 100th Anniversary Book, Yarakasukan (ed.), Yarakasukan, 1996
The Road to Basel, Helmut Schmid, Robundo, 1997
Japan Typography Annual 1998, Japan Typography Association (ed.), Graphic-sha, 1998
Typography Today New Edition, Helmut Schmid, Seibundo Shinkosha, 2003
Japan japanisch, Helmut Schmid, Robundo, 2012
Emil Ruder, Fundamentals, Seibundo Shinkosha, 2013
Typography Today Revised Edition, Helmut Schmid, Seibundo Shinkosha, 2015
ggg Books 119: Helmut Schmid, DNP Arts Communications, 2015
Typography (Japanese Edition), Emil Ruder, Born Digital, 2019

Independent publications

Typographic Reflections 1: 1989 11 09, 1992
Typographic Reflections 2: point line movement, 1993
Typographic Reflections 3: communal harmony, 1995
Typographic Reflections 5: democracy / hypocrisy, 2003
Typographic Reflections 6: arrange, select and explore, 2005
Typographic Reflections 7: toshiro mayuzumi's nirvana symphony composed on the hand press and, 2010
Typographic Reflections 8: project fukushima, 2012
Typographic Reflections 9: working with words, 2012
Typographic Reflections 10: type and illustration, 2014
Typographic Reflections 11: man made nature made, 2014
Typographic Reflections 12: a walk through the exhibition nippon no nippon, 2016
Typographic Reflections 13: Mit freundlichen Grüssen an alle, Kurt Hauert, 2017
Typographic Reflections 14: 2018 04 27, 2018

   * No. 4 is *The Road to Basel* (Robundo, 1997)

Journals   * Journal articles without an author's name are by Schmid himself.

«Typographie und Schriftdesign von Helmut Schmid» / "Type-Face and Script designed by Helmut Schmid,"
    Gebrauchsgraphik, Nr. 12, Verlag F. Bruckmann KG, 1971
"All art publications are subjected to the terror of an international codified layout," *Quad*, No. 4, Maarssen, 1982
"Design is Attitude," *Motif*, No. 6, Mudra, 1998
"Emil Ruder: Typography from the inside," *Baseline*, No. 36, Bradbourne Publishing, 2002
"Robert Büchler: Typography at the edge," *Baseline*, No. 42, Bradbourne Publishing, 2003
"Kurt Hauert: The line from the sound," *Baseline*, No. 45, Bradbourne Publishing, 2004
"Armin Hofmann: Compositions in typography," *Baseline*, No. 49, Bradbourne Publishing, 2006
"Helmut Schmid: The road after Basel," *Newwork Magazine*, No. 6, Studio Newwork, 2010

Typographische Monatsblätter

Nr. 5/6, 1965	«Profile junger Typographen: Helmut Schmid»
Nr. 3, 1971	«Emil Ruder, Rikiu der Typographie»
Nr. 8/9, 1973	«Japanische Typographie»
Nr. 1, 1975	«Mayuzumi»
Nr. 3, 1977	«Der Umschlag ist kein Tummelplatz für Dekorationen der Designer»
Nr. 3, 1978	«Ein Japanischer Wandkalender» / "A Japanese Calendar"
Nr. 1, 1980	«Kalender 1980; 15 Politypographien»
Nr. 2, 1981	«Typographie heute – Von den Pionieren zu den Heute kreativen Gestaltern» / "Typography Today – From the Pioneers to the Designers Now Active"
Nr. 5, 1986	«Helmut Schmid und Wolfgang Weingart: eine Korrespondenz entstanden durch das japanische typographie Jahrbuch» / "Helmut Schmid and Wolfgang Weingart: A Correspondence Prompted by the Japan Typography Annual"
Nr. 1, 1989	«Typographie von Helmut Schmid» / "Typography by Helmut Schmid"
Nr. 6, 1995	«Communal Harmony»
Nr. 3, 1998	«Der Weg nach Basel» / "The Road to Basel"
Nr. 1, 2000	«Eins zwei drei. Offenkundige Wahrheit» / "One Two Three. Obvious Truth"
Nr. 1, 2003	«Japanische Typographie und Schweizer Typographie» / "Japanese Typography and Swiss Typography"
Nr. 4, 2003	«Merci Jean-Pierre Gräber! Merci Jean-Pierre! Merci TM!»
Nr. 1, 2004	Hans Rudolf Bosshard, «Helmut Schmid Typograf»
Nr. 3, 2007	«Robert Büchler»
Nr. 4, 2014	«Danke Emil Ruder»

"Type and Typography," *Graphic Design,* No. 38, Kodansha, 1970
"Designer Interview: Helmut Schmid," *Lettering and Typography*, No. 3,
    Japan Lettering Designers' Association, 1971
"Designer Introduction: Helmut Schmid," *Typography Quarterly,* No. 6, Kashiwa Shobo, 1975
"The Rules of Typography are at Present Newly Valued," *Typographics ti:*, No. 27,
    Japan Typography Association, 1982
"From Orderly Typography to Organic Typography," *Typographics ti:*, No. 98, Japan Typography Association, 1988
«Entwurf einer Zeitschriftenanzeige,» *HQ,* Nr. 30, High Quality, 1994
"The Great 13: Asking Helmut Schmid about Emil Ruder," *JAGDA Report,* No. 160, JAGDA, 2000
"What's Next? Chapter 3 Letter: Helmut Schmid," *News and Report*, No. 90, Japan Package Design Association, 2005
"Interview with Helmut Schmid," *Studio Voice*, Vol. 379, July 2007, INFAS publications, 2007, licat
"Typography Designer, Helmut Schmid and Ryoanji," *Lmagazine*, December, 2007, Keihanshin Lmagazine, 2007
Nicole Schmid, Kiyonori Muroga, "Helmut Schmid and his education: Basel, Asia and Kobe,"
    Visual Design, No. 1, Sayusha, 2020

Idea Seibundo Shinkosha

No. 78, 1966	"Helmut Schmid, Young Designer of Typography" by Hiroshi Ohchi
No. 95, 1969	"Emil Ruder's Typography"
No. 103, 1970	"Emil Ruder"
No. 105, 1971	"Helmut Schmid and his Type Design (On Japanese Typeface Design)"
No. 142, 1977	"The SPD's election campaign" by Shigeru Watano
No. 146, 1978	"W. Weingart's Typography"
No. 147, 1978	"Printed Matters for the Citizen"
No. 156, 1979	"Serial Typography"
No. 168, 1981	"A Book for Seeing: Projekte Projects"
No. 175, 1982	*1979, A Kind of Story*: a new book by Hans-Rudolf Lutz"
No. 197, 1986	"Let's Remember Hiromu Hara as the Conscience of Japanese Typography and Graphic Design"
No. 283, 2000	"Wolfgang Weingart's (Typo)graphic Landscapes"
No. 296, 2003	"Typo Janchi, the Book"
No. 303, 2004	"Thank You, Prof. Hiroshi Ohchi"
No. 307, 2004	"The Visual Commentator Ahn Sang-Soo"
No. 322, 2007	"Helmut Schmid: Design is Attitude [exhibition preview]" by Victor Malsy and Philipp Teufel et al.
No. 323, 2007	"Comments on Wim Crouwel"
No. 329, 2008	"Sans Serif Does Not Represent the Final Stage – Karl Gerstner: International Designer, Artist and Author. New Books and a New Typeface."
No. 333, 2009	"Ruder typography Ruder philosophy"
No. 358, 2013	"Roy Cole: Typographer, Photographer, Typeface Designer"

Idea Special Issue: *Typography Today*, 1980
"Typography and Typography", *Idea* Special Issue: *Typography in Japan*, 1981
"El Lissitzky: the Pioneer of Visual Typography," "Jan Tschichold: The Conscience of Typography,"
    Idea Special Issue: *30 Influential Designers of the Century*, 1984

Helmut Schmid
Schmid Typography
Typografie

Editors:
Kiyonori Muroga (Graphic-Sha)
Nicole Schmid

Editorial Cooperation:
Hirofumi Abe
Chikako Tatsuuma
Fjodor Gejko
Fanny Rakeseder
Sumi Schmid

Photography:
Yoshihiro Asai

Books on Swiss graphic design
published by
Lars Müller Publishers:

Helmut Schmid, ed.,
Ruder typography Ruder philosophy,
2017,
ISBN 978-3-03778-541-6 (E/J)

Wolfgang Weingart,
My Way to Typography / Wege zur Typographie,
2014,
ISBN 978-3-03778-426-6 (E/G)

Lars Müller,
*Josef Müller-Brockmann:
Ein Pionier der Schweizer Grafik*,
2001,
ISBN 978-3-907078-59-4

Lars Müller,
*Josef Müller-Brockmann:
Pioneer of Swiss Graphic Design*,
2015,
ISBN 978-3-03778-468-6

Karl Gerstner,
*Designing Programmes: Programme as
Typeface, Typography, Picture, Method*,
facsimile reprint of the original (1964),
2019,
ISBN 978-3-03778-578-2

Karl Gerstner,
*Programme entwerfen: Programm als
Schrift, Typographie, Bild, Methode*,
Faksimile Reprint des Original (1964),
2020,
ISBN 978-3-03778-649-9

Lars Müller,
Helvetica: Homage to a Typeface,
2004,
ISBN 978-3-03778-046-6

Museum für Gestaltung Zürich, ed.,
100 Jahre Schweizer Grafik,
2014,
ISBN 978-3-03778-352-8

Translation (English – German):
Antoinette Aichele-Platen
Uta Hasekamp
Dieter Heil
Michael Pilewski (German – English)
Graham Welsh

Proofreading:
Sandra Leitte (German)
Stephanie Shellabear (English)

Cooperation:
Yu Adachi (hsdesign)
Mio Asai
Duncan Brotherton

Production:
Esther Butterworth

Design:
Nicole Schmid

Printing and binding:
DZA Druckerei zu Altenburg,
Germany

Paper:
Arctic Volume Ivory 1.1, 130 g/m^2

Lars Müller Publishers
Zurich, Switzerland
www.lars-mueller-publishers.com

ISBN 978-3-03778-739-7

© 2023
Nicole Schmid and
Lars Müller Publishers

No part of this book
may be used or reproduced
in any form or manner
whatsoever without
prior written permission,
except in the case of
brief quotations embodied in
critical articles and reviews.

Distributed in North America,
Latin America and the Caribbean
by ARTBOOK | D.A.P.
www.artbook.com

Printed in Germany

Originally published and designed
in Japan in 2022 by
Graphic-Sha Publishing Co., Ltd., Tokyo

© 2022 Nicole Schmid
© 2022 Graphic-Sha Publishing Co., Ltd.

German translation rights
arranged with
Graphic-Sha Publishing Co., Ltd.
through Japan UNI Agency, Inc., Tokyo
Foreign edition production
and management:
Takako Motoki
(Graphic-Sha Publishing Co., Ltd.)